RELAX
BABY
BE COOL

THE ARTISTRY AND AUDACITY OF
SERGE GAINSBOURG

[JEREMY]
[ALLEN]

RELAX BABY BE COOL
THE ARTISTRY AND AUDACITY OF
SERGE GAINSBOURG
JEREMY ALLEN

For Claire and Jean Genie.

A JAWBONE BOOK
Published in the UK and the USA
by Jawbone Press
Office G1
141–157 Acre Lane
London SW2 5UA
England
www.jawbonepress.com

ISBN 978-1-911036-65-4

Printed in the Czech Republic by PBtisk

1 2 3 4 5 25 24 23 22 21

TABLE OF CONTENTS

INTRODUCTION
THE CULT OF SERGE

March 1991. Things were changing in significant, imperceptible ways as the analogue world began to fall away. Tim Berners-Lee had recently trialled a browser for the World Wide Web at CERN for the first time; the first Gulf War had just come to a ceasefire; the jury of the Hillsborough disaster inquiry was about to return an accidental death verdict for ninety-six Liverpool fans crushed to death during an FA Cup game with Nottingham Forest; 'Do The Bartman' by The Simpsons was Britain's fictitious no.1, having knocked off '3am Eternal' by merry art-pranksters The KLF; Bret Easton Ellis's *American Psycho* was about to be published, on the way to causing shockwaves of controversy; and the biggest film in the UK, *Green Card*, was an incontestably non-controversial movie about an immigrant, played by the French actor Gérard Depardieu, attempting to outstay his welcome in the United States.

There was little room in the news in the English-speaking world for the death of a French singer. Serge Gainsbourg passed away at his home on the Left Bank in Paris after suffering a heart attack. At the time, he was perhaps regarded by the UK press as a musical footnote, having provided some erotic novelty value toward the end of the 1960s as the author of the UK's first ever foreign-language no.1, and the perpetrator of an international scandal twenty-two years earlier with his then partner, Jane Birkin. Across the channel, the news of Gainsbourg's death, aged sixty-two, was more akin to a national tragedy, with the whole country going into mourning. 'People remember where they were when they heard that Gainsbourg was dead,' says Birkin, sitting across from me in her bijou, boho, black-clad apartment in the sixth arrondissement of Paris. 'It's the thing that shocked people the most, like John F. Kennedy. Everything stopped. It was incredible.'

'I just happened to arrive in Paris early the day that he died,' says veteran music journalist John Robb. 'It was eerily quiet, and in those pre-internet days you could feel something had happened. The city felt spooked. Later on, I found out a national icon had died.'

While the streets were quiet, kids congregated outside the singer's apartment on Rue de Verneuil—a gathering not unlike the ones at the Dakota Building and Central Park, Manhattan, after the assassination of John Lennon. Candlelit vigils continued as the sun went down.

Jane Birkin and Serge's manager, Philippe Lerichomme, found it difficult to reach Gainsbourg's daughters, Charlotte Gainsbourg and Kate Barry (the daughter of John Barry, who Serge brought up as his own), inside the apartment. 'By the time I arrived at Rue de Verneuil with Philippe, a crowd was in the street, singing "La Javanaise". They'd blocked the whole street. The candles were out. It was quite extraordinary to try to get to the front door to find Kate and Charlotte and Bambou, who were closeted on the inside.' Caroline von Paulus, aka Bambou, was Serge's final partner.

The words 'he was our Baudelaire, our Apollinaire', from President François Mitterand, are oft quoted, given the elevation afforded the singer by France's longest-serving president. Though politicians are adept at wringing the auspices out of a good tragedy to help boost their own popularity, the high praise for Gainsbourg was seemingly genuine enough. 'He elevated the chanson to the level of art ...' These words would have particularly pleased Serge, were he still alive; he considered pop music a 'minor art'—or at least that's what he always maintained—and he regarded the vernacular tradition of the *chanson variété française* with only slightly less disdain. As a failed painter who'd been steeped in the music of classical composers like Chopin and avant-garde geniuses like Stravinsky and Debussy by a pushy, tyrannical father, Gainsbourg was disparaging about popular song to an extent that implied embarrassment. 'I practise a minor art that's supposed to be for young people,' he once said, sniffily.*

---

* 'Je pratique un art mineur destiné aux mineures.' Serge Gainsbourg, *Pensées provocs et autres volutes* (Librairie Générale Française, 2007)

'He was taken to the Mont Valerien just outside Paris, where they put heroes,' says Birkin, 'so people could walk past his coffin. I remember asking a man there whether he'd stay with him overnight to keep an eye on him, and he said it would be a privilege to. People were so kind and so terribly moved. The taxis came with flowers because he used to tip them five hundred francs at the end of each journey. The whole of France seemed to be in that cemetery. Catherine Deneuve read 'Fuir le bonheur de peur qu'il ne se sauve'. The words to 'Fuir le bonheur ...', recorded by Birkin on her 1983 *Baby Alone in Babylone* album, are as elegant and celestial—not to mention, respectable—as Gainsbourg ever got. 'There was no ceremony because Serge's sister Jacqueline didn't want him to be taken by any religion. And that day I've never seen anything like it, and I haven't since, apart from when Johnny Hallyday died.'

For a whole generation who embraced him when his own generation and the generation that came after had held him at arm's length, it wasn't Gainsbourg in that casket—it was *Gainsbarre*. Lucien 'Lulu' Ginsburg was born in 1928, an early entry into a demographic labelled the 'silent generation', and already an elder statesman of song by the time he was writing hits for *yé-yé* baby boomers while his own career was pushed to the peripheries. We can regard 'Je t'aime ... moi non plus' as an anomaly, a perfect storm of controversy that precipitated a massive international hit, even in places that at the time wouldn't normally recognise a song written in French (step forward the UK). Serge's musical career partially slipped back into the shadows following what was a commercial aberration, though he maintained a presence on French TV during the 1970s, begrudgingly tossing off witty songs for sundry light entertainers and chanteuses on Saturday-night telly.

It was reggae that saved Gainsbourg in the late 70s, just as Eurovision Song Contest winner France Gall had saved him in the mid-60s. Then, when he and Jane Birkin broke up, he invented Gainsbarre, a drunken doppelgänger he could brazenly parade around and blame all of his bad behaviour on. It was a Faustian pact that would have consequences. This alter ego, enshrined within another alter ego, would grow like a pernicious weed as he went in pursuit of ratings. But for more than a decade from his 1979 album *Aux armes et cætera*, which caused huge controversy by marrying the French national anthem to a reggae track, Serge enjoyed the adulation of Generation Xers who hung on his every transgressive word. He became a late-night TV fixture, bibulous and bellicose, spouting the supposedly unsayable in public with relish, and offending everyone's parents in the process. Burning a five hundred franc banknote on TV, humiliating Guy Béart on the arts talk show *Apostrophes*, calling Les Rita Mitsouko's Catherine Ringer a 'pute', telling *Champs-Élysées* chat show host Michel Drucker 'I want to fuck' Whitney Houston …

These were stunts designed to shock. To shatter the illusion of cosiness. To get people talking and seize the front page. Musician and pop impresario Bertrand Burgalat tells me about some of the differing generational perceptions from a French perspective: 'My father was born in 1919 and my mother in 1922, and for these people he really was a dirty man.' And Gainsbarre was impelled to up the ante wherever there was a spotlight. Jacques Wolfsohn, the mastermind behind Disques Vogue and one of Gainsbourg's best friends, told the writer Marie-Dominique Lelièvre, for her 1994 biography *Gainsbourg sans filtre*, 'Until "La Marseillaise" he was normal. A fairly standard carouser. After "La Marseillaise" he believed his own hype. He created this image and suddenly tried to become him.'*

This addiction to attention, even from behind the dark glasses of Gainsbarre, comes as little surprise to us today, in a celebrity-saturated twenty-first century where every two-bit pop star has assumed a persona. Perhaps more surprising is the fact the albums he is rightly exalted for now—*Histoire de Melody Nelson*, *L'homme à tête de chou*, *Initials B.B.*, and so on—were hidden from view for a lot of fans until after his death.

'When he died, only a few aesthetes remembered the earlier stuff,' says Burgalat. 'He became a huge and popular figure in France with albums that

---

* 'Jusqu'à "La Marseillaise", il était normal. Un joyeux fêtard normal. À partir "La Marseillaise", il a suivi sa légende. Il s'est créé une image et, tout à coup, a tenté de lui ressembler.' Marie-Dominique Lelièvre, *Gainsbourg sans filtre* (J'ai Lu, 1994)

were very different to those records. His early repertoire wasn't available on vinyl, and you had to find earlier songs on compilations.' Burgalat likens Gainsbourg's 80s popularity to another *chansonnier*, Claude Nougaro, who he says 'made some beautiful albums but then ended up broke. He went to New York with some stupid French jazz-rock musician, Philippe Saisse, to do an album called *Nougayork*. It's the worst kind of bad 80s funk done with a Yamaha DK7 … a huge success! Sometimes people in France become successful with their worst records.'

*

Long before Christan Marclay was proverbially dragging in people who don't normally go to art galleries to see his conceptual masterwork, *The Clock*, he was creating musical mélanges with turntables in homage to some of the greats. Turntablism began in the 1970s, with early practitioners like DJ Kool Herc, then became a central tenet of hip-hop in the 1980s; Marclay was recording without grooves, melding records together for a more dreamlike and abstract effect from 1979 onwards. He recorded some of these avant-garde experiments externally as he performed them live. In 1988, he made *More Encores* with tributes to Johann Strauss, Frederic Chopin, Jimi Hendrix, John Zorn, and Jane Birkin and Serge Gainsbourg. A note came with the album, to give the listener a tiny insight into his intentions:

> Each piece is composed entirely of records by the artist after whom it is titled. 'John Cage' is a recording of a collage made by cutting slices from several records and gluing them back into a single disc. In all the other pieces the records were mixed and manipulated on multiple turntables and recorded analog with the use of overdubbing. A hand-crank gramophone was used in 'Louis Armstrong'.

Naturally, the track 'Jane Birkin And Serge Gainsbourg' features a sample of 'Je t'aime … moi non plus', but there are other records that would have been more difficult to get your hands on outside of France in 1988: 'Panpan cucul', 'Ce mortel ennui', 'Pauvre Lola', 'Du jazz dans le ravin', and Birkin's 'Di Doo Dah', 'Yesterday Yes A Day', and 'L'Aquoiboniste'.

Jonny Trunk, a dedicated film music DJ, broadcaster, and owner of arcanum label Trunk Records, says he was on the floor in record shops in the late 80s, scouring for 'esoteric, odd stuff … TV music and what people would call easy listening' while others chose from the racks above. To Trunk and his coterie, 'Gainsbourg was a god … we all knew about him and we were hanging about at the Winchester Film Fair, which was on every three months, and Storey's Gate opposite Westminster Abbey, where there were loads of old codgers with Judy Garland pictures. And we were looking for anything interesting that came from the world of TV from the 60s and 70s, and Gainsbourg was a part of that as well.' Jonny picked up a copy of *Histoire de Melody Nelson* in 1990, after someone who worked at 58 Dean Street Records tipped him off that there would be Gainsbourg stock coming in that week.

'Three records arrived, and I'd already got two of them, but then there was this blue *Melody Nelson* album, so I bought it and took it home. And it's one of those records you put on and go, *This is nuts*. In a good way.' Trunk became one of the first people in Britain to write about *Melody Nelson*, in a column for *Record Collector*, as it had received little to no coverage on its release in 1971. 'I'm a big collector of sex and vinyl—not pornographic necessarily, but covering everything from the soundtrack to *Deep Throat* to Japanese pinky albums—and I thought that fitted in well, because he had that history with "Strip-Tease" and "Pauvre Lola" and all these sexy records. I remember in the 90s when I'd play it at dinner parties, which sounds much more fun than it was … basically you'd have four people around and you'd put it on in the background, and someone would say, What the fuck is this? It's amazing. And I'd go, Yeah, it is, isn't it?'

In 1991, an obscure Gainsbourg sample from his early jazz period turned up courtesy of alternative hip-hop legends De La Soul, who borrowed a trumpet top line from 'Les oubliettes' on their album *De La Soul Is Not Dead*. Simon Reynolds from *Melody Maker* asked about the recherché lifts, which included Gainsbourg, Frankie Valli, Wayne Fontana, and The Doors. Kelvin

Mercer, aka Posdnuos, replied, 'That delayed the album because a lot of what we sample was so old that it was hard to track down who owned the track, or whether they was even alive! A couple of the people we dealt with were sort of at the senile stage. They didn't even know what rap was!' In Gainsbourg's case, that would have been flagrantly untrue, given that he'd experimented with rap himself only a few years earlier.

Writing about the retrospective impact of Gainsbourg years later, UK-based French music journalist Pierre Perrone, sadly no longer with us, wrote in the *Independent*, 'Having dismissed Gainsbourg as the roué who led Jane Birkin astray with the suggestive chart-topper "Je t'aime … moi non plus" in 1969, the Brits developed a fascination for the enfant terrible of French pop after his death in 1991.' And, true enough, references to Gainsbourg started creeping into the music press in the early 90s, usually in articles featuring Jarvis Cocker or about his band, Pulp.

'Will the British never understand that by coming to terms with our seedy underside we may become humane individuals?' asked Pete Paphides in *Melody Maker* in 1993, as he witnessed Pulp confound an audience who'd paid their money to see Saint Etienne. 'Jarvis—Serge Gainsbourg in the body of Mr. Bean—should move to France immediately, with its risible military history, philosophers who claimed that the human soul was a pea-shaped tissue behind the nose (Descartes) and melancholy musical sleazes like Chopin and Gainsbourg. As tonight's baffled audience testifies, the British are just too damn repressed to deserve him.'

The following year, the *Maker*'s Chris Roberts mentioned this kinship with the French to Cocker himself, who had also been labelled 'quintessentially English' by some sections of the press. 'So I'm quintessentially French,' mused Jarvis. 'That's it, I'm a social chameleon. When we go to Germany I'll be quintessentially Kraut. Well, from what I know of the French music I like, it tends to deal with quite adult subject matter. Like, Serge Gainsbourg talking about having it off with his thirteen-year-old daughter is probably going a bit far, but there does seem to be a French disposition to lyrics which probe a bit.'

In 1994, the famous Michel Colombier-initiated repetitive loop heard throughout 'Bonnie & Clyde' formed the basis for two hit singles on either side of La Manche: 'Nouveau Western' by MC Solaar, and a self-titled track by Renegade Soundwave. The following year Serge was being sampled by alternative indie dance artists on the peripheries of the mainstream: Massive Attack took a bass line from 'Melody' for 'Karmacoma', while Black Grape made use of 'Initials B.B.' on 'A Big Day In The North'.

Paul Gorman managed to secure a small piece about Serge in *Mojo* in 1996—quite a feat in those days, according to the writer. 'Barney Hoskyns was the editor, he'd heard of him; you know, Barney is knowledgeable, but I couldn't get anything out of Serge's label in this country,' says Gorman. 'There wasn't anything reissued. I had to go to the ethnic or foreign-language sections in Piccadilly to buy up French releases. There was nothing released here. And I think I got a page.'

None of these artists or writers came to Gainsbourg with the dedication of Mick Harvey, guitarist with Nick Cave & The Bad Seeds. So captivated by Serge's music was he that, after a French friend shared a mixtape with him, he took it upon himself to reinterpret a whole album of covers in English in 1995, *Intoxicated Man. Pink Elephants* would follow in 1997, and he'd release two more Gainsbourg covers albums in 2016 and 2017 (*Delirium Tremens* and *Intoxicated Women*, respectively).

Harvey got to work long before the fruits of his labours manifested in the shape of a first album, spending the early part of the project attempting to figure out just how feasible translating material from French to English was for someone who didn't speak fluent French. Harvey asked himself, 'Can I get translations from these songs that I'm happy enough with that will work being sung? At that time there weren't really any available translations of his stuff. You couldn't even see bad literal translations online or anything. Nowadays there are loads of them, and Google Translate will give you some sense of what the person is trying to say.'

The musician formed a working relationship via fax with Alain Chamberlain, an Australian professor of French at the university of Brunei. The pair were introduced by Mick's friend Ed Clayton-Jones. 'So we struck up that conversation where the stuff would come through and then I'd have to start getting the rhyming schemes and shaping it at my end,' says Mick. 'I'd always ask for a literal translation, a straight translation, plus an explanation of where there were wordplays and jokes.'

Bertrand Burgalat was drafted in to arrange the strings for the early albums. 'Mick wanted to make Gainsbourg known outside of France,' he tells me. 'He didn't speak French and I don't know how he did it but he succeeded in translating his songs into English really perfectly!' B.B. laughs at the audacity of achieving such a seemingly insurmountable challenge. 'People like Mick, who tried to make his repertoire better known, were never helped at all by Lerichomme, Gainsbourg's manager. I think they were surprised afterwards.' Does Mick receive a Christmas card from the Gainsbourg estate? 'No. Nor a thank you card. And then it goes through the publishing—they have to approve the translations—and then they take all the money and don't give me a translator's cut. I think they probably think I'm a weird fan stalker. I'm not like that at all.'

Another artist whose head was turned by the music of Serge Gainsbourg was Northern Irish soundtrack specialist David Holmes, who paid homage to the Frenchman with the track 'Don't Die Just Yet' on his 1997 album *Let's Get Killed*. By that time, were music listeners starting to cotton onto Serge, and especially onto *Histoire de Melody Nelson*? 'No, nobody knew who he was,' says Holmes. 'I just stumbled upon *Histoire de Melody Nelson*, and that album blew me away. It's one of the greatest albums ever made.' Cornish electronic musician Luke Vibert also sampled Gainsbourg that same year, using musical scenery from 'Valse de Melody' and Dave Richmond's chunky bass riff from '69 année erotique' on his trip-hoppy breakbeat landmark *Big Soup*.

Paul Gorman says something changed in the mid-90s, when Gainsbourg started becoming better known. 'I was really into him in '95, and then that year I think Mick Harvey produced an album, Luna did a cover of "Bonnie & Clyde" with Lætitia Sadier of Stereolab. There was something very much in the air. And then that *Gainsbourg Forever* box set came out, and then you couldn't move for him, could you?'

INTRODUCTION

'If you think about *Melody Nelson*, nobody wrote about that record,' says Jonny Trunk. 'It was only in the mid-noughties really that people started saying, *Wow, this is a masterpiece*, and putting it in top tens. And we all knew about it years ago, but nobody took any notice of us lot …'

*

I discovered Serge Gainsbourg later than anyone I've mentioned so far. It was 2005 and my desk was deluged with polycarbonate plastic and folded paper printed with press releases nobody would ever read. I had become just another jaded features editor at an online magazine called *Playlouder*, drinking daily and hoping the old magic from when I first got the job would return. I'd been working as a music journalist for three years, and already all the things that seemed great about it at the beginning had become commonplace: free bars, Glastonbury every year, gigs every night, more free bars, trips to foreign festivals and less glamorous jaunts down to Guildford … it sounds ungrateful, but my life had become a slipshod blur of live music and passing out. The musical landscape itself was uninspiring and very safe—aside from all the heroin—and this was at a time just before record companies had got their heads around digital, meaning CDs piled up on my desk like the Tower of Babel, unplayed.

I dragged myself off to watch post-Libertines clones playing crack skiffle in porkpie hats, emoting purely in honking glottal stops. I would write stinking review after stinking review, wondering what it was doing to my soul. In and among all the shiny refuse came salvation. Somebody somewhere in an office or bureau had sent me a double DVD of *D'autres nouvelles des étoiles*, a posthumous collection of nearly a hundred Serge Gainsbourg videos mostly compiled from TV appearances over a thirty-year period. I'd heard talk about this Gainsbourg character and decided to put it on and see what the fuss was about. These two volumes, from nervy jazz chansons in black-and-white from 1958 to an inadvisable electro-tinged love duet with his daughter in 1984, had me hooked, enchanted, astonished, flabbergasted …

Serge hopped from jazz to pop and from symphonic funk to dub reggae with panache. He'd written songs for famous French actresses and chanteuses like Brigitte Bardot, Juliette Gréco, France Gall, Françoise Hardy, and Anna Karina. He wrote lyrics for his pals Jacques Dutronc and Alain Bashung. He wrote and produced entire albums for movie stars like Catherine Deneuve and Isabelle Adjani. And, most famously, he wrote for and duetted with Jane Birkin, who became an elfin foil to his raffish, open-shirted, Lee Cooper-clad, Repetto-wearing creation, and the pair of them have remained there in the collective imagination ever since. Serge and Jane actually broke up in 1980, and they both found new partners. But we never quite got over the idea that they weren't together anymore—and neither did they. He wrote *Made In China* for his later partner, Bambou, which captured neither the imagination of the public nor, from the sound of it, Bambou herself. I wouldn't have been surprised in the research for this book had somebody told me he'd composed an entire album for Birkin's pet bull terrier, Nana. There's almost too much to discover.

Out of all those songs, I fell hardest for the seven from *Histoire de Melody Nelson*. The album wasn't a hit when it came out in 1971, but I wonder if music that it influenced had primed me for it in 2005: Pulp's *Different Class*, Blonde Redhead's *Misery Is A Butterfly*, Portishead's *Dummy* … What really caught my eyes and ears initially were those kitsch, raunchy pop videos made for a Christmas special with the French TV director Jean-Christophe Averty, with the work of the surrealists brought to life and hanging behind Serge and Jane as they performed before a blue screen. But it wasn't just *Melody Nelson* that had so beguiled me; from the off, I was completely transfixed by everything Gainsbourg wrote and performed, and it was a little baffling that he'd evaded me for so long, hiding in plain sight.

Sure, I'd heard of this arrogant Frenchman, and I'd heard 'Je t'aime … moi non plus'; I knew he'd asked Whitney Houston to fuck him on live TV; I even had some Dublin drinking buddies who spoke of him in hushed whispers when I visited, though I didn't take much notice at the time. It was ironic that, all of a sudden, Serge was speaking to me directly, because I could barely understand a word he was saying. I wanted to know what all the dirty things he was singing about meant, so I enrolled in French classes. Six weeks of lessons later, I realised I still couldn't speak French and that it might take a bit longer than I'd planned.

My love of Gainsbourg became a gateway to French culture. Paris is practically on our doorsteps, save for a stretch of water, and yet we've roundly ignored this rich cultural heritage for centuries, sometimes defiantly. Large swathes of the English have declared an open hostility to 'foreign' influences, slamming the door on a continent many of us have grown up feeling very much a part of. As the crow flies, the French capital is only fifty miles further from London than Manchester in the other direction, and yet if you spent all day listening to The Smiths, Joy Division, and The Fall, you wouldn't be accused of being a *mancophile*, because that word doesn't exist. It's not just the language barrier—other issues are at play too. Xenophobia is the worst part, but an inherent distrust and embarrassment of culture itself, a deplorable trait in the British, is almost as sad.

Gainsbourg soundtracked my life and became a companion, inspiring me and being there during the good times and the difficult ones, too. When I gave up smoking, I vicariously puffed through Serge, who always had one lit. When I gave up drinking—which was more problematic—I vicariously drank through Serge, the 'Intoxicated Man' of his own chanson. My life had become unmanageable because of alcohol, and I decided to get sober, whereas Gainsbourg never quit anything in his life.

*

As *Histoire de Melody Nelson* surreptitiously crept into the pantheon, well-known artists showed their appreciation for Gainsbourg via a series of compilations made in homage to him, from ambient jazz and electronic artists to alternative rock and indie stars. John Zorn produced a 1997 compilation called *Great Jewish Music: Serge Gainsbourg*, which was part of a series on his Tzadik Records label exploring *Radical Jewish Culture*. The initial idea sprang from the New York avant-garde scene of the early 90s, and culminated in collections covering the work of Burt Bacharach, Marc Bolan, and other pop geniuses besides. Gainsbourg tributes include Mike Patton's 'Ford Mustang',

Blonde Redhead's 'La Chanson de Slogan', and Marc Ribot bringing to life a particularly melancholy rendition of 'Black Trombone'. Given Zorn's indifference to publicity, these tracks have remained largely under the radar.

In 2001, it was electronica's turn, with reimagined ambient dub remixes of tracks by the likes of The Orb and Howie B for the *I ♥ Serge* compilation. His lounge-pop leanings translate well to the world of ambient electronics, with the breakbeat jazz of 'Aeroplanes (Readymade's Bold Mix)' in particular proving to be a revelation. The album came out on CD but never made it onto vinyl. Alex Paterson of The Orb told me, 'That track only came out on a compilation; it's a bit like our Louis Armstrong remix, you can only find it on Christmas editions!' The West Norwood ambient pioneers gave a very Orb-like treatment to the already mesmeric 'Requiem pour un con' by stripping most of it away: 'We did a new track and put the vocal over the top for that one, basically. That was the fun of what we were doing in the 90s: we couldn't get into those big studios unless we were doing a remix, so we'd say, *Let's do a track and put whatever we have to do over the top*.' It turns out 'Requiem pour un con' wasn't their first choice for the compilation. What had Alex wanted to do instead? 'There's that album with the teddy bear and the bird on the cover,' he says, referring to *Histoire de Melody Nelson*. 'That's iconic, that's a fucking brilliant album. We were hoping we'd get one of the tracks off that, but we didn't. That's what normally happens when you've got a big catalogue to get through.'

In 2002, Beck took 'Cargo Culte' and reworked it on his introspective *Sea Change* album with the new name of 'Paper Tigers', and in 2003, Danger Mouse and Jemini sampled the Dvořák-penned chorus from 'Initials B.B.' on 'Live On Both Sides', a year before Danger Mouse, aka Brian Burton, broke through with the zeitgeist-y bootleg *The Grey Album*; Gainsbourg has proven to be a recurring sonic influence in the starry careers of Beck and Danger Mouse. In 2006, a collection of artists from the indie fraternity: Franz Ferdinand, Placebo, and The Rakes, and American rock stars like Michael Stipe and James Iha, recorded versions of Serge's songs in English; Franz's take on 'Sorry Angel' is especially good. Cat Power, Jarvis Cocker, and Nina Persson also got in on the act, as did Portishead, Tricky, and Faultline. And there were also those personal connections: Jane Birkin (duetting with Alex Kapranos), Marianne Faithfull, and Sly & Robbie also took part in what was a reckoning of recognition. Most of the chansons were translated by Alain Bashung's celebrated lyricist, Boris Bergman.

Other unlikely sources of Sergophilia have included the great Iggy Pop leaving his comfort zone to record a French language version of 'La Javanaise' in 2012 for his sixteenth studio album, *Après*, and the not so great South African hip-hop duo Die Antwoord desexing 'Sea, Sex And Sun' on their squeaky 2014 number 'Sex', but perhaps the biggest tacit acknowledgement that Serge had finally gone overground came in 2007, when samples from two of his songs were used on 'Sensitized' by Kylie Minogue, from her million-selling album *X*. Loops from 'Bonnie & Clyde' and 'Requiem pour un con' feature strongly throughout, meaning Serge Gainsbourg was suddenly collaborating as a songwriter from beyond the grave with wildly successful twenty-first-century writers like Guy Chambers and Cathy Dennis. Some may sneer at this appropriation from beyond the grave, but I suspect it would have pleased him greatly. It's not like he didn't do that kind of thing all the time himself, using chunks of melody from Chopin, Dvořák, and Beethoven.

In the last ten years, Serge Gainsbourg has increasingly become more visible outside of France, albeit as one half of a famous couple of yore, with Jane Birkin. *Plus ça change, plus c'est la même chose.* Theirs is an idealised relationship that captures a moment, and they share a chemistry that's not easy to put your finger on, but very easy to market. They're alternative enough to namedrop, and analogue enough to feel nostalgic about, a Kodachrome fantasy of the perfect couple in vintage threads with authentic filters and the *mise en scène* of Paris behind them. 'And he was actually really handsome at that point,' says London musician Baxter Dury, an artist whose muttered estuary poetics juxtaposed by a dulcet female accomplice have drawn comparisons with Gainsbourg and helped make a career for him in France. 'He's got this weird, amazing face. Him and Jane together, imagery wise and music wise, are so powerful, and they don't want to dismantle that. If you look on any French girl's Instagram who's between the ages of seventeen and twenty-three, they'll have a picture of those two on it. Every single one of them will.'

Saying that Gainsbourg went 'overground' might be a little *de trop*, but the legend of Serge and Jane has been transferred to high-end perfume adverts where Natalie Portman cavorts in black-and-white to 'Je t'aime … moi non plus', and boutique handbags go by the brand name Rue de Verneuil—the street Serge and Jane lived on—with the strap line 'elegance and refined anticonformism'. When I'm in London I can drop his name and elicit conversation from ageing hipsters and music journalists, and in France everybody has something to say about Serge, but when my hairdresser in Surrey asks me what I've been up to and I tell her I've been writing a book about a dead French singer, his name draws a blank. When I lived in Paris, it was quite the opposite: it's impossible to escape Gainsbourg there. He seeps out of the walls and fills the air with his sounds, his face peering out of windows on posters and in the shape of his latex rubber puppet from the recently retired satirical show *Les Guignols de l'info*. He's everywhere and nowhere, if you discount his plot in Montparnasse Cemetery, where fans leave cigarettes, metro tickets, and cabbages in tribute; the Jardin Serge Gainsbourg, over near Lilas; and his waxwork of dubious similitude at the Musée Grévin.

Let's also be clear, there's been plenty written about Serge in French, some of which I've read, though my second language is still a work in progress. If there's not that much more to be said about him *en Français* then I believe there's plenty more to add in English, with books written about him being few and far between. I devoured Sylvie Simmons's *A Fistful Of Gitanes* (2001) when I found it, but a lot has happened in the world of Gainsbourg in the twenty years since that was written, even if the man himself continues to repose in Montparnasse. Hers is a slender book based loosely on the writings of Gilles Verlant and an extensive interview with Jane. I wanted to interview as many people as I could, from well-known modern music fans to acolytes of his, and try to get to the bottom of what made him tick or how they perceive him, and I wanted to fill the book full of opinions—sometimes opposing, often passionate.

As well as the ever-growing cult of Serge, the way we view material from another era is changing too. Should we look back with opprobrium? Or, given that so much of what he did is deemed unacceptable, especially in these chastened times, does that make its transgressive power yet more pleasurable? Serge always said he was *amoral* and not *immoral*, and while that probably wouldn't work as a Get Out Of Jail Free card these days, do we need to judge their standards by our standards? And, when we're talking about art, do we even need to judge at all?

On a practical level, I had little luck finding those who were around in 1958, for obvious reasons, whereas there's plenty of testimony from the 1980s. And speaking to the London-based session guys from the 1970s was a delight, though they played on so many records that nailing down memories of specific songs other than 'Je t'aime … moi non plus' was all but impossible. Serge is much more than just 'Je t'aime' or an incident on live TV with Whitney Houston, or even the lover of Jane Birkin, even if people of a certain age are unaware of the rest of his illustrious catalogue or any of the other gobsmacking stunts he pulled.

It's a cliché that the subject of a biography is a wealth of contradictions, but with Serge it's definitely true. There's Gainsbourg and Gainsbarre, a split personality that's easy for the observer to compartmentalise; two distinct works of artifice that the general public understood. Gainsbarre was a construction designed to deflect the blame from Gainsbourg, though Gainsbourg was a work of fiction too, albeit with more recognisable traits from his creator. Born Lucien Ginsburg and nicknamed Lulu, he'd tried on other lesser-known personae in his past: Julien Grix, the unsuccessful jazz sideman and barfly who first started depositing songs at SACEM (the French equivalent of PRS) in 1954; and Lucien Guimbaud, the name given to him on falsified papers to help him evade the Nazis during the Occupation. Serge was a whole collection of people.

Furthermore, Gainsbourg became a proper pop star at the ripe old age of forty, and a superstar aged fifty. Success had evaded him for long periods before and between. He was, as Jane's brother Andrew Birkin told me, incredibly sophisticated and childlike at the same time. He wrote songs that referenced Chopin and Beethoven and others that were scatological and borderline paedophilic. He loved to surprise people, and yet his songs were almost entirely devoid of middle eights. He was brilliantly creative and also a thief of intellectual property; a master and a dilettante all at the same time. People kept telling me *Serge didn't give a fuck*, and yet at times he clearly appeared to care far too much about what people thought of him. He was well known for his largesse among his friends and with cab drivers, and yet he stinted on writing credits, often taking sole responsibility for songs that were penned by his arrangers. He was sweet and sensitive, and an alcoholic abuser. In most cases I leave you to draw your own conclusions.

And then there's another paradox for us, the listeners. The Francophone artists I spoke to all mentioned an amazement at Serge's lyrical dexterity, and it's this legacy that holds strongest in his native France. Many Anglophonic listeners miss out on the deftness of his lyrical touch, where so often he could present ostensibly simple ideas—snappy and topical—with more complex, implicit meanings waiting in the wings, ready to deliver a sucker punch. You can hear the spectre of Alan Parker's guitar style on Baxter Dury's *Prince Of Tears*, or a decent impression of Jean-Claude Vannier's quixotic strings on Angel Olsen's *All Mirrors*, and yet his *jeu de mots* are lost on most of us. Lyrically, there's nobody like him in the English-speaking world. Musically, he's clearly strong enough, and yet there's this whole other facet lots of us are missing out on.

As well as his elusive meanings, there is also so much music. And when you've listened to that, there are the films, the TV shows, the interviews, and all the books in French to try to read. I remember looking at Jane Birkin after our meeting, slightly flabbergasted, and admitting to her that there was a lot to cover. It suddenly felt like a big responsibility, but at the same time I can let myself off the hook a little bit with an artist like Gainsbourg, because you're never going to get everything in.

This book started out being called *Intoxicated Man*, but that felt like a cliché—not that it would have done when Mick Harvey used the title twenty-five years ago. The recovering alcoholic in me is fascinated by a man who refused to slow down or attempt to regulate his self-destructive impulses, and yet there are plenty of other areas of his existence that are positively fecund to mine. 'Rich material!' said eighty-five-year-old German electronic pioneer Roedelius, when I told him about the book I was writing over WhatsApp. 'Erotic material!'

It also laboured under the misnomer *Bad News From The Stars* in the very early days, which felt too negative very quickly. I settled on the name *Relax Baby Be Cool*, borrowed from a lesser-known track from his first reggae album, *Aux armes et cætera*, because it's rhythmical and has a breezy universality to it. It's a song with very few lyrics, with the words 'Relax Baby Be Cool' repeated like a mantra, contrary to the anxieties of the verses. It encapsulates Serge's childlike and elementary grasp of the English language, which he loved despite his limitations (something I can relate to, inversely). It became my own mantra when I was approaching the deadline, and also something I could tell my two-year-old when he'd lost his favourite train. 'I think it's cool because you can understand this in every country,' says Françoise Cactus of Stereo Total, whose band memorably covered the song. 'It's perfect for us, because we are an international band.'

For this book, I've taken each studio album in sequence, but the text itself is not necessarily linear: I wanted to grab what was pertinent to the theme when it occurred, rather like Gainsbourg himself, grabbing sources from everywhere to make a Dadaist *papier collé* of sound. We start with a chapter on Gainsbourg's first four jazz ten-inches, starting with *Du chant à la une !...* in 1958, and we conclude with a chapter on decline pegged to *You're Under Arrest* in 1987, with tales from across his life threaded into the narrative. For instance, Lucien Ginsburg lived through the Occupation as a child of World War II and was made to wear a yellow star, a humiliating badge of identification imposed on Jews by the Nazis; Gainsbourg wrote about his childhood experiences on his 1975 concept album *Rock Around The Bunker* in his typically irreverent way, and it seemed more germane to examine those experiences within the context of that album than somewhere near the front of the book, thus hopefully avoiding the plodding and predictable chronology of some music biographies in the process.

It was my intention to delve deeper than any English language Gainsbourg biography has done so far, exploring the music and the lyrics as much as possible, and taking a closer look at what influenced him: his political leanings, his aesthetic passions, his amorality and complicated sexuality, his highbrow pilfering from art and literature and the popular contemporaneous sounds that he flagrantly assimilated into his own act. He was an acutely postmodern figure way ahead of his time, though viewed today he's as much a visionary as an anachronism.

Gainsbourg was a self-mythologist and media manipulator who often stirred up France—a country that is orderly and, dare I say it, rigidly conformist in some ways—by shocking his compatriots with material that would be cancellable now. Stealing drum rhythms from African percussionists and tunes from long dead classical composers was forward thinking—irrespective of your feelings about appropriation—but writing lasciviously about pubescent girls confirms the past is a foreign country.

In Britain, Gainsbourg is often perceived as a caricature enforcing French stereotypes, a grotesquery that wasn't ameliorated by Johann Sfar's 2011 biopic *Gainsbourg (vie héroïque)*. Thirty years after his death, and half a century after *Histoire de Melody Nelson* was released, I wonder if it was such a heroic life after all, and whether the fact Gainsbourg became trapped in a self-made creation which then devoured him whole is really something to be celebrated—presuming you're evolved enough not to buy into the myth of the tortured genius sacrificing himself on the altar of his artistic ambition.

And yet, it's this wealth of contradictions that make him such a fascinating subject to write about, and these failings and foibles that helped foster the stunning artistry and audacity of Serge Gainsbourg.

JAZZ BEGINNINGS

DU CHANT À LA UNE ! ... (1958)

NO.2 (1959)

L'ÉTONNANT SERGE GAINSBOURG (1961)

SERGE GAINSBOURG NO.4 (1962)

> My first record came out too soon. It was dark. Too dark. And nobody wanted it around the house.*

Who could have predicted Serge Gainsbourg would become one of the great legends of French pop when his first recordings appeared in 1958? He could clearly write songs, but there were thousands of singers with better voices who were more natural performers, with pulchritude and panache, making him look stiff and agitated by comparison. His early appearances on TV were nervy, and they conveyed no indication that the man onstage would eventually threaten to become the most recognisable Parisian singer in the world, vying to one day surpass Édith Piaf. Even the style of music he chose to carry his idiosyncratic talents, jazz, was looking *dépassé*, with rock'n'roll kicking the doors in. The yéyé wave would soon subsume France, and Serge was still on the beach having sand kicked in his face.

---

* 'Mon premier disque, c'était trop tôt. C'est noir. Trop noir. Et personne n'a envie d'avoir ça chez soi.' Gilles Verlant, *Gainsbourg* (Albin Michel, 2001)

A lack of stage presence compounded by sickening stage fright surely meant a career as a leading man in show business would be over before it had really started. The few column inches he received focused on his appearance, and were at best mocking, at worst antisemitic: 'We know his songs, he sings them himself with a thin reed of a voice, without gestures, a melancholy and indifferent air, two big dreamy eyes and two big flying elephant ears,' said *Les Beaux-Arts Brussels*, in one of his earliest reviews.* Then there was his ulterior desire to be a painter, and a supercilious attitude toward popular song.

The Gainsbourg of the popular imagination is at ease with himself. He's unshorn and disreputable and usually half cut, perpetually holding a lit cigarette. There's the tousled hair around the ears, the soft canvas Repetto shoes, and the Lee Cooper jeans that make him such a dishevelled 70s archetype. Serge is a rock star, even if he rarely played rock. He's a rebel and a *poete maudit*, cut from the same foppish cloth as Thomas Chatterton, who he'll later sing about. To the unreconstructed Anglo Saxon, there's something about Serge that is tacitly understood where so many of his compatriots and contemporaries get lost in translation.

'I think I know why that is,' says Canadian composer, sometime rapper, and pianist Chilly Gonzales. 'I think he fits to a tee the foreigner's vision of what a Frenchman should be. He's a little bit of a dirty old man; he's charismatic but not handsome. The smoking and the drinking and the non-apologetic womanising and sexism makes him the embodiment of a cliché. If you just added a beret, a striped shirt, and some cheese, then you'd pretty much have the cartoon version of Marcel from your language books growing up. He's not far from that.'

During the mid-50s, Serge scraped by as a sideman, playing guitar for the jazz chanteuse Michèle Arnaud at the bohemian cabaret club the Milord l'Arsouille, and as a pianist and musical arranger at the drag club Madame Arthur in Pigalle, a job he inherited from his father. His real name is Lucien

* 'On connaît ses chansons, il les chante lui-même avec un filet de voix, sans gestes, un air mélancolique et indifférent, deux grands yeux rêveurs et deux grandes oreilles d'éléphant volant.'

Ginsburg, but the first songs he wrote were under the alias Julien Grix, a composite of his literary fictional hero Julien Sorrell, from the Stendhal novel *Le rouge et le noir,* and a cubist painter, Juan Gris, who he was rather partial to—Gainsbourg's first creation wouldn't become a breakout star. After the name he was born with and its diminutive, Lulu, and the name that was thrust upon him as a child of the Occupation hiding from the Nazis, Lucien Guimbaud, he became Julien Grix through choice. It was his third incarnation, and he began registering songs at SACEM from August 1954 onward.* He'd ditched his own name, Lucien, because he thought it sounded too much like the name of a hairdresser, though, to be honest, Julien Grix doesn't sound unlike a hairdresser.

Importantly, in 1958 Gainsbourg met Boris Vian, who provided him with an epiphany and became his mentor. Vian, the polymath musical man about town, was good at just about everything … except performing. It was apparently Vian's perspiring upper lip and lack of ease with a crowd at the Cabaret Milord one night that gave Serge the self-belief he could stand up there and be equally as awful.

To understand Serge's 50s musical milieu, we need to meet Vian. In the post-war years, he inhabited the Left Bank with pals such as Simone de Beauvoir and Jean-Paul Sartre, who allowed him into their literary clique around 1945. He would hang around the Deux Magots café, writing poems, radio plays, and reviews, when he wasn't working the day job as an engineer. He was a fine trumpeter, and he became a *grand fromage* of the Paris jazz scene, a jolly and sometimes silly intellectual, tickled by the spectre of surrealism.

He wrote many well-received novels, including *L'ecume des jours* (*Froth On The Daydream*). It was eventually turned into the so-so 2013 Michel Gondry fantasy film *Mood Indigo*, which may have caused Vian to turn angrily in his grave, such was his violent antipathy for mediocre interpretations. '*L'écume des jours* is often seen as a quintessentially post-war book, flush with the sense of woozy, magical freedom that filled Paris after the liberation put an end

---

* SACEM is the French equivalent of PRS, with a difficult entrance exam, and one which the great George Brassens failed on his first attempt.

to the worst years of privation,' wrote Alexandra Shwartz in the *New Yorker* in 2014. 'Thanks to a new edition brought out in the sixties, it became a favourite among the *soixante-huitards*, the revolutionary students of 1968, who superimposed their own utopian aims onto Vian's apolitical surrealism.'

J'irai cracher sur vos tombes (*I Will Spit On Your Graves*), the book that immediately followed, was a noir that saw Vian sued for indecency by right-wingers, and featured a strangling scene that was circled in red pen by a copycat killer who left the book at the scene of a Montparnasse hotel murder. The hubbub caused by these newsworthy controversies helped the book to become a bestseller and propelled Vian to a strange kind of celebrity. That he could write one book full of surrealist whimsy and another filled with darkness in the same year—and all the while carry out all his other various activities—must have given an impressionable Gainsbourg ideas about the possibilities of production from the one artist.

Serge's song 'Intoxicated Man', from LP *No.4*, may never have come into being had he not heard Boris Vian's 'Je bois' ('I Drink') first. 'Je bois systématiquement,' sings Vian on the big-band swing number, 'pour oublier les amis de ma femme' (or 'to forget the friends of my wife'). Given that his first wife, Michelle Léglise, had a sexual relationship with Sartre, it's perhaps not difficult to guess where the inspiration might have come from for that song, other than the bottom of a bottle. Free love in the liberal Left Bank bubble paid its toll on Boris and Michelle's marriage, and they divorced in 1951. Meanwhile, Vian had met the Swiss ballet dancer Ursula Kübler at a party in 1950 and was carrying on himself (he and Kübler married in 1954).

Gainsbourg's 'Intoxicated Man' is musically groovier than 'Je bois', with tom toms and jazz organ and a lyric that projects the hallucinations of the alcoholic into chanson; seeing pink elephants, a spider crawling on his smoking jacket and bats on the living-room ceiling.* From the off, Gainsbourg wasn't

---

* *Seeing pink elephants* is a euphemism for the visions of a drunk, which first appeared in Jack London's 1913 autobiographical novel *John Barleycorn*. Mick Harvey used it for the title of his first Gainsbourg covers album, and he and Bertand Burgalat composed the instrumental title track as an orchestral homage to open the album.

afraid to parade his influences in public, or borrow something he liked and pass it off as his own. His debt to others was often great, and these liberties taken would sometimes test friendships and even end up in court.

Vian was flattered by the tribute. Another string to his bow was criticism, and he raved about his protege's first album, *Du chant à la une! …* (*Singing On The Front Page*), in *Le canard enchaîné*, a century-old French newspaper that's often been compared to *Private Eye*. A review so effusive might have shown up in the *Eye*'s 'Streets Of Shame' section were it written now, given the close bond between critic and singer: 'Empty your pockets and run to the record shops and demand that the owners give you a copy of the new Philips B 76447 B. This is the first 25cm 33rpm from a funny guy named Serge Gainsbourg, born in Paris on 2nd April 1928 … You might come back to me and say this boy is a sceptic, that he's wrong to see things in such dark terms, that it's not constructive (yes, yes, you can say that if you like). To which I will reply that a sceptic who builds words and music like this deserves a second listen before you write him off as just another disenchanted soul of the new wave.'* He goes on to call 'Le poinçonneur des Lilas' 'sombre, feverish and lovely', and 'Ce mortel ennui' a triumph of 'phrasing, style and cadence'.

Vian and Gainsbourg had a great deal in common, aside from being nervous performers: both were fine musicians with cultivated, voracious intellects and a playful ease with words. They'd both been sickly children, too, and both were afflicted in later life with the incurable literary illness of punning. In fact, Vian had been driven by a knowledge from childhood that his lungs weren't fully functional, suffering a pulmonary edema in 1956. He might have raved some more about Serge in the press, but in 1959, aged just thirty-nine, he dropped

---

* 'Tirez deux sacs de vos fouilles et raquez au disquaire en lui demandant le Philips B76447B. C'est le premier 25 cm 33 tours d'un drôle d'individu nomme Gainsbourg Serge et ne a Paris le 2 avril 1928. … Vous viendrez aussi me dire que ce garçon est un sceptique, qu'il a tort de voir les choses en noir, que ce n'est pas "constructif" … (si, si, vous dites des choses comme ça). A quoi je répondrais qu'un sceptique qui construit des paroles et des musiques comme ça, faudrait peut-être y regarder à deux fois avant de le classer parmi les désenchantés de la nouvelle vague.' Gilles Verlant, *Gainsbourg* (Albin Michel, 2001)

dead from a heart attack while shouting at the screen at the premiere of *I Will Spit On Your Graves*, a distressing interpretation that he clearly didn't approve of. He'd once predicted he'd die on his fortieth birthday, but he checked out 261 days early.

Vian was a funny guy with a serious mind who took jazz, above everything else, seriously. He once admonished the Americans for 'not tackling the challenge of jazz in the same way as they treated the challenge of the bomb'. And it was true: the French appeared to accede to jazz's exotic charms long before the country that birthed it, beginning with American GIs during the First World War and then Josephine Baker at the Folies Bergère. Black Americans living in Paris at various periods during the jazz years, from James Baldwin to Miles Davis, often spoke of the emancipation they enjoyed, but the reality, as always, is complicated. Paris might have been freer than Illinois or Harlem, but there were some still pervading, populist ideas that were anything but progressive. 'As Josephine Baker, the living embodiment of modern primitivism, was taking Paris by storm with her music-hall hit chanson "J'ai deux amours" and her slave-chic attire, the Institut Pasteur hosted a conference on so-called racial hygiene that explained the public health problems of the immigrant population in France,' writes Dr. Carole Sweeney in *From Fetish To Subject: Race, Modernism, And Primitivism, 1919–1935*. 'Most striking of all perhaps is the fact that a popular cultural negrophilia existed alongside a gradual resurgence of aggressively xenophobic nationalism.'

Jazz in France in the 1940s has come to be associated with La Resistance, but it was never banned in the Occupied Zone, or anywhere else for that matter. It was certainly looked upon as insubordinate enough by the Nazis that artists like Django Reinhardt would need to submit song titles of an evening before playing them, even when most of, or all of, the set was instrumental. Two men, Hughes Panassié and Charles Delauney, founded the groundbreaking Jazz Hot Club in 1931 and followed it with a magazine, *Jazz Hot*, in 1935 (now printed in Marseilles, it's the world's oldest jazz mag). Together, they aided the development and dissemination of jazz in Paris, with Delauney also managing Reinhardt. Alongside the virtuoso violinist Stéphane

Grappelli in the Quintette du Hot Club de France, Reinhardt led the first homespun jazz band, playing a take on American music that they made very much their own. The hot jazz that originated in New Orleans and the more metropolitan, modernist bebop even became competitors in Paris, with this territorial rivalry doing wonders for the collective scene. By 1947, you couldn't move without hearing one or the other reverberating up through a ventilation shaft in the street.

Gainsbourg was a fan of Reinhardt and attempted to emulate his style in his early days as a guitarist in clubs. The story goes that he was taught to play by a Romani boy while still studying art in 1946, which may be true or may have been a tale he told to add bohemian authenticity to his guitar-playing status at the time. He stuck with his painterly dreams until 1957, and he appeared to tire of guitar around the same period. There's now little photographic evidence of Gainsbourg holding a guitar. It's possible that, like with the painting, he expunged his strumming days from his own official history, another story of frustration at not being quite good enough. He's rarely seen in public with a guitar, except for an informal Luc Fournol beach shot from 1970, where's he's serenading Jane under a windbreak with shades on, and a performance in 1966 at the 36th Gala of the Union des Artistes in front of Princess Grace of Monaco, where he appears to loop all of the instruments live onstage, including the drums, the bass, the guitar, and the piano. Otherwise, he'd give the instrument a wide berth, perhaps conscious of the fact he'll never be Django Rheinhart, despite having more fingers.

A love of jazz was inculcated further into the French way of life during the 1950s, culminating in the 1958 Louis Malle film *Ascenseur pour l'échafaud* (*Lift To The Scaffold*), which married the atmospheric trumpet playing of Miles Davis with the French new wave and Jeanne Moreau, and is rightfully regarded as having one of the greatest soundtracks ever recorded. Furthermore, the New Orleans soloist Sidney Bechet moved to Paris in 1950, and, flushed with success after years as a temperamental journeyman, he stayed in the city until his death in 1959. Bechet had been in France during the 1920s, playing with Josephine Baker and others, but he'd been deported back to the States

RELAX BABY BE COOL

after being jailed for eleven months when he accidentally injured a woman in a shootout, according to his colourful and sometimes creative memoir, *Treat It Gentle*. He was thrown out of Duke Ellington's band in 1924 because of his uncompromising lifestyle, which was some going, given Ellington's reputation for magnanimity and equanimity.

Bechet's final nine years back in Europe proved a period of salvation, with his songs 'Petite fleur' and 'Les oignons' becoming big hits of their day in France. 'Bechet achieved a careful balancing act,' writes Andy Fry in *Paris Blues: African American Music And French Popular Culture, 1920–1960*. 'He was a New Orleans jazzman but also a Creole who had, in a sense, come "home" to France and was happy to play a Gallic-inflected repertoire.' The fact he could speak French and had also been a contemporary of the legendary Buddy Bolden bolstered a connection between France and *La Nouvelle-Orléans*, bringing a tacit authenticity, and even a sense of ownership, to the French jazz scene. Following his death from lung cancer at his home in Garches in 1959, his funeral brought thousands of mourners out onto the streets of Paris.

Gainsbourg's emergence as a songwriter and performer in the late 50s happened to coincide with the rise of cool jazz. It was well timed in that the new strain became the perfect vehicle for his talents: elegant, tuneful, with enough virtuosity and outréness required to make his classical and avant-garde training worthwhile. It was also a kind of jazz that lent itself to hybridisation with samba, bossa nova, and other Brazilian and neighbouring dance genres—a situation that Gainsbourg took full advantage of, particularly on *No.2* and *No.4*. Cool jazz mixed with the French variations gave him the foundation to find himself, even if the popularity of jazz itself was waning by the time he was finally getting into his stride.

As well as Boris Vian, Serge had other influential music-industry luminaries in his corner: Denis Bourgeois, the man who signed him; and Bourgeois's boss, Jacques Canetti, the celebrated talent agent who opened the famous Théâtre des Trois Baudets in Pigalle in 1947, and who looked after a number of legendary artists at Polydor and later Philips, including Marlene Dietrich, Piaf, Charles Trenet, Maurice Chevalier, and Louis Armstrong, and later Jacques

Brel and Juliette Gréco. Canetti and Bourgeois saw things in Gainsbourg that others didn't, and Bourgeois's faith remained steadfast. He would later be the man to hook Serge up with France Gall.

In Canetti's autobiography, *On cherche jeune homme aimant la musique*, Gainsbourg gets only a passing mention, perhaps because Serge had hit a creative impasse in 1978, when Canetti's book was first published, or more likely because he was really Bourgeois's man. Canetti describes Bourgeois succinctly as 'my deputy and my veritable shield; a calm, well-organised man with many an ungrateful task to carry out' who 'displayed the patience of a spider to help [Gainsbourg's] breakthrough. Then, quickly, Gainsbourg was free from the constraints of the scene, finding interpreters for his songs instead'.[*]

Canetti had expected his man Jacques Brel to be a behind-the-scenes figure writing songs to order, then he had a massive hit in 1957 with *Quand on n'a que l'amour*. It would be Serge who'd end up as the man in the shadows, writing chansons for artists like Juliette Gréco. 'The personal contact I had with Gainsbourg often persuaded me that behind his aggressiveness, his desire to shock, his quest for originality at all costs, was a great hidden modesty,' Canetti writes.[†]

*

With his thirtieth birthday just over a month away, Serge Gainsbourg demoed 'Le poinçonneur des Lilas' at Studio Philips on Rue Blanqui on February 17 1958. He also recorded four other songs: 'Ronsard 58', 'La recette de l'amour', 'Douze belle dans la peau', and 'Friedland'. Four of these songs would appear

---

[*] 'Mon véritable bouclier, homme calme, actif, organisé, a la tâche souvent ingrate … Denis Bourgeois, qui déploya une patience d'araignée pour l'aider a percer. Puis, rapidement, Gainsbourg devait se libérer des contraintes de la scène pour trouver des interprètes à ses chansons.'

[†] 'Les contacts personnels que j'ai eus avec Gainsbourg m'ont souvent persuadé que son agressivité, son désir de choquer, sa recherche de de l'originalité à tout prix, étaient la masque cachant une grande pudeur dont il se défend.'

on his debut ten-inch album, *Du chant à la une!* ...—his first four albums came out on ten-inch before he gravitated to the more grown-up twelve-inch long-player. These songs also carry a distinctive songwriting quirk that continued throughout his career, eschewing middle eights for straightforward verse/chorus economy.

'The middle eight and the bridge are designed as relief from the repetitive nature of another verse, and then another verse and then another verse,' says Mick Harvey, who spent many hours taking Gainsbourg's songs apart and putting them back together again. 'And he just doesn't use it because he makes the melody good enough that you don't get bored of it. I think that's a very deliberate decision by him: *I don't need to do that, it's bullshit.* If it's strong enough ...'

Bertrand Burgalat, the orchestral arranger on Harvey's first two Gainsbourg albums, was surprised when he noticed Gainsbourg's bridge aversion: 'When I got to work on those songs, it was something I'd never spotted before. Because that guy wanted to be so efficient and straight to the point: little intro, verse, chorus, second verse, chorus, maybe a little instrumental part, final chorus ... incredible!'

Gainsbourg was paralysed by his own lack of self-confidence when he demoed the tracks on piano, many of which had been written in the first place for Left Bank chanteuse Michèle Arnaud. Arnaud was the first to identify the makings of a rich talent. She discovered Lucien was writing songs on the quiet and coaxed them out of him, finding they were surprisingly good. He was a married man at that point, but he was surreptitiously obsessed with the singer. She showed an interest in his songwriting prowess, and evidently saw herself as a 'big sister' figure.

Nine years his senior, Arnaud was out of his league. She attained two degrees in philosophy, had represented Luxembourg at the first Eurovision Song Contest in 1956, and an illustrious career in production for television lay ahead once she finished her studies. Arnaud was Serge's earliest musical champion, and she would continue to bolster his career throughout the 60s as a TV producer. She would later persuade the film director Pierre Koralnik to put him up after he left his second wife, Françoise-Antoinette Pancrazzi (known as Béatrice), in 1966. Béatrice was an Italian heiress who gets short shrift in the Gainsbourg story on account of the fact she was, by most accounts, pathologically jealous.

In the tell-all memoir *Lise et Lulu*, named after their nicknames, his first wife, Elizabeth 'Lise' Levitsky, paints a picture of Arnaud as an adversary vying for Lucien's attention. According to Levitsky, Lulu (she always called him Lulu) goes from being, in Arnaud's eyes, 'the little pianist who accompanies me' to 'the nice pianist who is in love with me'. One night, Levitsky is thrown out of the Milord for mocking François Mitterand, who turns up to watch Arnaud sing. The future president of France is a high-ranking politician in the war cabinet during the Algerian conflict. Mitterand drools and Lise openly laughs at him. She soon has her collar felt. Lucien stays put while his wife is sent packing.

Lise is from the period of Gainsbourg's life where the desire to be a famous painter possesses him. She and Lucien met at art school in 1948, and he had been very clear of his ambitions from the beginning. 'Lulu is convinced that he will be the greatest artist of the century, that he will go down in history. I'm just as sure of it as he is, by the way,' she writes.* And Arnaud represents the *chanson*—a very different, less solitary world that threatens to steal him away from her. While Lise is in the audience at the Milord one night, listening to Arnaud singing Serge's composition 'La recette de l'amour fou', she is taken aback by the finale, with a lyric that roughly translates as 'get the fuck out of here'. Lise has an epiphany at that moment and decides to get the fuck out of the Milord, and Lucien's life, once and for all.

Back to that afternoon in February '58, and despite his obvious nerves, Gainsbourg's audition at Studio Philips was a hit with recording executives. Listening to the demos now, it's striking how together they were before the orchestral arranger Alain Goraguer brought his consummate contribution to

---

* 'Lulu est persuadé qu'il sera le plus grand artiste du siècle, qu'il entrera dans l'histoire. J'en suis tout aussi certaine que lui, d'ailleurs.' Elisabeth 'Lise' Lévitzky with Bertrand Dicale, *Lise et Lulu* (First, 2010)

the songs. The first recorded fruits of his musical endeavours come almost fully formed, with cascading jazz piano and his voice sounding strong despite any wobbles. The striking saxophone and twangy guitar narrative is missing from 'Le poinçonneur des Lilas', but Serge's busy piano plays most of the parts that will eventually make it onto the record. A faint double bass, presumably by a session man, can be heard too. The half-hearted attempt at rock'n'roll on 'Ronsard 58' would later be smoothed out by Goraguer. The swift tempo changes in 'La recette de l'amour fou'—the first of his songs interpreted by Arnaud—are all present and correct, and 'Douze belles dans la peau'* benefits from not having a novelty hoedown violin at its conclusion, like on the record—a moment on the first album that smacks of farce.

Goraguer had been working as an arranger with Boris Vian before he met Gainsbourg properly, and it appeared to make sense for them to work together, a partnership that lasted for six years despite some bad feeling about the fact Gainsbourg was parsimonious with his accreditation. 'Goraguer was basically a very nice man who was affiliated with Boris Vian,' the revered arranger Jean-Claude Vannier told me when I met him at the Place des Vosges near his home in Paris in 2019. Vannier was Gainsbourg's musical foil on *Histoire de Melody Nelson*, among other collaborative works. 'Vian is very famous in France, and he was a very good writer, musician, and poet. Gainsbourg asked Goraguer to work with him through that association. From then on Serge was a little dishonest.† Goraguer said Gainsbourg was dishonest with him, so he went away.'

'He liked the idea of going with the trend, and exploring all these black music ideas,' says Bruno Blum, who created dub remixes of all of Gainsbourg's reggae songs in 2003. 'So he probably would say, I want some merengue, or do something Cuban, or do a samba, while he was focusing on the songwriting. So he gave his arrangers a direction, but he didn't do it himself. In fact, Alain

---

* 'Douze belles dans la peau' is a pun on the idiomatic 'douze balles dans la peau'—or twelve bullets in the skin—dating back to the Napoleonic wars.

† Vannier used the French word 'malhonnete'.

Goraguer, who was his arranger for years, complained a lot that he never got the credit for the music that was his.'

Goraguer had first noticed Serge by chance at the piano while on vacation in 1956, observing him playing to a room full of holidaymakers in a northern French resort. Serge stuck out from all the other pianists. He told Gilles Verlant, 'I was at Le Touquet as a tourist and I took an apéritif and there he was sitting outside playing the piano. Usually you don't notice a bar pianist unless they play very well or very badly. But I noticed him because of the choice of his songs, which were nothing but very beautiful American standards sung in a very murmured way. And I was struck by his face … he had an air of real melancholy.'*

As well as working with Gainsbourg and Vian, Goraguer has provided sweeping musical landscapes for Nana Mouskouri, Sasha Distel, Jean Ferrat, and many others, and he's been known to release the odd novelty record too: 1976's 'Sexy Dracula' by Monsieur Goraguer was a cult hit in Japan. His arrangements and the role of *Alain Goraguer et son orchestre* cannot be underplayed where Serge's early career is concerned, especially as he wrote much of the material. The credits don't do him justice, and this was the case for most of the arrangers Gainsbourg worked with.

Goraguer is officially ascribed as composer on 'Indifférente', which may leave you feeling just that on a first listen, but a closer examination reveals some of Serge's best lines, including the glibly hilarious 'In your eyes I see my eyes … It gives you a glimmer of intelligence'† and the oft quoted 'Whatever the weather, whatever the wind, better your absence than your indifference'.‡ He also gets a credit for 'Les femmes c'est du Chinois', which features some

* 'J'étais au Touquet en touriste, je prends l'apéro et lui etait la, en plein air, avec son piano. Souvent, un pianiste de bar, on ne le remarque pas, a moins qu'il ne joue très bien, ou très mal. Mais lui, je l'avais remarqué a cause du choix de ses chansons, rien que de très beaux standards américains chantés d'une façon très murmurée, déjà. Et j'avais été frappé par son visage, son air de grande tristesse.' Gilles Verlant, *Gainsbourg* (Albin Michel, 2001)
† 'Dans tes yeux je vois mes yeux … ca te donne des lueurs d'intelligence.'
‡ 'Qu'importe le temps, qu'importe le vent, mieux vaut ton absence que ton indifférence.'

pentatonic scales in that lazy way records used to to denote that we're supposed to be somewhere vaguely in the Far East. (See also: Carl Douglas's 'Kung Fu Fighting', Aneka's 'Japanese Boy', David Bowie's 'China Girl', Siouxsie & The Banshees' 'Hong Kong Garden', Alphaville's 'Big In Japan', and so on.) Perhaps worse than the lazy orientalism, 'Les femmes c'est du Chinois' makes reference to Jujutsu and kimonos, both Japanese, sending a clear message that 'this'll have to do'.

Goraguer wasn't required for the stripped-back *Gainsbourg Confidentiel*, but he was back overseeing the Ethno-jazz experiments of *Gainsbourg Percussions*, and, significantly, he's the man responsible for those descending violins on 'Poupée de cire, poupée de son', France Gall's winning entry at the 1965 Eurovision Song Contest—written, of course, by Gainsbourg.

Alain Goraguer was supposed to be the first interviewee for this book. From a personal perspective it would have been gratifying not only to go tête-à-tête with a man who was there at the start of Gainsbourg's recording career, but also to meet the composer of the soundtrack to René Laloux's *La planète sauvage* (or *Fantastic Planet*) from 1973, which for my money is one of the finest symphonic rock scores ever composed and performed. I reached as far as the front door of Goraguer's second floor apartment in the sixteenth arrondissement, accompanied by Guillaume Le Disez from Les Disques Des Culte, acting as chaperone. Guillaume's label had issued Goraguer's last record, 2018's *Musique Classée X*, a compilation of funk soul tracks collected from pornographic films recorded during the 1970s. After the soft-core success of *Emmanuelle* in 1974, porn soundtracks became lucrative for French artists, and musicians got their action where they could, whether it was hard or soft. *Musique Classée X* is a collection of tracks from the sex films of Brigitte Lahaie— who would later go on to make a career as a controversial radio phone-in host in France. The tracks are named after their respective films: *Swinging Couples Cruise, Private Nurses, A Foreign Girl In Paris*, etc …

Sadly, Goraguer failed to answer the door. He didn't pick up the phone either. Guillaume put it down to the eighty-eight-year-old's deafness, and we had to trail away and grab a coffee around the corner to commiserate. What sense I would have gotten out of him it's difficult to say. I'd been warned that 'oui' and 'non' might be the best I could hope for, though either would have been better than an immovable door. For purely selfish reasons, a nod of the head, a handshake … these would have helped connect me to those early recordings.

*

Despite his lyrical dexterity and originality, the French music press at first wrote Gainsbourg off as a mini-matryoshka version of the gangling chanteur Philippe Clay, who had a hit with the tack-piano chanson 'La goualante du pauvre Jean' in 1954 and a similarly knockabout 'Le danseur de Charleston' the following year. Clay was six foot two to Gainsbourg's five foot nine, both men were Jewish, and it's true that there was a passing resemblance and their voices had a similar timbre. At worst, the inference was that there wouldn't be enough room for another Jew in the higher echelons of light entertainment. Vian said both men had a 'tense and biting quality', but for some there was no need for a counterfeit Clay with an existential twist.

The revue *Arts* didn't hold back, delivering perhaps the world's harshest backhanded compliment. Titled 'Gainsbourg: Uglier Than Clay', the piece read, 'Ears perpendicular to his head, huge eyelids, miserable arms … but as is the case with Philippe Clay, so much horror on the face highlights the singer's sensitive soul. This hack predicts that Serge will eventually become as famous as his song "Le poinçonneur des Lilas."'* In 1975, Clay recorded 'Les Juifs', a thoughtful riposte to antisemitism that imitated the casual racism he encountered and included lines like 'It's not that I don't like them, but …' and 'Well, what about Christ?'† Gainsbourg would challenge antisemitism in his own way years later.

'Le poinçonneur des Lilas' was a hit in as much as it gained Gainsbourg

---

* 'Gainsbourg: plus laid que Clay … Oreilles perpendiculaires à la tête, paupières énormes, bras misérables. Mais comme dans le cas de Philippe Clay, tant d'horreur sur le visage n'est faite que pour mieux montrer une âme sensible. Pourtant l'auteur prédit que Serge sera bientôt aussi célèbre que sa chanson Le poinçonneur des Lilas.' Gilles Verlant, *Gainsbourg* (Albin Michel, 2001)
† 'C'est pas qu'on ne les aime pas, mais …'; 'À propos … et le Christ?'

exposure, received radio play, and garnered a couple of jumpy television appearances, all despite its bleak subject matter. The lyrical inspiration came from a conversation Serge had with a ticket inspector working the Paris Métro. Having struck up a brief conversation, Gainsbourg casually asked him what he had planned for the rest of the day. The *poinçonneur*—or ticket puncher— quipped that his one aim was to 'see the sun'. The chanson became about a depressed underground employee who lives 'in the heart of the planet',* who never sees the sky and spends all day punching tiny holes in tickets while dreaming of punching a giant hole in his own head to end it all. 'Hello le soleil brille' by Annie Corby it isn't.†

It was quickly covered by Les Frères Jacques, a French barbershop quartet, and Hugues Aufray, a chansonnier and Spanish-language specialist who made a career out of covering Bob Dylan songs.‡

In Serge's early days as a performer, Hugues Aufray was that rarest of things: a Gainsbourg fanboy. Perhaps he was the first? He failed to communicate with the singer, not because of any language problems but because of shyness. Little by little, Julien Grix came out from behind the artist he was playing sideman to, and Serge Gainsbourg emerged tentatively into the spotlight. When he

---

* 'Je vis au cœur de la planète …'

† Annie Corby spent twenty-six weeks at no.1 in 1958 with 'Hello le soleil brille', a French version of a tune published in the first year of the World War I—'Colonel Bogey March'— perhaps made more famous by its cruder World War II iteration, 'Hitler Has Only Got One Ball'.

‡ Grateful that a Frenchman was covering his material, Dylan befriended Aufray, though their inability to communicate made this long-standing association awkward, according to Tony Frank, Gainsbourg's go-to photographer from the mid-60s through to the mid-80s: 'Sometimes Dylan plays in Paris and Hugo is like a child—he's ninety years old but he's a big fan where Dylan is concerned. We'd go backstage and say hello, and I think Dylan has had enough of it, because Hugo doesn't speak a word of English. He keeps whispering to me: *Say this to Bob*. And Dylan doesn't see many people. When he's finished singing he usually gets back on the bus. The last time we saw him was maybe fifteen years ago at the George IV, and Dylan, myself, and Aufray walked down Avenue Georges IV to the Seine; it was early evening and there was a lot of traffic. And Dylan said, I want to buy a house here. I told him I'd drive him around, but another time because there was too much traffic even to get a taxi. And then we went back to the hotel and we didn't see Dylan again.'

was onstage, Aufray would creep into the shows and mingle anonymously, scribbling down copious notes that he'd then take away and work out how to play for himself. His faithful rendition of 'Le poinçonneur des Lilas' is a testament to a pair of receptive ears. It's a chanson that mainly grew in status because of the number of versions that were made by other artists.

In 1978, Lyon-based punks Starshooter exemplified the blue-collar essence of the song with their angry, shouty version. Serge casting a critical eye over the insanity of the rat race might have seemed to the listener, as might some of the songs of Ray Davies, like the detached observations of a witty poet insulated from such toil himself. Starshooter brought something visceral to it, and the spiky London indie four-piece The Rakes transferred the action to the London Underground and renamed the song 'Just A Man With A Job' in 2006. As a group that sang a fair bit about the mundanity of one's *metier*, they brought some lower-middle-class veracity to it. I'm not saying I don't prefer Gainsbourg's version, I'm just saying it's hard to imagine him standing around gloomily punching tickets.

So why did Serge choose Lilas? It's a good question. One subconscious reason might be that the closest metro station to his family home on Avenue Bugeaud, Porte Dauphine at the conclusion of Ligne 2, is at the opposite end of the network to Mairie de Lilas at the terminus of Ligne 11, and therefore represents escape, or at least somewhere far enough away to project the fantasy of the song onto without straying from Paris itself. Another is that Gainsbourg was playing with the double meaning of 'lilacs', a colloquial nickname for *billets* because of their colour. Whatever the reason, Serge would no doubt be honoured and delighted to learn that a new station in Lilas, opening in 2023, will be called the Métro Serge Gainsbourg. A bronze statue has been mooted too.

The other classic song on *Du chant a la une! …* that has endured, despite its emo-like melancholy, is 'Ce mortel ennui' ('This Mortal Apathy'), a song with a slow-burning menace and stealthily addictive melody. A video for the song was shot by Radio Télévision Suisse, paying homage to new-wave auteur Alain Resnais's surrealist masterpiece *L'année dernière à Marienbad* (*Last days In Marienbad*), featuring lots of moody shots of models stood on steps and staircases looking in various directions. Filmed in 1965, it came some seven years after the song was first released, which is an impressive extended lead time compared with today's PR campaigning.*

'Ce mortel ennui' is a no-strings-attached manifesto, with the lone piano top line jarring with notes on the way down as if to signify the loveless humping that's in store if you get with Serge. It's lyrically misanthropic and borderline misogynist. In 1968, a compendium of Gainsbourg lyrics up to that point was published, a 'livre de chevet' or bedside book called *Chansons Cruelles*. He gifted a leather-bound book to Jane Birkin when they met, perhaps to annoy her or perhaps to impress her, or maybe a little of both. Once they'd got over their mutual enmity, he inscribed it with her middle name, Mallory, and wrote that it was missing a poem to 'Melodie Nelson', which he was yet to write.

Jane diligently sat down with a French dictionary to pore over his words. One wonders what she would have made of lines like 'Of course there's nothing to say horizontally / And we can't find anything to say vertically' from 'Ce mortel ennui'.† 'En relisant ta lettre' from *L'etonnant Serge Gainsbourg* certainly did impress Birkin, and I know this because she told me so. In the song, the protagonist receives an epistolary *cri de cœur* from a lover saying farewell, which he proceeds to pedantically tear apart, pointing out grammatical errors and misuses of punctuation. It's brutal but also wickedly amusing. 'En relisant ta lettre' is one of those songs that is sadly lost on many English-speaking listeners, whether performed by Serge or later by Barbara. Birkin tells me she feels her last important job on Earth is to find someone with the ability to translate into English Serge's *paroles*, so simple and yet so complex at the same time, without losing too many of the multiple meanings or the humour. She came up with a good example of his lyrical complexity, but not before conceding the difficulty of the task at hand.

'I tried to translate "Fuir le bonheur de peur qu'il ne se sauve" myself. I

---

* *L'année dernière à Marienbad* has influenced everyone from Federico Fellini to David Lynch, Karl Lagerfeld to Blur (the latter created a pristine pastiche for their 'To The End' video in 1994).
† 'Bien sûr il n'est rien besoin de dire á l'horizontale / Mais on ne trouve plus rien à se dire á la verticale.'

was stuck immediately. I wasn't able to do it. My brother Andrew had a son, Anno, who died. But before he died, I'd asked him to translate everything of Serge's, because he was a poet himself, and a rather *chivalresque* poet at that. So I thought, *He'll know how to translate Serge, being an adolescent*, and yet he was very worldly: he knew Shakespeare, he was very well-educated, and he'd be able to do it, but he didn't have enough time. The last album Serge wrote for me, *Amour des feintes*, means *love of feigning* in French, but it's also *love of the dead*. It referenced *Pavane pour une infante défunte* by Ravel, which was some of the music that Serge loved the most. That's why he's complicated, because it's love of feigning, love of the dead, and *infante défunte*. But someone could do it,' she adds, wondering how translators have brought Guillaume Apollinaire to life in English but haven't managed as easily with Serge.

'His lyrics have been translated in quite a beautiful way by some artists,' says Serge's daughter, Charlotte Gainsbourg, speaking on the phone from her home in New York, 'but I think you do miss out on the double meanings of some words. There's no way of transcribing it. But it's like translating poetry: you can come close, and it's the same for us when we read English poetry. So I think you miss out on some of the meaning, but I also think you can get a sense of who he was; his character, his past with his parent's immigration and the Jewish part of his life. I think everyone can understand that.'

*

'There's plenty of footage in the Inathèque of Gainsbourg standing very stiffly and singing into a skinny microphone and then getting off stage again in three minutes. He's not this master of the television yet,' says Jonathyne Briggs, French pop historian at Indiana University Northwest.[*] 'What's he doing here? He's not having much commercial success. But he's still being rolled out onto television when his records come out.'

---

[*] The Inathèque is the consultation service of the audio-visual archives of the Institut National de l'Audiovisuel, or INA. It was set up in 1974, and much of its archive material can be found online.

[41]

Du chant à la une! … didn't sell particularly well. The Academie Charles Cross saw its worth, though, awarding it the Grand Prix du Disque of 1959. Gainsbourg was clearly a rare and exciting talent with a great future ahead of him as a songwriter. He'd probably need to cheer up a bit, though. As Serge said himself, it was 'too dark and nobody wanted it around the house'.

He returned to Studio Blanqui in 1959 to record what Sylvie Simmons correctly describes as a mutant jazz record. The opener on *No.2.*, 'Le claqueur de doigts', slowly swings and smoulders, jiving and changing keys while fetishising that all-American invention, the jukebox. Alfred de Musset's 'La nuit d'Octobre' gets treated to flutes and brass and emphatic congas, a chapeau tipped to the literary greats distinguishing Gainsbourg at this point from all the cheap acrobats jumping on the yé-yé wagon—the bubblegum pop movement that sought to emulate *Les Beatles* with an inevitable, often feminized, French twist. Naturally, Serge would soon jump on the yé-yé wagon.

Elsewhere on the record there's mambo and cinematic jazz and big band and rock'n'roll, all audaciously fused together throughout. And on the cover, Serge leans nonchalantly with a gun and some roses, hinting that the man singing is a ladykiller, irrespective of those dumbo-ears. But the record-buying public remained largely unmoved. 'He's like the guy who's wandered onto the set, picked up the stuff and is pretending to be James Bond, but he's not James Bond,' says Jonathyne Briggs. 'But he will be James Bond.'

In 1960, Gainsbourg diversified slightly. The song 'L'eau à la bouche' came from the film of the same name, and it could be described as Gainsbourg's first proper hit, as well as his first foray into film, registering a respectable one hundred thousand sales. It'd be another nine years before he clocked up those kinds of figures again. It must have felt like a boon, a glimmer of hope that would turn out, as usual, to be a dying ember. What's more, he'd have to share the publishing with Goraguer, having tossed him a rare credit. It was money well spent, though, given that the door was now ajar, and Serge would take full advantage, writing soundtracks and asking for cameos that would take him to plenty of exotic locations around the world in the coming years.

A third album was released in 1961, but *L'étonnant Serge Gainsbourg (The*

Amazing Serge Gainsbourg) is sadly anything but. There's a chance the singer had had his head turned by film and took his eyes off the prize: as well as the *Eau à la bouche* soundtrack, he also wrote the music for *Les loups dans la bergerie* with Goraguer in 1960. These outings alerted the new-wave auteur François Truffaut to his talents, and Gainsbourg nearly ended up doing the music for *Jules et Jim*, though for whatever reason the job eventually fell to the composer Georges Delerue. Gainsbourg was suddenly very busy, playing residencies at the Milord and the Trois Baudets, and picking up an acting part in *La revolte des esclaves*—one of three sword-and-sandal pictures he'd do in his early career—playing a baddie. There was also a small role in *Voulez-vous danser avec moi?*, which is where he first met Brigitte Bardot.

Anyone coming to *L'étonnant …* via the mesmerising opener, 'La chanson de Prévert'—an elegiac waltz with duelling Spanish guitars set against Gainsbourg's dulcet croon—would have been sadly let down by an album of dolorous, mid-paced chansons. There are a plenitude of literary references and words purloined (Victor Hugo here, Gérard de Nerval there), and some uncharacteristically dreary crooning. Serge was being repositioned by his label at this stage as a brooding troubadour. The original cover even had the words 'great for dancing'—the handiwork of executive producer Jacques Plait, and a move that would have only intensified the feelings of anticlimax that lay ahead once the ten-inch hit the turntable. For 'La chanson de Prévert', Serge lifted words from the famous screenwriter and absurdist poet Jacques Prévert's *Les feuilles mortes*, as well as from Paul Verlaine's *Chanson d'automne*. Verlaine was dead, of course, so no permission was needed there; he did meet up with Prévert, and the pair got drunk together over some convivial breakfast champagne.

Short of material on an album with just eight tracks on it, Gainsbourg revived one of his very first compositions, 'Les amours perdues', which he'd originally written for Michèle Arnaud. And while the previously discussed 'En relisant ta lettre' lands a few glances, the overall mood is a little despondent, and some of the songs definitely feel phoned-in. There would be many a Gainsbourg album that would deserve the epithet *L'étonnant* in the future, though *L'étonnant Serge Gainsbourg* isn't one of them. At this point, he felt cut adrift from the concomitant yé-yé scene, a youthquake of French rock'n'roll in thrall to Britain and America. He was nearly a decade and a half older than the *jeunesse dorée*—Johnny Hallyday, Sylvie Vartan, Françoise Hardy—which was reason enough to reject what was emerging. *L'étonnant Serge Gainsbourg* is a doubling down on the traditions of la chanson variété—the weightier musical vernacular tradition in France that often prioritized poetic meaning over melody—referencing the literary greats and biting a thumb at the pernicious yanks. He's enthralled by America, too, but maybe he's also concerned that French culture is about to be washed away by the expanding cultural hegemony of the United States.

The monolithic culture of France began to change after World War II, opening up to outsider influences—especially American ones. Jazz couldn't just be jazz, though: it had to be intellectual, existential Left Bank jazz; rock'n'roll in the form of yé-yé might have been dumb, but it wasn't as dumb as its New World counterpart, and certainly not when Gainsbourg got on board. In cinema, Jean-Luc Godard would take the American gangster genre and help kickstart the *nouvelle vague* with *Breathless*. But why were young French people embracing ideas from elsewhere, when their parents and ancestors had always been so proudly and fiercely protectionist?

'For the want of a better expression, the French did not come off well at the end of the Second World War, despite their best propaganda efforts,' says Jonathyne Briggs. 'There was an insecurity about what the French had done during the war. A lot of them sat it out, or engaged in activities that they would rather have forgotten about. The generation that was coming up in the 50s and 60s—and you see this too in West Germany and Denmark and Norway, even—said, We're not going to have the same values as the older generation because to us they didn't really do what they were supposed to do. In America we call it the Greatest Generation, and in Britain too you celebrate the valour of surviving the Blitz and being the last bastion of democracy in Europe. They don't really have that in France, and so this opened the younger generation up to different cultural ideas and a quest for different cultural values.'

Another reason for this heightened American visibility was the financial capitulation of the French state. Up until World War II, the law decreed that only 188 non-French language films could be distributed in the country during any calendar year, and during the Occupation, nearly all of the films watched in France were French- or German-made. In 1946, in order to eradicate nearly three billion dollars in debt that the French had accumulated by borrowing from the Americans for war provision during two world wars, a treaty was signed between the two countries to open up the distribution channels, meaning more American goods could be sold in France: the Blum-Byrnes Agreement, which came two years ahead of the Marshall Plan, allowed more free-market competition, particularly within the film industry.

US movies would have more parity with domestic ones. France's impecunity after the war was suddenly held up in stark contrast to the glitz of Hollywood. The projection of wealth onto the screen would no doubt have had a giddying effect on theatre audiences living vicariously through the lives of their richer, more glamorous transatlantic cousins, and young French girls and boys began to covet an idealised lifestyle. Gainsbourg's nod to the literary greats was intended as a rejection of Anglophonic influences.

Serge said popular song was as pointless and decorative as jewellery, so bringing these giants of French culture into his work meant he was aspiring to elevate the popular song to something more worthy. He said himself that he had been called to activity as a reaction against 'the poverty of contemporary lyrics'. He felt it was his duty to write well, and he wasn't going to demean himself by reciting lowest common denominator glossolalia. There'd be plenty of time for that (and even Gainsbourgian glossolalia is smarter than most people's erudition). 'French chanson is not dead,' he was still telling people in 1963. On the show *Discorama* he informed Denise Glaser that 'it must evolve and not hitch itself to America's wagon'.[*]

'The *Anglais* don't really understand the heritage of the 50s and 60s in

---

[*] 'La chanson française n'est pas morte, elle doit aller de l'avant et ne pas être à la remorque de l'Amérique.' Gilles Verlant, *Gainsbourg* (Albin Michel, 2001)

France—the chansons and so forth—and Gainsbourg was a very clever writer,' says Jean-Claude Vannier. 'Serge's lyrics were incredible, but the English probably don't really get them. He mined the heritage of the nineteenth-century writers so well.'

When Gainsbourg and Vannier worked together in the 1970s, they held up one chanson as a benchmark by which everything else should be judged. '"Les petits pavés" was a very nice song because of the lyrics,' he says, 'and Serge and I, when we were writing a song, we'd always asked ourselves, Is it as good as "Les petits pavés"?'

Vannier is correct. It is hard for a *rosbif* to figure out what it is exactly about 'Les petits pavés' that elevates this premeditated murder ballad above other chansons, although one assumes it was extremely daring performed during the *Belle Époque* when it was written. Claude Nougaro—a popular crooner in the early 1960s—performed it, as did Prévert-interpreting, high-minded chanteuse Cora Vaucaire. There's footage of Serge singing it on television in 1962, looking more awkward than usual in a mask and dinner suit, wielding a cane like Arsène Lupin, 'the gentleman burglar', as part of a cabaret setting intended to evoke the Roaring Twenties. Nope, me neither. There's probably little for the Anglophonic listener beyond curiosity value watching Serge performing 'Les petits pavés' at a masked ball, and the same is even more true of Claude Nougaro. It's a part of French culture that we'll probably just have to take Vannier's word on.

'Claude Nougaro was an artist who did jazz in French using very literate lyrics,' says Bruno Blum. 'I never quite liked Nougaro, but he was very good at what he was doing. And there were others, too, but Serge Gainsbourg's power came from his main influence, which was Boris Vian. Gainsbourg and Vian both transmitted a love of the French language. It's easier to sing black American music in English—it's truly a challenge to do it in French.'

*

The year 1962 saw the release of the fourth and final ten-inch record, imaginatively titled *No. 4*. If Gainsbourg had dropped the ball with the previous record, this was a scintillating return to form, though the music-buying public remained just as disinterested. It opens with a minimalist sea shanty, 'Les goëmons', which is the French word for seaweed, though the lyrics are more metaphorical and poetic than the irritating marine algae might imply. There's a droning, slightly mystical energy to the song, and it again proves Gainsbourg was unafraid to try something different.

'It's not a famous one … it's one of the older ones, but the melody and the words always really touch me,' says SebastiAn, the Franco-Serbian Ed Banger producer and foil to Charlotte Gainsbourg on her brilliant 2017 album *Rest*. 'In the lyrics he talks about floating around in the sea like a piece of seaweed; it's poetic and very, very sad, but there's this glimmer of hope too. I really, really love this song. And there's something oriental sounding with violins or strings which perhaps comes from his Russian or Slavic background. It keeps appearing in his music and I love it.'

The music journalist Yves Salgues was also a fan of 'Les goëmons', which touched him on a spiritual level in the most dramatic fashion. 'One particularly hot summer, I almost died at the cold end of a course of self-annihilation,' he wrote in 1989, giving an honest account of his life-threatening addiction to drugs. 'The kidneys were blocked, my breathing sagged, and the heart pump was only sending weakened pulses into my blood flow. I was only a few seconds away from the eternal night. Then I was resuscitated with a dose of morphine that would have killed a dray horse with immediate effect.'* The ambient qualities of 'Les goëmons' and the familiarity of Serge's voice brought him sustenance in that moment of near dispatch.

Opener 'Baudelaire' offers a tantalising glimpse into the future as Serge speaks the words from the poet's 'Le Serpent qui danse', dropped over bossa-

---

* 'Un été particulièrement caniculaire, je faillis mourir au terme frileux d'une cure d'anéantissement. Les reins s'étant bloqués, ma respiration s'affaissent et la pompe du cœur n'envoyait plus dans ma géographie sanguine que des pulsations ralenties. J'étais à quelques poignées de secondes de la nuit éternelle. L'on me réanima avec une dose de morphine telle qu'elle eût abattu sur-le-champ un cheval percheron.' Yves Salgues, *Gainsbourg ou la provocation permanente* (JC Lattès, 1989)

flavoured, easy-listening bars, not growled or lascivious or close enough to the microphone to trigger autonomous sensory meridian response but half-whispered nonetheless, some six years before he'd begin to adopt this kind of delivery as his calling card. 'Baudelaire' was also the final redouble on French literary heritage in a last-ditch attempt to stave off the American invasion. Charles Pierre Baudelaire was an important reference point for Gainsbourg: the poet's *Les fleurs du mal* explores decadence and eroticism, two of his favourite subjects, and even Serge's appropriation of lines from *The Raven* much later in the song 'Initials B.B' relates back to Baudelaire, who was Edgar Allen Poe's first French translator. It's as if he's waving into the past to a fellow rapscallion, identifying a lineage from him to the symbolists that he hopes will continue against the onslaught of globalisation.

Elsewhere, 'Black Trombone', is a parpy, breezy number with a swing beat and delicate brushes. The tipsy brass call-and-response juxtaposes against Gainsbourg's lyrical bleak beauty: 'Black trombone / Monotone / It's the autumn of my life / Most people don't surprise me / I'm giving up / It's over.'[*] And then, on 'Quand tu t'y mets' ('When You Get Down To It'), he's enticed into bed by rock'n'roll and seduced once and for all, and he likes it so much that he follows it up with 'Requiem pour une twister', a double-bass slapping, snare thwacking, North American slang-copping two fingers to *l'Académie Française*, the preeminent council concerned with preservation of the language.

No.4 signals that the future might not be jazzy. The playful fusion of styles demonstrates a yearning to explore and exploit the new pop wave then enveloping France. Jazz will always remain Gainsbourg's first love, even if he plays it less and less as time goes by. It's interesting to imagine where he might have gone had he not jumped ship and continued to play within the same genre, evolving as jazz itself evolved. Might he have made an avant-garde jazz record like Miles Davis? Or imitated the spiritual jazz of Alice Coltrane or Don Cherry? Transcendental Gainsbourg is a tantalising idea, and one that

---

[*] Black trombone / Monotone / C'est l'automne de ma vie / Plus personne ne m'étonne / J'abandonne / C'est fini.'

requires a stretch of the imagination, though his lack of political will and distrust of spirituality might have deterred him from going down that route. It's academic anyway—on his next record he'd strip jazz down to its essentials, and then he'd move away almost entirely from it, save for a few tracks on *Gainsbourg Percussions*. He'd need other genres to help him to get to where he wanted to go, and he'd need other people, too, to project him into the spotlight. Women, mostly.

'In his early jazz career he's copying people around him and trying to find his style,' says Jonathyne Briggs. 'Especially in his piano playing style, he's trying to fit in a little bit. He's obviously very interesting lyrically and has this instantly recognisable lyrical style, but in terms of his music, I think those early albums are a lot of failed attempts to be innovative in ways that he couldn't quite manage yet. It was when he started to write for other people that he began to take off and become an in-demand songwriter, such as with France Gall.'

If the first four records are perceived as stepping stones, a metamorphosis as Gainsbourg finds his way as a performer, those albums still have plenty to recommend them, and they're not without their fans, either. 'I really love the jazz period of Gainsbourg,' says Hervé Carvalho of Acid Arab. 'I just love the vibe of *No.4*, I like his voice, and I like the lyrics.' His bandmate, Guido Minisky, says it wasn't until he heard the jazz records that he realised Gainsbourg was truly gifted. 'When I was sixteen and I was looking at him on TV and thinking, *Who is this old, fucking disgusting guy? Why? Why?* Then in the late 80s they released this huge box set of all his music, and for my generation it was the first time we heard something different than the hits of that period. It was a real shock. When you heard his young voice on jazz music and listened to his first lyrics, which were so great, slowly, a lot of people from my generation started to realise, *So it's true, he really is a genius. It's not just something older guys say.*'

The bellicose publicity machine Gainsbourg would later become is a far cry from those edgy performances where he's standing hoping the ground will somehow envelope him. 'But he was good at it!' argues Johnny Hostile, the

French musician and Savages producer. 'People say he wasn't good to begin with, but even in those days it was interesting seeing him being shy and a bit gloomy, you know? He was the only one doing that.'

'When he started out, his hair was clipped very short to his head, so he had big sticky-out ears that looked quite funny,' says Jacqueline Ginsburg. Jacqueline is Serge's older sister, born in 1926, who we'll meet properly in the next chapter. Did she think he'd become a legend of French pop? 'Not at all! I was really surprised. He started writing songs and was suddenly appearing on television, but he was thirty years old by then. I thought he was going to be a painter, so it was a complete surprise to me ...'

Later, Jacqueline dropped me a mail to clarify her thoughts on how she felt about her brother's potential all those years ago: 'But as soon as we heard his first songs, we found them extraordinary.'

2

PERFORMANCE

GAINSBOURG CONFIDENTIEL (1963)

[I think I have the soul of a teenager. It's this weakness that makes me strong.*]

Juliette Gréco cut a dash on the Parisian scene in the post-war years. Her bohemian aura and rich contralto captivated everyone from Germanopratin intellectuals to members of The Beatles. She was a muse of Cocteau's and a lover of Miles Davis's, and Jean-Paul Sartre said her voice contained 'millions of poems not yet written'.† Looking back in 1982, Gréco admitted to being aware of the seductive powers she exuded: 'In my tight black dress with my hair undone and my deep voice, I was a violent image, a scandal … forbidden!'‡ It's perhaps unsurprising, then, that Gainsbourg was a little fazed when he was invited around one evening to her home at 33 Rue de Verneuil.

Gréco and Gainsbourg would eventually become neighbours. In 1962, their mutual respect and awkward acquaintance would yield one of the finest numbers in the whole of the Gainsbourg songbook, after a night of heavy drinking and dancing to classical music. Gréco had an eye for interesting

---

* 'Je pense que j'ai l'âme d'un adolescent. C'est cette faiblesse qui fait ma force.' Serge Gainsbourg, *Pensées provocs et autres volutes* (Librairie Générale Française, 2007)

† 'Gréco a des millions dans la gorge : des millions de poèmes qui ne sont pas encore écrits, dont on écrira quelques-uns.' Jean-Paul Sartre, in the sleeve notes to *Juliette Gréco chante ses derniers succès*, for her first 33⅓ LP, from in 1952.

‡ 'Dans ma robe noire moulante, les cheveux défaits, la voix grave, je suis une image violente, un scandale, un interdit!' Jonathan Faiers (ed.), *Colors in Fashion* (Bloomsbury Academic, 2016)

young songwriters and had recorded an EP of Serge's earlier work. *Juliette Gréco chante Gainsbourg* from 1959 was made up of chansons that had already been recorded by Michèle Arnaud: 'Il était une oie …,' 'Les amours perdues', 'L'amour à la papa', and 'La jambe de bois (Friedland)'. Gréco, Gainsbourg, and some friends downed champagne at her soiree and danced into the night. That could have been the end of an uninteresting story, but the following day, Serge popped around again with a bespoke three-minute masterpiece.

In 1954, while still operating under the nom-de-guerre Julien Grix, he'd been unable to disseminate his wares any further than the transvestite bars he played, like Madame Arthur, the underground cabaret joint where he'd started as a proxy for his pianist father. Now, suddenly, he was hanging out with *La Muse de l'Existentialisme*, drinking her bubbly and writing songs made to order. By 1962, he had some magnificent chansons under his belt, and Gréco's exquisite bohemian aura would help provide him with his most magnificent yet. Her classy rendition of 'La Javanaise' must have made him doubt his future as a performer. Michèle Arnaud had sung some of his songs beautifully, but Gréco slipped them on and wore them like mink. She purrs her way through 'La Javanaise' and is in no hurry to wrap things up, and nor is the listener.

When Serge recorded the song himself, with the Harry Robinson Orchestra, in 1963, they wisely differentiated his version from the one Gréco had started to perform by upping the syncopation and turning it into a more swaggering waltz with backing singers. On the same EP were versions of 'Vilaine fille mauvais garçon', which he wrote for Petula Clark; 'L'appareil à sous', which he wrote for Brigitte Bardot; and 'Un violon, un jambon', largely unloved by other artists and made two-years later into a corny western promo by Jean Bacqué, though why seems to be lost to the mists of time.

Another curiosity is the fact Harry Robinson made this record, rather than Serge's usual wingman, Alain Goraguer. Robinson started life as Harry Robertson but changed his name when he was paid a rather large cheque for an orchestration at a time when he was broke, and realised it'd be easier to change his name than get the cheque made out to the correct person. The Scot used both names during his career. Harry was an in-house arranger at the

Philips studio under Stanhope House next to Marble Arch, which Gainsbourg favoured and used for many sessions. Recording there in 1963 is earlier than many might have supposed, having assumed he'd been lured to London thanks to his relationship with Jane Birkin. One of the reasons French singers sought out studios in London was for its musicians; the other, less discussed reason, was for the hardware, much of which wouldn't have been available in Paris at that time.

'Take Rickenbacker guitars,' says Jonathyne Briggs. 'Young people in the suburbs just didn't have access to those. They weren't really imported into France because there wasn't considered to be a market there. So how did they make the sound of the Rickenbacker? And then, when people got successful enough, they'd either go to work in English studios, where they'd have access to all these things, or they'd get foreign producers to come over and bring some of these instruments with them.' Hardware limitations are not normally considered as a reason for the differing timbre of rock'n'roll and yé-yé records, but Briggs makes a valid point here. Gainsbourg still hadn't made the leap over to becoming a full-time yé-yé writer for hire yet, though casing out London studios and arrangers might suggest it's something he was considering when he entered Studio Fontana with Harry Robinson and Jacques Plait in January '63.

As for what was spoken between Serge and Juliette at 33 Rue de Verneuil that night, might I suggest that it was more argotic than erotic? When I spoke to Anna Karina at the Brasserie Vagenende in Saint-Germain in May 2019, she told me that Serge was a big fan of deploying dexterous wordplay from the streets, which would be used to confound the older generation, of which he was one. 'We had lots of fun speaking slang that nobody else could understand,' remembered the late, great *nouvelle vague* actress. 'Then we'd be laughing and screaming. With Gainsbourg it was always really very enjoyable.' There are many virulent strains of French street vernacular: *Louchébem* ('the Butcher's slang'), *Verlan* (where words are inverted), or their version of Pig Latin (where the syllables are transposed); Saint Denis street walkers became a *cause célèbre* in the 90s, when it had been proposed that they be moved on, mainly because Parsians wanted to preserve the exotic argots passed down through generations.

'La Javanaise' references the Java dance that was popularised in 1920s Paris. Its legend is enshrined in the beautiful art deco building La Java, a former haunt of Edith Piaf and Django Reinhardt, which lies tucked away down a staircase in the tenth arrondissement. Boris Vian's 'La Java Javanaise' from 1957 wouldn't have been impervious to Gainsbourg's ears, either; it was inspired by the *javanaise* argot that did the rounds in the 50s, where *ava* sounds are inserted between syllables to obscure meaning and create an indecipherable code for the uninitiated. Gainsbourg's 'La Javanaise' doesn't sunder any words, but it does use *av* as an assonant motif throughout.

Bruno Blum, who made dub versions of Gainsbourg's reggae songs and remixed and extended the 1979 live album *Enregistrement public au Théâtre Le Palace* for a 2006 re-release, explains, 'La Javanese is like Cockney rhyming slang, but you put *ava* between every syllable. You don't say *bonjour*, you say *bon-java-jour*. If you build a sentence doing this, no one understands what you're talking about, only the people who are conversant. It's a mental trick, and you have to practice it. If you listen to the song, he's got the syllable *av* all the way through, but he's not singing in the slang, he's using real words: *J'avoue j'en ai bavé pas vous, mon amour* … So it sounds a bit like Javanese, but it's really French. It's clever—it's typical of him doing really clever stuff. And so this is embedded in French culture now. Anyone who attempts a play on words in any way is going to be compared to Gainsbourg. It's been very influential in French songwriting for fifty years now.'

Gainsbourg uses repetition in the chorus, with the use of the reflexive verb *s'aimer* doing half the work for him. 'We are in love for the length of a song' is a winsome idea, but it sounds much prettier in French ('Nous nous aimions le temps d'une chanson.')

*

Serge looked to shake things up on 1963's *Gainsbourg Confidentiel,* a critically-acclaimed first full-length 33 1⁄3rpm album that sold just 1,500 copies on its release. Serge's new 30cm LP (we're dealing metrically, *naturellement*) stripped back the frills for a playful avant-jazz offering that sought to increase his own rhythmical language while daringly dispensing with the percussion and brass. *Confidentiel* is a transition album that barely gets talked about now, but it acted as a showcase for what Serge was capable of, ably backed by a crack duo of virtuoso musicians: the Hungarian gypsy-jazz guitar maestro Elek Bacsik (a cousin of Django Reinhardt), and the hardy, capable double bass exponent, Michel Gaudry. The trio provided Serge's newest songs with a slickness and intimacy, especially when performed live. Opener 'Chez les yé-yé' threw down a gauntlet—or perhaps threw in the towel—declaring his own version of Tin Pan Alley open for business:

> Neither the tom-toms of the yé-ye-ye,
> Nor the gris-gris that you wore,
> Or the 'Da Doo Ron Ron' that you listened to,
> At the Dunun ball where you hit the floor ...*

Serge had finally adopted the nonsensical language of the yé-ye, which in turn copied the repetitiousness of American rock'n'roll, but he was also deliberately referencing the charms and the hoodoo and the percussive instruments of Africa to infer that beneath the veneer of childish echolalia there'd be a deeper undercurrent of knowledge regarding where the music actually came from. It's a fascination that would lead him on a voyage of discovery into the heart of Africa on his next album, *Gainsbourg Percussions*, like one of his heroes, Arthur Rimbaud—and while he wouldn't be gun-running like the great symbolist poet (Rimbaud's last job before he died of gangrene aged thirty-seven), he would be making off with the sonic loot like a colonial frontiersman.

The extra layer that Gainsbourg added to many of his lyrics would often be lost on the audience—and sometimes on the singer, too. The most famous example of this came in 1966, when he gave the unsuspecting France Gall a

---

* 'Ni les tams-tams des yé-yé-yé-é
Ni les gris-gris que tu portais
Da doo ron ron que tu écoutais
Au bal doum doum où tu dansais.'

cutesy song full of innuendo in the priapic shape of 'Les sucettes'. Gall was reportedly mortified when she missed the double meaning of a song about sucking lollipops and being in the throws of ecstasy when the aniseed-scented goo hits the back of her throat.*

'Obviously, "Chez les yé-yé" is very rhythmically different from what he was doing before, but it's placing him lyrically in a different place too,' says Jonathyne Briggs. 'Rather than doing these character studies, he begins to inhabit the characters himself as a singer. That's the transition. On the surface it's jazzy, but it's really something else. He's no longer positioning himself as a chansonnier, a Brassens or a Léo Ferré, and instead he's trying to figure out something else to do. And when he sees these young people singing nonsense and making hit records he thinks, *I can do that.*'

Perhaps he sees a new artfulness in phonetic absurdities, as well as the potential to earn money for old rope—the early Dadaists at the Cabaret Voltaire were no strangers to echolalia, after all. 'He finds a voice that is a lot more playful,' says Briggs. 'He's not playful on his earlier records. They're very serious records, and he's singing about serious subjects. Here there's a tension between trying to be playful and serious, so this is why *Gainsbourg Confidentiel* is such a weird transition record.'

'Chez les yé-yé' also sees the emergence of a *Lolita* figure, and she will come to feature in, and define, so much of Serge's work in various forms. He makes no secret of his love for the novel by Vladimir Nabokov, or the Kubrick film version, which came out in France in 1963. He begins to pepper his work with more contemporary references, too, while his formal, superannuated dress sense lags behind, and he has the air of a square older boy playing a song from the hit parade on the church organ when the vicar is out of earshot. During a video for 'Scenic Railway', directed by Léo Quoilin, he climbs a staircase in a stiff shirt, loafers, blazer, and chinos. He cuts an avuncular figure, ill at

---

* 'Parfumé à l'anis
Coule dans la gorge d'Annie
Elle est au paradis …'

ease as Gaudry's bass wanders and Bacsik's hallucinatory guitar at the end of each verse threatens to take us to flashback. In the song, he chases the girl in question all the way to the Russian Mountains, but here, without any kind of budget, the spiral staircase would have to do.

There's another reason for Serge's discomfort. A certain prop is conspicuous by its absence throughout the clip. As Gainsbourg slowly ascends the stairs it becomes evident that he doesn't have a cigarette in hand. There's little footage anywhere of Serge without cigarettes, but here we have a full two and a half minutes of sharp relief for his besieged lungs.

The art critic Franck Maubert later commented on the fact that Serge was without a cigarette at the Louvre when the pair visited the museum together. 'He had spent thirteen years of his youth dreaming of being a painter,' he writes in *Gainsbourg à rebours*. 'He suggested that we go together to the Louvre, where, as an apprentice painter, he copied masterpieces. Once at the museum, he could easily deprive himself of cigarettes.' The absence of smoking tobacco is such that it deserves comment, as does Gainsbourg's immense knowledge of the Louvre's interior. 'He noted how certain works had been moved from other rooms, as well as the absence of others. He was inexhaustible, bewitching. He amazed me.'*

In another Léo Quolin video likely shot on the same day, Serge has taken off his blazer and is standing in someone's front room, lamenting the passing of the yoyo while reluctantly accepting that the time of the yé-yés is upon us (the bubblegum pop fad would soon fade, while the toys of antiquity would enjoy a huge seventies resurgence). 'Le temps des yoyos' is a maudlin number, but more upbeat and fun is 'Elaeudanla Téïtéïa', a phonetic reimagining of the name 'Laëtitia', who Serge is pining for as he taps out her name over and over on a Remington typewriter. His playfulness with words even stretches as far as playing with the letters within the words themselves.

---

* 'Il avait passé treize ans de sa jeunesse à rêver d'être peintre. Très vite il m'a proposé que nous allions ensemble au Louvre, là où, apprenti peintre, il exécutait des copies. Au musée, il pouvait bien se priver de clopes. Il notait le changement de salle de certaines œuvres, l'absence d'autres … Intarissable, comme envoûté. Il m'épatait.' Franck Maubert, *Gainsbourg à rebours* (Fayard, 2013)

It's this playfulness that inspired the singer/songwriter Francois Guernier to devise a theatre show called *Gainsbourg For Kids*, where children get to sing along to the songs of Gainsbourg. My first thought when discovering this troupe was in existence was that his songs would be wholly unsuitable for children, but then I remembered the 'Shebam! Pow! Blop! Whizz!' onomatopoeia of 'Comic Strip' and I began to revise these initial assumptions. Songs in the set include 'Harley Davidson', 'L'ami caouette', 'La jambe de bois (Friedland)', and 'Elaeudanla Téïtéïa'.

Guernier tells me by email that none of the lyrics have been changed, though obviously songs like '69 année érotique' don't quite make the cut. Was Gainsbourg a naughty boy himself, I ask Francois? 'At the core of his work,' he writes back, 'one can imagine or perceive an injured child.' I then ask if the show is provocative, but without the obvious adult themes. 'Our show is not at all provocative,' he says. 'Above all, it's unifying.' I wonder if there are cultural differences that would make singing certain songs more acceptable to French children than their English counterparts. I sense a tone of annoyance from Guernier's follow-up reply: 'No, this show is really intended for all children, and I repeat, there is nothing provocative about it.'

One of the more curious tracks on *Confidentiel* is 'No, No Thanks, No', an ironic ode to abstinence, written with a simple, hymnal backing that evokes the prairie songs of rattlesnake-dodging, foot-washing protestants, with a chord progression worthy of Tom Waits. 'No, No Thanks, No' joins 'Le talkie-walkie', 'Scenic Railway', 'Negative Blues', and 'Maxim's'* (with a possessive apostrophe), signifying English-language armageddon is upon us. Serge might have seen himself as the heir to *poètes maudits* like Baudelaire, but he doesn't appear to be shackled to French in the way that many of his literary songwriting contemporaries are—a contributing factor to his international popularity where so many gallic chansonniers are dismissed, perhaps?

---

* Maxim's is named after a plush, pricey *art nouveau* restaurant that was a favourite of Serge's. He and Birkin made friends there after a fraught first week of filming for *Slogan*, and later Birkin would be rumbled stealing cutlery while the pair were on a date (the knives and forks tumbled out of her wicker basket when she put it down to sign an autograph).

'There were the serious dudes like Léo Ferré and Georges Brassens who were literary figures, but nobody outside of France really cares about the music or talks about it,' says Chilly Gonzales. 'The melodies aren't necessarily banging pop melodies as we'd conceive them. They're literary figures and troubadours, lyrics first 100 percent. And then there was novelty music, which might incorporate *en fait la twist* or some such shit. Gainsbourg kind of married those two, and that's why it's more fun to listen to. You hear his playfulness with the words without having to understand it, and he sacrifices the literary quality so that it would just be super-playful, fun, and hitting you in a way that goes straight to your child's mind. The literary stuff can't translate well to a foreign audience with a lack of melody and groove as well, because the literary writers aren't really concerned with groove either. At best, there's a lilting waltz by Brassens or something, but it's not party music, it's not fun. So the fact Gainsbourg can internalise the aspects of American music that are all about fun, groove, party, catchy, and be just literary enough to have the respect of that audience as well, was a masterstroke that made him.'

*

Serge Gainsbourg was born Lucien Ginsburg at 4:55am on April 2 1928 at Hôtel Dieu, Paris, to Olga and Joseph Ginsburg, two Russian émigrés who'd crossed the Mediterranean from Istanbul to the port of Marseille seven years earlier. They came from what is now the Ukraine, East Slavic Ashkenazi Jews who'd fled pogroms and persecution before eventually arriving safely in Paris. The Ginsburgs would enjoy nearly two decades of peace before persecution would pursue them again, though a young Lucien experienced antisemitism at school, from his contemporaries and more often his teachers. In a perverse way, Serge must have benefited as a songwriter from his feelings of outsiderdom, even if he would have preferred acceptance from his peers and his professors at the time.

'And maybe this is where the Ukranian thing comes into it,' says Gonzales, real name Jason Beck, who is the son of Ashkenazi Jews who were forced to flee to Canada from Hungary during World War II. 'He wasn't actually French in the same way that Azanavour wasn't French, and so he was constantly out to prove himself as an outsider. Often, it's foreigners and immigrants who have a certain kind of drive, and I saw that with my dad. It's a kind of drive that isn't there when you're a few generations in, and perhaps that enabled him to somehow internalise something about American music and also the literary tradition which other singer songwriters were unable to do so well, except in a very superficial way.'

Gainsbourg's parents met and fell in love in the Crimean Black Sea town of Feodosia in 1915, when Joseph was hired to give Olga singing lessons. He was two years her junior, and accordingly Olga always maintained a subtle seniority in their relationship. The course of true love certainly wouldn't run smooth, as was the case with many young couples during the war years. They'd be forced to take a long, arduous, and sometimes dangerous journey across Europe, but not before Olga—or Olia as she was nicknamed—had moved to Petrograd in 1917, to serve at the newly opened Anglo-Russian Hospital (the Tsarina Alexandra and two of her daughters had attended the opening ceremony the year before). Olga managed to find Joseph work at the hospital as a secretary, and her then-seventeen-year-old boyfriend had to travel for three days and nights by train in his music student's uniform with one loaf of bread to keep him going. 'Bolshevik and Menkovic soldiers would come onto the train looking for young men to kill,' Serge's surviving sister, Jacqueline Ginsburg, tells me. 'My father hid himself under the dress of a peasant woman who took pity on him.'

Joseph Ginsburg and Olia Besman were married in Petrograd, the former St Petersburg, in 1917. It would soon become Leningrad, following the October Revolution. A prewar boom had attracted investors to the city, but the disparity of wealth under the Tsar had created societal divisions and desperation among the proletariat, with long queues for food for the poor and high culture for the rich. Jacqueline: 'In Petrograd, people were suffering from hunger, typhus, and cholera, and my parents' wedding meal consisted of potatoes and some meat taken from the officer's canteen. But people continued to go to the opera to hear Feodor Chaliapine singing Boris Godunov with the sound of gunfire in the background. How very romantic!'

Once the Communists had toppled the Tsar, the Ginsburgs fled the city and returned to the Crimea in order to prepare to go west. They sailed to Batoum, Georgia, where they stayed for more than a year, with Joseph making money playing in bars, and they then headed on to Constantinople, where they found life difficult. 'Crossing the Black Sea was extremely dangerous at the time,' says Jacqueline, 'because there were so many pirates. Turkey was full of refugees, and making a new life there was impossible, so they managed to forge some documents and head for Marseille to seek refuge.'

They arrived in Paris in 1921. It was a city that it made sense for them to seek refuge in, given that Olga already had a brother there, working for the Louis Dreyfus Company transporting cereals and grains. Quickly their lives changed beyond all recognition as they entered into *l'esprit du temps* during what was a cultural boom time for the city. 'Joseph found cabarets to play piano and earn his living in while Olga spent her time visiting exhibitions, going to concerts, and seeing ballet. At this time, Paris was the artistic centre of the world, with Diaghilev and the Ballets Russes and the whole avant-garde scene,' says Jacqueline. The Ginsburgs lived in working-class Menilmontant in the contemporarily 'bobo' eleventh arrondissement, not far from Joseph's idol, Frédéric Chopin, reposing in the nearby Père Lachaise Cemetery. They would move to Rue Chaptal when Lucien was four, in closer proximity to the bars Joseph played at in the evenings.

Ginsburg's first born sadly died in infancy. 'We lost our oldest brother, Marcel,' says Jacqueline. Marcel Ginsburg was born in 1922 and died of bronchitis when he was eighteen months old. 'I arrived in 1926, and then our mother fell pregnant again, though my parents didn't want more children at that time. And so, out of desperation, she visited an abortionist. The twins, Liliane and Lucien, nearly never arrived, though Olia saw the rusty instruments and squalor and couldn't go through with it. The doctor then informed her that two babies were on the way. In 1928, Liliane arrived first, and my mother started crying, *I'm going to have two daughters!* And then Lucien popped his head out.'

A picture of little Lucien hangs on the wall of Jacqueline's apartment, behind the family's grand piano. The chubby-cheeked devil is aged nine, and he's sat attentively on the edge of a table with a book in his lap, his famous ears protruding from under a neat side-parting. Adorning the piano in the room are music scores and publicity pictures for Charlotte and Jane. The interior is decorated throughout in rich, comforting autumnal browns and oranges, with artefacts of French pop history dotted around the place: Serge's guitar which he played at the Milord; a ceramic pot under a coffee table that he gave to Jacqueline on her wedding day in 1945, with a painting on the pot of her and her husband, the family resemblance between Lucien and a young Jacqueline unmistakable. There's also a self-portrait hanging in the hallway of Serge aged nineteen, looking quizzically out from the watercolour as if posing for a selfie. The portrait was restored by specialists at the French National Museums and exhibited at a big Gainsbourg exhibition at Cité de la Musique in 2008. It now lives in Jacqueline's hallway, on the way to the kitchen.

In 1946, the Ginsburgs moved from 11 bis Rue Chaptal in the ninth arrondissement to Avenue Baugard in the sixteenth, a sign that Joseph was going up in the world as a night-time minstrel.* The family stayed at this address for years, and Serge would spend time there even after he moved out and got married (twice). Brigitte Bardot often visited the apartment during their affair, and she got on famously with the family. Jacqueline reacquired the apartment in 1986 and has been living here ever since. When I contact Jacqueline via email, she's immediately witty and likeable, and clearly in possession of all her marbles. ('Cher Jeremy,' she writes, 'I'm not sure why we say *cher* when I haven't met you, but we shouldn't dispense with convention I suppose.') Her stipulation for a visit is clear, and I never question the reason why: Jacqueline tells me I'm welcome provided I don't bring a tape machine or record the conversation. I'm forced to scribble notes in French as best I can with a pencil, though about halfway through Jacqueline takes pity on me and breaks into perfect English now and again when she sees I'm struggling.

By Parisian standards it's not a small flat, though the grand piano is the

---

* 'Bis' denotes a partition at a French address, so 5 bis would be the equivalent of 5a in Britain.

unmistakable centrepiece of the lounge, taking up a good deal of the space. 'We all played the piano,' says Jacqueline. 'I felt so sorry for the neighbours! Our father would have the three of us playing one after the other, throughout the day, and our neighbour would suffer it out. But if we went a minute past ten o'clock at night he'd be banging on the door.' Tales of Joseph's authoritarian piano lessons are legendary. 'We'd always have a hanky at the ready because lessons with our father were tough. I was the best player amongst us, which meant I got into trouble the least.' Joseph schooled his younglings with classical heavyweights—the preludes and the etudes of Chopin, and the avant-gardism of Igor Stravinsky. Away from his father, Serge secretly enjoyed the uncomplicated chansons of Charles Trenet—a big formative influence—and those of the chanteuse Fréhel, who he met once when she was wandering out of a bar.

'Learning the piano for him was a very traumatic episode in his life,' says Charlotte Gainsbourg. 'His father taught him classical piano, and it was torture for him. He always shared the memories of having to sit down at the piano with his father, which always ended in tears. He hated everything about it, but he then—as his father had—became a pianist in bars.' Serge would be bullied as he attempted to scale the heights of Beethoven, Bach, and Mozart, and he admitted in an interview in 1989 that when he stayed awake composing until his fingers bled, it would bring back memories of the pain inflicted on him by his father as a little boy.

'Sometimes our father would lock him in the cupboard,' titters Jacqueline. 'Lucien was afraid of the dark, but there was actually a switch in there that he'd secretly turn on. He'd come out in tears but then we'd all start laughing. He wasn't very courageous when he was younger.' Jacqueline, perhaps of a generation where such behaviour was the norm, makes light of the treatment Lucien received, but there's little doubt that he was abused by his father physically and mentally in ways that would have possibly attracted attention from the authorities, were it going on today. The sisters were left out of this habitual cruelty, meaning the little boy took the brunt of the punishment while they could only watch.

Jacqueline and Serge have both painted Joseph as a sensitive and caring father (his twin, Liliane, rarely goes on the record), though Serge did let his guard down when talking to biographer Gilles Verlant late in his life: 'I could have almost admired this disciplinarianism, but what I found intolerable was that in the evening, when we sat down for our family dinner, he'd apologise for his brutality. In my little bird's head, I would have much preferred it to be hard and for it to stay that way.'* Joseph appears to have been one of those abusers who keeps saying sorry to excuse himself, his actions eroding trust and fostering feelings of confusion and betrayal in his poor, tyrannised son.

Lucien found solace in playing the fool when his father was out playing at night. 'He was a clown. A clown!' repeats Jacqueline. 'He made everybody laugh so much. He had a brilliant sense of humour. Often there would be tears of laughter from my sister and me.' Any amateur psychologist can draw the dots between the abuse little Lulu internalised and the sad clown act that he performed so often. Sometimes Serge was more comedian than musician, particularly with the public outbursts, with an underlying pain almost detectable in the boozy vapour. The clown act was something he called upon when he did military service in 1948, discovering that he could make everybody roar with laughter when he'd had a few. That's when the drinking started in earnest.

His earliest performances as a musician came when he joined his father at the Casino Balneum in Dinard for summer season in 1939, with L'Orchestre Gilbert Gosse. The work would often dry up in Paris, and the Ginsburgs would go to northern French resorts, where Joseph would find jobs playing in the casinos. Lulu would have been only eleven years old at the time, making this a blooding in an elegant seaside town in anticipation of a career playing tenebrous joints in Paris one day. Though he had aspirations to be a painter, it was prudent to have something to fall back on, and so it proved.

'Our father often played in the resorts during the summer, which was a

---

* 'J'admirais ce côté disciplinaire mais ce que je trouvais intolérable c'était que le soir, au dîner familial, il s'excusait de sa brutalité. Dans ma petite tête d'oiseau, j'aurais préféré qu'il soit dur et qu'il le reste.'

beautiful time for the family,' says Jacqueline. Her sister, Liliane, failed her sixth-grade entry exam when asked what her favourite season was, and jokingly replied that it was the season at Trouville. 'Her teacher wasn't amused and marked her as a fail,' says Jacqueline. 'My parents tried to protest this ridiculous decision, but in the end it meant we went to Dinard for the best part of a year, from 1939 to 1940. It was a very happy year for us, like a long holiday.'

I sought out the Casino Balneum, or what was left of it, following 2019's La Route du Rock festival in Brittany. Dinard is just across the river from the pretty tourist destination of Saint Malo. Google led me to a whitewashed wall down a hill toward the seafront, though it's more likely Maps was taking me to the recently defunct Balneum Restaurant, which had gone south five years earlier. All we have to go on now is the testimony of people like Andrée Audrin, Serge's childhood friend, who many years later told the Brittany local paper *Le Télégramme* all about her friendship with the youngster.

'We met on the beach. My dad was also employed at the casino and our beach tent was close to the Ginsburgs by the lifeguard tower. His name was Lulu,' said eighty-five-year-old Andrée in 2011. 'He prevented other children from throwing water at us. Lulu was a very shy and caring little boy. He watched over us and his sisters. To us, he was almost a girl.'*

Jacqueline says summers spent in Brittany were dreamlike, but then things started to change: 'Being children, we weren't really aware of the dangers. We'd go to the market square to see trucks arriving, and I remember seeing refugees in the marketplace with their animals, their horses and bicycles. It was a terrible sight, and it felt like you were looking at a human zoo.' On a beautiful summer's day, the ferry to La Baie de Prieuré from Saint Malo is an unforgettable experience, with dolphins chasing the boat and frolicking in the cerulean waters. In 2019, it has an idyllic shoreline full of super-yachts, and

---

* 'Nous nous sommes rencontrés sur la plage. Mon père était également employé au casino et notre tente de plage était proche de celle des Ginsburg, sous le poste de secours. On l'appelait Lulu. Il empêchait les autres enfants de nous lancer de l'eau. Lulu était un petit garçon très timide et tellement attentionné. Il veillait sur nous et ses soeurs … Pour nous, il était presque une fille!' *Le Télégramme*

you can go and enjoy piano recitals from Florence Delaage. Dinard has also been hosting a British film festival every year for the last thirty years—a fairly benign invasion, one assumes. Eighty years ago, it was a more fearsome foreign force alighting on the seaside town. 'I remember there being a thick black cloud coming over from Saint Malo after the British set fire to the petrol reserves,' Jacqueline says. 'And then one day we were playing in the marketplace and a figure loomed in the distance, and as he came towards us, we realised he was a German soldier. We'd see many more in the coming years.'

*

Serge Gainsbourg played a critically well-received residency at the Théâtre des Capucines throughout October 1963, ably assisted by his two musicians at that time, Gaudry and Bacsik. Booze had its part to play, too. He let *Pilote* magazine in on his secret a year later: 'I'm off my head on bourbon ... now I'm swinging! It's much better than my early performances, where I used to give people the fear.'* Despite the excellent reviews he received in the Paris broadsheets, as well as up to four hundred people coming to see him and his stripped-back band each Tuesday, more indifference and ultimately disappointment was around the corner. *Gainsbourg Confidentiel* sold very badly, and the gigs got worse.

He was offered a support slot by Barbara, a literate singer of great finesse, on the cusp of superstardom at that point, who sang her own compositions as well as some notable Léo Ferré chansons. Barbara and Gainsbourg had much in common as Jewish singers with ancestors connected to Odesa who both had to hide during the German Occupation. Both suffered abuse from the press, too: 'We had met at a gala the day after a journalist had said we were both very ugly, which was nice,' said Barbara. 'I thought he was very handsome, and we both suffered from similar anxieties: we're both skinny, we both love black ... I asked him to do a tour with me, which he very kindly accepted. I didn't consider myself the headliner: both our names were on the poster.'

---

* 'Je me dopais au bourbon ... Maintenant, je m'en balance ! Ca vaut bien mieux que l'agressivité de mes débuts. Les gens avaient peur.'

She added, 'His stage fright and his great shyness could make him sick before going onstage.'*

Gainsbourg was scheduled to do ten dates, though he was heckled at a few of the early shows, causing him to drop out of the tour altogether. Barbara begged him to see it through and conquer his stage fright, and she even went onstage to rebuke her fans, but he decided to back away, and he would soon retire from touring altogether. 'He suffered from terrible nerves, but I think my mother had stage fright too,' says Charlotte Gainsbourg, who remembers watching from the wings. 'I saw this because I was backstage with them, and my mother would be on the verge of fainting. He had to drink a lot because otherwise he didn't have the courage to go on. It's funny when you imagine him being so provocative because he needed to be pushed, and he was really terrified.'

If his career as a performer wasn't exactly taking off, as a writer, things were improving. At the end of 1963, Denis Bourgeois introduced him to a singer he would later admit saved his life. 'I had the pleasure of asking Serge to write for France Gall,' said Bourgeois. 'He'd hitherto stayed in his corner, writing for cabaret-style artists like Juliette Grèco, Michèle Arnaud, or Isabelle Aubret. He'd never written for young singers and this huge new wave. As soon as he got down to it, he cracked on and started writing classics!'† Gainsbourg's first song for the sixteen-year-old was the biting 'N'écoute pas les idoles' ('Don't Listen To Your Idols'), a clever lampooning of the new pop fad, and a very

---

* 'Nous nous étions rencontrés lors de ces galas au TEP au lendemain desquels un journaliste avait dit que nous étions très laids, tous les deux, ce qui était agréable … Moi, je le trouvais très beau, nous étions assez proches dans nos angoisses, nos maigreurs, notre amour du noir. Je lui ai demandé de faire avec moi une tournée: avec une extrême délicatesse il a accepté. Je ne considérais pas qu'il faisait ma première partie: nous étions tous deux à la même affiche … Son trac, sa grande timidité pouvaient le mener jusqu'à la nausée avant de monter sur scène.'

† 'J'ai eu une initiative heureuse, c'est de demander à Serge d'écrire pour France Gall. En fait, il restait un peu dans son coin: quand il écrivait pour les autres c'était surtout pour des artistes de cabaret style Gréco, Michèle Arnaud ou Isabelle Aubret. Ce n'était jamais pour les jeunes, pour cette vague immense. Dès qu'il s'y est mis, il s'est défoncé, il a écrit des classiques.' Gilles Verlant, *Gainsbourg* (Albin Michel, 2001)

meta offering for 1963. Better still, 'Laisse tomber les filles' juxtaposes world-weary lyrics with an undulating groove and a sassy top line sung by an ingénue; melancholic pop at its best.

Gainsbourg's smart, multi-layered version of yé-yé was unlike anything else around. With demand for his songs beginning to grow, he provided Brigitte Bardot with 'L'appareil à sous', a swinging, *jeux de mots*-laden chanson about playing someone like a slot machine. Bardot would be impressed enough to call upon his services again for *Le show Bardot* in 1967. He gave Greek superstar Nana Mouskouri the magnificently moody 'Les yeux pour pleurer', and English singer Petula Clark 'La gadoue', a turgid number about kicking around in the sludge that's only nominally better than its English near-namesake 'Agadoo'. Even a chirpy mid-90s ska version by Jane Birkin with Les Négresses Vertes couldn't quite save it. The point is clear, though … demand for Serge's songs had never been greater, and it would increase exponentially after his Eurovision success.

Over the years, Gainsbourg wrote songs for as many as fifty female artists, and lots of those women had a number of hits with his songs. Given the prolific nature of his work and the abject failure of his own music at the time, and also the fact he'd inject ideas into chansons that even those singing were unaware of, the epithet *svengali* began to be mentioned in the same breath as the name Serge Gainsbourg. The word svengali has passed into modern usage—a mild barb aimed at any controlling figure in the music industry with perhaps a tinge of admiration too—but it's worth noting that it has antisemitic provenance dating back to the late nineteenth century.

Franco-British writer George Du Maurier, cartoonist for satirical magazine *Punch* and later grandfather of Dame Daphne, caused a publishing sensation in 1896 when his gothic novel *Trilby* was first serialised in *Harper's Bazaar*. Trilby O'Ferrall is a beautiful artist's model living *un style de vie bohème* in a Parisian garret, idling her days away smoking cigars and drinking chianti and generally promoting a proto-feminist way of life that captured the imagination of women on both sides of the Atlantic. The heroine accidentally hooks up with a 'very shabby and dirty' but charismatic musical genius who aids her in becoming a singing sensation in the theatres of Paris by putting her in a hypnotic trance. Svengali's dark arts elevate her above her squalor, though it's a Faustian pact with grave consequences, made with a sinister and controlling hypnotist who, as was pointed out by Professor Gayle Wald, fits the stereotype of the 'cultured Jew as musical parasite' posited by Richard Wagner in his 1850 pamphlet *Das Judenthum In Der Musik* (*Judaism In Music*), where he attacks competitors like Felix Mendelssohn and the German-Jewish bourgeoisie in general.*

'He went by the name of Svengali, and spoke fluent French with a German accent and humorous German twists and idiom, and his voice was very thin and mean and harsh, and often broke into a disagreeable falsetto,' wrote Du Maurier, echoing Wagner's bizarre claims about song being an extension of speech, and Jews being unable to find their own voices and apparently only capable of imitating the speech of the European nation states they were residing in (a recurring antisemitic trope about 'not belonging'). As for Svengali's physical appearance, he has 'bold, brilliant black eyes, with long heavy lids, a thin, sallow face, and a beard of burnt-up black, which grew almost from under his eyelids and over it his moustache, a shade lighter, fell in two long spiral twists.'

Trilby became a popular girl's name when *Trilbymania* swept Victorian Britain, and a very popular, narrow-brimmed fedora still worn today was named after the lead character. Trilby O'Ferrall is largely forgotten, though. 'Svengali' retains very specific usage, and the causal antisemitism in the name is still at the core of the coinage. It has come to us losing most of its dark connotations along the way, although the 1931 film and the 1954 film, both called *Svengali* rather than *Trilby*, traded on caricaturish stereotypes, faithfully recreating the novelist's character descriptions, with John Barrymore and Jeremy Brett, respectively, adopting Yiddish accents and wearing prosthetic noses. What's more, svengali might be a word used to describe Simon Cowell nowadays, but more traditionally it would be specifically used for managers and hitmakers such as Brian Epstein, Phil Spector, Malcolm McLaren, Larry

---

* Gayle Wald is a professor of English at George Washington University, Washington DC.

Parnes, Lou Pearlman, Albert Grossman, Peter Grant, Andrew Loog Oldham, and so on.

So should we continue to use the word svengali? Here's a suggestion: in traditional Japanese puppet theatre, the puppetmaster is called a bunraku. Bunraku is dressed in black, and while he's clearly visible to those watching, the audience adjusts to the idea and almost forgets he's there. It could take some getting used to, but as a term it's less problematic than svengali, should an epithet be needed at all.

As we leave 1963, it's worth remembering Serge did another song with Juliette Gréco: 'Strip-Tease', from the soundtrack of the Jacques Poitrenaud film of the same name. *Strip-Tease* starred a young Nico, fresh from *La Dolce Vita* and an affair with the French actor Alain Delon, which bore her a son. It would be a few years before she met Andy Warhol and the New York Factory set, or The Doors' frontman Jim Morrison, who convinced her to start writing her own songs.

Curiously, a frame from the film of Nico appears on the cover of the EP sung by Gréco, and Nico recorded the song herself—it's her version that's playing during the scene when she performs a striptease. It's likely that the Cologne-born singer's version of 'Strip-Tease' is her earliest surviving recording. It didn't make it onto the EP, though, and it wasn't released until 2001, on the compilation album *Le cinéma de Serge Gainsbourg*, some thirteen years after her death. It's an interesting exercise to play Greco's version against Nico's version, if only to compare the light and shade and the warmth and coolness, with one very French version and the other very, very German.

'Strip-Tease' was a great example of a Gainsbourg song that could be widely interpreted by diametrically different singers, though it would have sounded faintly ridiculous had he recorded it himself. At this stage in his career, there still weren't too many people in the world clamouring for Serge Gainsbourg to perform his own songs at all, and his decade-and-a-half vanishing act from the stage wouldn't untowardly bother anyone, either. Except for maybe himself.

3

APPROPRIATION

GAINSBOURG PERCUSSIONS (1964)

[I'll steal something from the classics like Benjamin Constant. Herman won't notice, poor idiot. He's an ignoramus.*]

When Serge Gainsbourg performed 'New York USA' in 1964, he might as well have been singing about the moon. In fact, the lunar surroundings would have been similarly exotic compared with the extravagant Lower Manhattan Financial District in the mid-60s, given that the first skyscraper at La Défense, la Tour Nobel, didn't appear in the Parisian financial hub until 1966. 'J'ai vu New York,' he sang, apparently suspended from a high-rise, made possible by a blue screen in a French TV studio. 'Oh! C'est haut, c'est haut, New York …'

In reality he would've had no first-hand experience of the city, with the impressions he did have built up from books, newspapers, cinema, and TV. He admitted as much when asked on television; what transpired was a titter, an amused shrug, a slight look of embarrassment, although not too embarrassed as you didn't really get to go to America in those days, unless you were Édith Piaf.

> 'Empire States Building, oh! c'est haut / Rockefeller Center, oh! C'est haut / International Building, oh! c'est haut, Waldorf Astoria, oh! c'est haut, Pan American Building, oh! c'est haut, Bank of Manhattan, oh! c'est haut …'

---

* Gainsbourg as Stan in *Charlotte For Ever*.

[71]

Like many stars of his generation, Serge was enchanted by America: the glitz, the Cadillacs, the Pop Art, the movies, and the rock'n'roll. As mentioned previously, a post-war agreement between the president of the provisional government, Léon Blum, and the US Secretary of State, James F. Byrnes, had allowed a wave of American films to flood French cinemas in order to erase significant debts from two world wars, much to the chagrin of the conservatives and also the communists. Goods and lifestyle were exported from the New World, altering the cultural output of France's glitterati. Johnny Hallyday, Les Chaussettes Noires led by Eddy Mitchell, and Dick Rivers's Les Chats Sauvages made livings performing knocked-off rock'n'roll and rhythm & blues songs from across the Atlantic translated into French.*

Gainsbourg went further. He was capable of experimenting with the sounds around him and curious about the sonic praxes of other territories, too, and he had the talent and the vision to bring disparate worlds together. 'The most important Gainsbourg music that I ever got into was the *Percussions* album,' says Joseph Mount of Metronomy. 'That's the brilliant thing about him—you can think you've heard all the good stuff. My girlfriend played me that "New York USA" song, and it's so good. And he's just singing about buildings. It's such a nice simple way of thinking about lyrics.' 'New York USA' isn't just a Frenchman's fantasy about the Big Apple, it's undercut with percussion from a Nigerian musician called Babatunde Olatunji. Not that Olatunji knew much about it—well not to begin with, at least. Three songs were lifted from his *Drums Of Passion* album and used as the basis for three songs on *Gainsbourg Percussions*, the other two being 'Joanna' and 'Marabout'.

This is no dubious case of drawing inspiration from a percussive backbeat in the way that Robin Thicke's 'Blurred Lines' paid homage to Marvin Gaye's 'Got To Give It Up' (Thicke and Pharrell Williams paid almost $5 million for the privilege). 'New York USA''s reliance upon 'Akiwowo (Chant To The

---

* Halliday picked up the nickname 'the French Elvis' and the less catchy 'the biggest rock star you've never heard of' (the latter epithet assumes you're not from one of the twenty-nine countries that recognises French as a spoken language).

Trainman)' is startling. Gainsbourg hadn't just used the rhythm as backing track, he'd pinched the tune and replaced the words with his own.

'Eyi lo poro!'—the cry of a famous local train conductor, Guard Akiwowo, known by the passengers on routes from Lagos to Idogo, and Ibadan to Kano— was transposed over a rhythm that simulates the sound of the locomotive. He was also known for his apparently humorous catchphrase, 'Do you call this having an easy time?' You probably had to be there.

'That's a Juju album,' said Afrobeat drumming legend Tony Allen, when I met him at the BMG offices in London in early 2020, 'and what they did was very different to what Fela Kuti and Africa 70 were doing. They make more money than us because what they do we don't do. We don't flatter people— singing in praise of somebody. As soon as they know your name, the man is going to be singing your name, in the club or the party. They sing your name and you'll say, *I've got to give money to the bandleader*. It's showing off. We were just playing music in Africa 70 where we don't praise nobody, we attack them!'

When the album *Drums Of Passion* was released in 1960, it would have been borne of a new enthusiasm for a fledgling republic, free of the shackles of British occupation. 'Akiwowo' is the ecstatic sound of a young country set free. It mines the traditions that would have been a part of Olatunji's upbringing in the small fishing village of Ajido, which, even today, is little more than a slender dirty track running through a series of corrugated iron shacks flanked by palm trees. It's situated along the coast from a less than inviting sounding Snake Island, while Lagos is three and a half hours away in the car. The Gulf of Guinea laps into shore a stone's throw from where Babatunde grew up.

As a child in Ajido in the 1930s, he'd go with his great aunt Tanyin to hear the drumming of the townspeople at night and witness the spinning wicker rotundas of the zangbetos, or nightwatchmen, patrolling and dispensing their apotropaic magic. At other times he'd listen to the women sing at their weaving frames, having returned from the markets in Lagos or nearby Badagry after the rains had dissipated. 'It was in this way that drum rhythms became part of Babatunde,' writes Akin Akiwowo in the sleeve notes. 'In many places he has travelled in Africa; how often he must have heard the continuous beats of gangan, dundun, omele, bembe, kiriboto, agidigbo, sakara, go je konnongo, gbedu, igba—to name a few types of talking drums that are common in West Africa, and beyond, even today.'

That all said, *Drums Of Passion* isn't, as some might have assumed, the sound of a primitive percussionist captured by some benevolent ethnomusicologists with handy tape machines driven by a sense of noblesse oblige. It's a fastidious cataloguing of sonic tradition by a virtuoso musician, a loving act of preservation, as Olatunde began to notice the sounds and practices of his youth disappearing. What's more, it was actually cut in the United States, the first album by an African artist to be recorded in stereophonic sound, with three other drummers—Baba Hawthorne Bey, Taiwo Duval, and the Jamaican jazz percussionist Montego Joe—and a chorus of nine singers.

The record executive John Hammond signed Babatunde to Columbia after hearing him play in 1957, and his hunch that Western audiences would respond to the music was astute: *Drums Of Passion* can be regarded now as the foundation stone of world music—that catch-all term for 96 percent of the music made on planet Earth.* It sold five million copies worldwide and became popular among beatniks and bohemians; John Coltrane and Carlos Santana were two certified apostles. The record had come into Gainsbourg's possession via his frenemy, the crooner Guy Béart, who'd been introduced to *Drums Of Passion* by Harry Belafonte while he was over in New York. Béart played Gainsbourg the record back in Paris, and Serge acted quickly, working with Goraguer to stitch it together. Béart was irritated by his acquaintance's underhand actions but resolved to keep his mouth shut.

Guy Béart and Gainsbourg had started out on Philips around the same time, and they toured together throughout France and Italy as part of Jacques Canetti's stable in 1959. They had a lot in common, and yet a discrete, unspoken, and simmering dislike for one another finally boiled over on the

---

* 'It's a label for anything at all that is not sung in English or anything that doesn't fit into the Anglo-Western pop universe this year,' wrote David Byrne in his 1999 *New York Times* piece 'I Hate World Music'.

Boxing Day edition of the late-night talk show for artists, *Apostrophe*, in 1986. Béart, who'd recorded some hits in the late 50s and early 60s before reinventing himself as a television personality, was on the receiving end of one of Serge's famous late-night verbal assaults. As the discussion heated up, Gainsbourg scowled passive aggressively from behind a piano, and for some reason called Béart a 'badger'.

The disagreement? Béart took to defending all art as significant, while Serge repeated his long held view that the chanson is a minor art, belligerently demonstrating the difference between a three-chord trick and something more high-minded requiring significant legerdemain, with exaggerated bridged hand shapes to prove it. Béart tries to make the case for everything being art, even cooking. Gainsbourg then belligerently calls him an arsehole ('connard'). This farcical and childish altercation gets repeated on French TV most Christmases, and it did the rounds on the internet when Béart died in 2015.

Some might suggest Béart was angry because he didn't think of doing the same thing himself, or even that he was planning something similar but Gainsbourg beat him to the punch. Unlikely. To take Babatunde's songs and build entire chansons around them was so audacious that it could have only come from Gainsbourg. Serge adapted and often set musical trends, whereas Béart rather got left where he was standing in 1958. A career in light entertainment beckoned. Some years later, Béart admitted he'd been hurt by Gainsbourg's unprovoked attack.

Laying ethics aside for a moment, what Gainsbourg did in 1964, with *Percussions*, was a remarkable leap into the future. Musique concrète pioneers like Pierre Schaeffer and Pierre Henry had composed with found sounds in the form of tape loops long before the term *sampling* was coined, but to adopt another artist's oeuvre and make something entirely new from it was Gainsbourg at his most cubist, borrowing from an African aesthetic and creating collage from disparate media—Picasso's *L'art nègre* in musical form. Widespread adoption of backing tracks from other sources would become commonplace in hip-hop during the 1980s, but in 1964 it was new. Paul Simon, who went on to record *Graceland*, had just made the slow-burning folk classic 'The Sound Of Silence'; he was more than twenty years away from mining the musical resources of black South Africa. *Percussions* was also released fifteen years before Brian Eno and David Byrne started recording the ethnomusicologist's disco of *My Life In The Bush Of Ghosts*, and fifteen years before Eno and John Hassell's *Fourth World*, which was the name for their own musical aesthetic fusing primitivism with futurism.

Innovative yes it was, but it was also made at a time when France's colonial hold overseas was shrinking like a lasered tumour. The Algerian War of Independence had come to a brutal finale two years before, and France was having to come to terms with some changes. Ingrained attitudes, especially about former 'glories', are hard to eradicate, and even in April 2020 there were French doctors on TV causing controversy when they suggested coronavirus vaccines should be trialled in Africa.

Colonialism enjoyed a second flourish in France in the late nineteenth and early twentieth centuries, with the lessons of Napoleon's 'French Period' unlearned. Pierre Paul Leroy-Beaulieu's *De la colonisation chez les peuples modernes*, first published in 1874, stated that imperialism was an inevitable by-product of economic, political, and cultural development.* With cultural development also came a sense of *noblesse oblige*—or privilege entailing responsibility. It's a foundation stone of 'Frenchness' that contradicts the postcolonial melancholia that was to follow. There's no melancholia, colonial or otherwise, on *Percussions*. The plundering is seen as fair exchange for services to betterment. It looks ugly now, but it isn't entirely surprising:

'And then I was listening a lot to this album of ethnic music: cynically, I stole two or three tracks,' Gainsbourg told Verlant.† He was laughing too, according to the writer, but it's not clear exactly what it is he's laughing about, or whether it's embarrassed laughter, genuine amusement, or the titter of someone who thinks they've got away with something.

---

* J.P. Daughton, *An Empire Divided: Religion, Republicanism And The Making Of French Colonialism (1880–1914)* (Oxford University Press, 2006)
† 'Et puis j'écoutais beaucoup un album de musiques ethniques: aux Africains j'ai piqué deux-trois plans, cyniquement, au noir. Hé hé hé …'

'In the mid-60s, it was very common,' Mick Harvey told me in 2014, in an interview for *Fact* magazine. 'Stuff wasn't nailed down quite as permanently as it is these days, and people could claim to have written all sorts of stuff. The Stones and even Led Zeppelin did a bit of that stuff in the late 60s, just putting their name to songs. It was pretty common. I think in the case of that African guy, percussion is pretty hard to copyright. To identify. It's not necessarily tonalities or chordal movements that can be identified quite so specifically.'

'That was all it was,' says Nigerian-born drummer Tony Allen, 'because it was a different era. It's just a question of dedication and music is a dodgy business in the first place.'

I put the theory of this new-frontierism in copyright to Jean-Claude Vannier and suggested there may have been fewer rules during the 1960s. 'There were rules,' says Jean-Claude, shaking his head. 'There should have been legal questions asked at the time. He had a lot of people after him. A lot of legal cases. There was a trial in France. Serge took off the voices and just left the rhythms and wrote his own lyrics over the top.'

Naughty though this might have been at the time, it looks very ahead of its time, given that so much of hip-hop would be built on samples from other records twenty-five years later. 'Yes, but you have to pay for it,' counters Vannier. 'Well, you don't necessarily have to pay, but you have to ask for authorisation to do it, which is something that Gainsbourg didn't do.'

In for a centime, in for a franc, Serge went seven thousand kilometres south, to South Africa, for the instrumental melody for 'Pauvre Lola', a revisiting of Nabokov's *Lolita* with an uncredited cameo giggle from France Gall at the start of the song. Also uncredited is the great debt owed to Miriam Makeba's 'Umqokozo', which first appeared on *The Many Voices Of Miriam Makeba* in 1962. The unmistakable bass from 'Pauvre Lola' bears an uncanny resemblance to the main guitar line running throughout 'Umqokozo'. It's a clear interpolation of a melody that loops through both songs, yet Gainsbourg got away with this one. When Mama Africa came to re-record 'Umquokozo' in 1968, on *Makeba!*, the new version was faster, and, as if to prove a point, sounds more like the Gainsbourg version. 'This is by far the most African of her recent releases,' writes A.B. Spellman in the liner notes. 'Here she is working in a purely African environment, and all the elements of her style are brilliantly focused.' Ironic, given the hint of the Frenchman's pace and percussion mirroring his update—a case of fighting fire with fire, perhaps?

Ever the upcycler, Serge reused France Gall's laugh from the intro of 'Pauvre Lola' for the Jean-Claude Forest hipster sci-fi cartoon *Marie Mathématique*. Mathematique was the little sister of Barbarella, living in space in 2830, with Gall's distinctive giggle. *Marie Mathématique* enjoyed six outings on French TV in 1965 and 1966 as part of a new magazine programme called *Dim Dam Dom*, with the songs in the cartoon performed by Serge on an acoustic guitar—a surprisingly anachronistic timbre, given that the cartoon was set nearly eight thousand years into the future.

Serge turned his attention to Africa one more time in 1983, when he made his second feature film, *Equateur* (don't worry, we'll visit his first feature film, *Je t'aime moi non plus*, in the next chapter). Based on the Georges Simenon 'colonial noir' novel *Coup de Lune* (or *Tropic Moon* in English), it was shot mostly on location in Gabon. Starring French theatre actor Francis Huster and German actress Barbara Sukowa in what promised to be a hardboiled erotic thriller, it fails to live up to its description on any level, and, worse still, it enforces stereotypes of the entire African continent as a primitive backwater waiting to be civilised.

There are so many audio and visual clichés that should you alight on this film any time during its eighty-five minute duration, you will almost certainly be aware that you are in Africa: Huster dresses in a white linen suit and Sukowa wears a white pith helmet, their faces glistening with sweat; there are sounds of tribal instruments, noble savages in the courtroom, and township children singing freely in the background as the star crossed lovers shag under white mosquito nets. All that's missing is someone with a bone through their nose. Worst of all is an excruciating *Heart Of Darkness*-style ride down a swampy river on a canoe propelled by tribal, shirtless oarsman. it's a sequence that endures for a mosquito's lifetime.

Gainsbourg, behind the lens, took the book's internal anxieties and turned them inside out, while turning the sublime scenery into bromide. The racial stereotyping in the film is cringeworthy, though fetishizing disparate cultures was always a feature of his work. Jane willingly and dutifully played *la petite Anglaise*, and Bambou more reluctantly took part in his exotic China-doll orientalist fantasies, irrespective of the fact she was born in France. He even gave her a song—'China Doll'—on her solo album *Made In China*. Like most of the Gainsbourg women, Caroline von Paulus was brought close to the mic, singing in a higher than natural register to portray vulnerability. A first attempt at making her record at Alan Hawkshaw's studio in Hertfordshire didn't come to anything. 'All she did was laid down beside the swimming pool outside the house,' says Alan Parker. 'She didn't do much apart from that.'

Eventually, the record was made with the American musicians Billy Rush, Curtis King Jr., and keyboard player Gary Georgett. According to Gilles Verlant, when Bambou finally came to the studio, once the music was recorded, she barely knew which way around to put on her headphones. Serge lashed out in frustration in the studio like his father lashing out during piano lessons. *Made In China* is lacklustre, a hostage situation set to music. It does feature one curio, though: a first and last in Serge's canon, according to Gary Georgett. 'Making Bambou's album was a blast! Billy Rush and I had a little more control over it. Serge is strictly verse, chorus, verse, chorus … and we finally talked him into making a bridge with the title track. An interlude. We fought tooth and nail to put in a bridge. He was such a fish out of water with that. He let it go—it was just the one song …'

*

You probably don't need me to tell you that the history of appropriation in popular music is complicated. Seen in black and white, limeys like The Rolling Stones and The Beatles took black music, etiolated it, repackaged it, and turned it into a global phenomenon. On the other hand, music is viral and addictive, and it seems churlish to put limitations defined by borders and ethnicity on one of life's true pleasures. Furthermore, the back and forth between cultures is symbiotic. The birth of the blues in the nineteenth century had been painful, and the midwife was the harmonica, a nineteenth-century Viennese invention. Twelve-bar progressions are a European idea, while pentatonic scales have been utilised by a variety of cultures independently over many millennia. Music isn't invented; it hangs in the air, waiting to be plucked from the sky.

Nowhere is impermeable. Even two centuries ago, when travel between continents across the Atlantic was infrequent. Take Appalachian folk, which draws variously from the musical traditions of Cherokee Indians, African American blues, English ballads, and Celtic folk. Musical crossbreeding makes a mockery of definitions. Just ask Kentucky-born Will Oldham, who writes folk songs and country songs for a living: 'I don't know that those terms mean anything to me at the end of the day, because I listen to the music I listen to and experience the life I experience and then translate it into music. If my music ends up being more confrontational or more experimental, does that mean its leapt all of a sudden out of the boundaries of those genres you've just described?'

That's not to say that because jazz is played on the saxophone, white Europeans can claim it as their own. Adolphe Sax might have been a white dude, but jazz, like the blues, is born of the African American experience. But that shouldn't occlude, say, the French, who embraced jazz like no other nation on Earth and brought their own experience and cultural understanding to it. And so too, later, did Serge Gainsbourg. Hybrids are inevitable if you have ears. Keith Richards and Paul McCartney had to invest their hard-earned money and wait for records to arrive on ships so that they could then take them home and be inspired. The *musiques sans frontières* nature of the internet means these geographical restrictions are negated almost entirely, and sound itself becomes fair game. Which doesn't mean that major labels marketing white artists doing black music to the hilt because they sell more records than black artists (George Ezra, Rag'n'Bone Man, Hugh Laurie!) isn't cynical and depressing.

Gainsbourg was inspired by black music his whole creative life. He liked hot jazz and cool jazz, Latin jazz and bossa nova, Jamaican reggae and ska, Nigerian percussion and South African township folk. His Carnaby Street-centred Swinging London phase was based on the British interpretation of the blues and rock'n'roll that was coming out of America, while yé-yé bypassed the Anglo Saxon influence and went straight for the source, as did his 50s doo-wop rock album about the Nazis, *Rock Around The Bunker*. Even the symphonic rock of *Melody Nelson*, with all its propinquity to progressive rock and the classical European composers, was underscored by a deep funk groove, but *Rock Around The Bunker* and *Melody Nelson* were performed by white, mainly British musicians.

Chilly Gonzales argues that Gainsbourg wasn't appropriating black music when he was making jazz or American funk, he was just channelling the dominant musical ideas of his day. 'With all due respect, because American black music is the music that dominates on an international level, if you're a musician and you're not doing that—or you're not inspired by that music—then you're not doing it right. Maybe in France that was something that hadn't been done, other than in a superficial way by novelty hitmakers of that time, but when I say Gainsbourg internalised American music, I'm saying black music, because there is no other American music than black music. Even country is black in some way; it's just blues for white Southern people.'

Gainsbourg had much in common with David Bowie. A pair of sonic Dadaists working independently in different countries, they were both magpies making collages with shiny objects, flying vertiginously to retrieve ideas from high culture and swooping the depths of trash culture too, making musical melanges like photomontage pioneer Hannah Hoch. It didn't matter where it came from as long as it was a good idea, but both were vociferous readers and art fanatics, leading to more variegated palettes and more arcane references that wouldn't necessarily be immediately identifiable to a listener with mainstream tastes. 'His music kind of reminds me of Bowie in its inventiveness,' says Baxter Dury, 'but done in a French way where they're still clapping on the one and the three. It's wrong and it's out of tune, and there's a punkness to it.'

Gainsbourg paid tribute to the Dame in song with 'Beau oui comme Bowie', featuring an amusing titular pun that warrants more quizzical punctuation ('Beautiful, Yes? Like Bowie?'). The song was sung by Isabelle

Adjani on her 1983 *Pull Marine* album. Serge references Oscar Wilde's *The Picture Of Dorian Gray*, a smart choice given that a beautiful twentysomething actress is the manifestation of the collaboration, while the old grotesque who masterminded the songs hides from view behind a recording desk. This creative duality would certainly not have been lost on the author. Serge also owns up to a kind of professional jealousy, which, sung by Adjani, sounds more like fan worship, particularly when talking about Bowie's androgynous beauty and icy cool. 'Beau oui comme Bowie' is meta, witty, playful, androgynous … an underrated gem from the Gainsbourg songbook.

Another inspiration that was ripe with possibilities to rip off was punk, and, as the writer Greil Marcus contended, punk was merely a continuation of Dada by way of the Situationists anyway.[*] Gainsbourg and Sex Pistols manager Malcolm McLaren were fond of one another, and the casual exchange of ideas may have influenced British and French culture more indelibly than is supposed. They identified fellow travellers in one another, and the influence of McLaren almost certainly altered Gainsbourg's trajectory. 'Malcolm moved between celebrity dinners with his fellow practitioner of musical outrage, Serge Gainsbourg, and hanging out with transvestites in Pigalle,' wrote punk icon Jordan in her memoir, *Defying Gravity*.[†]

MacLaren recalled Serge drinking twenty-six Bloody Marys to his five over the course of a couple of hours drinking on the Champs-Élysées, and, as they departed, Gainsbourg uttered the words 'I love Sid Vicious'. Serge kept two framed pictures on his Steinway piano: Chopin and Sid, the latter of whom had recently died from a heroin overdose. 'Malcolm and Serge got together in the late 70s and were planning to work together at one point,' says McLaren biographer Paul Gorman. 'Gainsbourg was a fan of punk, definitely, and Malcolm was a fan of Paris. He'd been going there a lot by that time, and so I think it was just that thing where two brilliant people pick up on the same ideas, not necessarily copying each other, but mining the same reach.'

---

[*] Greil Marcus, *Lipstick Traces: A Secret History Of The 20th Century* (Faber, 1989)

[†] Jordan with Cathi Unsworth, *Defying Gravity: Jordan's Story* (Omnibus Press, 2019)

APPROPRIATION

When Malcolm had returned to Paris in 1978, following the Sex Pistols' split, he found refuge in a city he'd spent lots of time in the past. He'd been there in May '68, for the student uprising, and five years later he was hanging out in Les Halles with decadent writers from France's music papers, taking notes and eventually making off with their ideas.

'I wouldn't be as bold as to say the French invented punk,' says Bertrand Burgalat, chuckling, 'but when Malcolm McLaren came to Paris with the New York Dolls in 1973, he met this clique of rock aesthetes such as Yves Adrien and Philippe Manœuvre. Britain and America may have had the bands, but Paris had the writers. Adrien and Manœuvre were imagining punk through the Stooges before punk arrived in Europe. Malcolm, who was clever, totally got this bloody thing!'

Punk musicians in Paris—and there were a few—were demonstrably more louche and chic than their future UK counterparts. McLaren met The Stinky Toys, led by the impossibly good-looking couple Elli Medeiros and Jacno, future electronic-pop pioneers. Malcolm had been particularly taken with the way Medeiros's clothes were hung together with safety pins, a cheap accoutrement that became emblematic in the punk movement. 'He arrived in Paris dressed like a teddy boy and went back to London dressed like a punk,' says Burgalat.

McLaren was also heavily influenced by the Situationists, who Gainsbourg kept his distance from because of affiliations with communism (he had deep anxieties about *la menace rouge*, which we'll look at in more detail later). 'Serge liked strolling around and seeing what would happen,' says Gorman. 'He wasn't a Situationist, not politically, but I think he came from that same Baudelairian tradition, which involved sitting outside the Café de Flore pissed out of your mind and seeing what happens. They were kindred spirits, and I know Malcolm liked him very much.'

Gainsbourg attended the filming of Sid Vicious's 'My Way' at L'Olympia, and apparently stood at the back clicking his fingers, saying the word *classe* over and over. Julian Temple, who directed *The Great Rock And Roll Swindle* (from which the song is taken), said, '[Serge] got the idea to do the "Marseillaise" [as "Aux armes et cætera"], the reggae version, through hanging out with the Pistols and through seeing Sid."* We know Gainsbourg was a Jimi Hendrix fan—a cassette of the American guitarist still sits in Rue de Verneuil, adjacent to the ashtray full of Gitanes butts that he'd been smoking the night he died. Hendrix and the Sex Pistols had something in common—they'd both subverted their respective national anthems and turned them into works of rebellion. Hendrix played 'The Star-Spangled Banner' at Woodstock, an excoriating napalm version that howled with disapproval at the ongoing Vietnam War. The Sex Pistols released their own version of 'God Save The Queen' (although a different song) in the Silver Jubilee year. Two years later, Gainsbourg would cause unholy controversy with a reggae version of 'La Marseillaise' on the hit single 'Aux armes et cætera'. A Jew recording the national anthem with a troupe of Jamaican musicians was all too much for most racists.

'I have no doubt that he was following the lead of the Sex Pistols and Hendrix at Woodstock,' says Bruno Blum. 'I mean, Serge was really into the Sex Pistols. He wore a Sid Vicious T-shirt, he spoke about them in interviews, he understood the whole provocation aspect from Malcolm McClaren, which he started doing after that.' *Quid pro quo*, Gainsbourg may have been an influence on McLaren—albeit indirectly—with *Gainsbourg Percussions*.

When McLaren managed Adam & The Ants for a time in the late 70s, he charged Adam Ant a thousand pounds for the pleasure. Some hoodoo came with the service. And the story goes that Malcolm divulged a two-word secret that he promised would make the singer huge: 'Burundi beat'. A 1971 single by the French musician and producer Michel Bernholc, 'Burundi Black' was recorded under the alias Mike Steiphenson. It's essentially a piano piece on top of the sound of Burundi drummers, taken from a field recording made by ethnomusicologists in 1967 called *Musique du Burundi* on Radio France's field music label Ocora. Adam & The Ants diligently copied the tribal rhythms from the record with two drummers and became the pop sensation of early 80s Britain. Malcolm had been proven right; the formula worked again for Bow

---

* Emily Mackay, the *Guardian*, April 12 1999

Wow Wow, who McLaren also managed. The pop trend even received a name: *the new tribalism.*

'Malcolm was recovering from the post-Pistols fallout in Paris,' writes Jordan. 'The city was full of his old friends at the time, including his art college comrade Robin Scott, now working with his brother Jullian at Barclay Records. Robin had been producing some African musicians with a heavy drum sound called the Burundi beat, which immediately grabbed Malcolm's attention.'

'Adam Ant's first album was released on my label [Do It] in the UK, and there was some speculation as to who sowed the seeds in Adam's mind to adopt the Burundi beat,' Robin Scott, the artist formerly known as M (of 'Pop Muzik' fame), tells me when I contact him via Messenger. 'Eclecticism followed the commercial collapse of punk in the record industry, and Malcolm and I advocated the practice. So who knows?' Years later, McLaren claimed he'd discovered the original recording by the drummers from the Bukirasazi region of central Burundi while at the Kandinsky Library at the Centre Pompidou, and had approached the librarian and asked her to play 'Tambours Ingoma', mainly because he fancied her. She apparently played it at 45rpm instead of 33rpm, setting off lightbulbs in McLaren's head, thus changing the course of British pop in the process. The chances of McLaren alighting on the very same obscure library track that Michel Bernholc had had a UK hit with in 1971 seems fanciful even by McLaren's standards, though it is possible.

In 1981, Rusty Egan of Visage remixed 'Burundi Black', and it became a dance-floor hit in the UK. 'This latest "Burundi Black" is glitzy pop-schlock, a throwaway with a beat,' wrote the *New York Times*. 'But its perpetrators are making money with it, and so is Mike Steiphenson, who has held on to the "Burundi Black" copyright.' Indeed, Steiphenson, or Michel Bernholc, was profiting from the toil of some uncredited African drummers and coining in the publishing with every record sold, like Gainsbourg did in '64.

I ask Robin Scott who the artists were 'with a heavy drum sound' that Jordan refers to. 'I produced a number of acts in Nairobi where many musicians had found safe refuge from neighbouring states,' he replies. 'This was prior to recording *Jive Shikisha*, a collaboration between myself and the South African female vocal trio of the same name in 1982. Malcolm and I shared a lot of ideas in Paris, where he frequented the Barclay label, who signed the Pistols for France. World music was more current in Paris than the UK.' It'll probably come as no surprise that 'Burundi Black' was released by Barclay Records. Scott's interest in the Burundi beat, which began with 'Burundi Black', may have rubbed off elsewhere; Jean-Marie Salaun, who Scott played with in the art-rock band SpionS for a short while, also used Burundi drumming on the 1981 Afro-cosmic 'Tam Tam', using the moniker Codek.

Did Gainsbourg and McLaren speak about *Percussions*? Who knows? His influence is more likely unavowed and indirect. If he copied Michel Bernholc, which is likely, it's also highly likely that Michel Bernholc copied Serge Gainsbourg. Their paths would have almost certainly crossed during the making of Françoise Hardy's 1973 album *Message Personnel*, where Gainsbourg was a writer working with Vannier, and Bernholc was orchestrating the songs of Michel Berger. Furthermore, Michel Bernholc was a Gainsbourg fan. He recorded all of the tracks for the soundtrack for the 1978 French comedy *Les Bronzés* but one: 'Sea, Sex And Sun'. Inviting Gainsbourg onto the soundtrack was a gamble, as he was commercially in a rut at the time, but Bernholc's patronage paid off. The film was a big hit in France, and 'Sea, Sex And Sun' was played everywhere as a result, even if Gainsbourg disliked the comedy (he went along to the cinema to see his song on the opening credits, then promptly left).

Bernholc knew the *Percussions* record, and without it there's a strong possibility he would never have had the idea to do 'Burundi Black' in the first place, which then set off a chain of events that precipitated the new tribalism in British pop in the early 80s. I would have liked to have asked Bernholc himself, but he committed suicide in 2002. The same imperialist sense of entitlement that 'Burundi Black' reeks of begins with *Percussions*, but both records opened up possibilities of crossover between cultural styles. Paris is the greatest place on Earth to buy records, and part of that is thanks to the public's acceptance of musical *métissage*—an attitude that these records helped to foster.

'France is at the centre of the global musical map, and close to the centre of Europe,' Finders Keepers label founder Andy Votel told me when I interviewed him for the *Lonely Planet* in 2017. 'So many so-called ethnological records sat in the bargain bins untouched for years. Now France is the go-to place for Lebanese, Moroccan, Egyptian records, which share the racks with European soundtracks and a wealth of American free-jazz musicians that visited France in the 70s … then there's punk, synth-pop, and yé-yé. It's a hotspot with a great pop-cultural history.'

Whether Malcolm knew about *Percussions* or not, it was a precursor to the new tribalism, helping to make the mingling of ideas from various cultures a more acceptable practice. It's hard now to imagine how radical Adam & The Ants sounded in 1980, or otherworldly, given the frequency with which records nowadays take freely from within the globalised community, thanks to the internet. 'You can either call it stealing it and being a twat, or making it universal in a way,' says Joe Mount from Metronomy about *Percussions*.

What was a sonic shock for many in the UK had become commonplace in France thanks to records that had dared to explore and draw on the heritage of non-native societies like *Percussions* and 'Burundi Black'. Blighty's backwardness—as it had been with the Renaissance—meant that while continental types were all enjoying the Day-Glo Latin-tinged *jouissance* of Les Rita Mitsouko's 'Marcia Baïla' in the mid-80s, we were importing dreary *Schlager* nonsense like Opus's 'Live Is Life' in the name of exoticism.

In 1983, McLaren made his own montage album of borrowed rhythms from around the world, taking in South African Mbaqanga and New York hip-hop, and then spliced them together with Trevor Horn. *Duck Rock* is a joyous melange on the whole, with critic Robert Christgau writing in the *Village Voice*, 'McLaren knows how to record African music for Western ears, and the ebullient tunes he's collected here more than make up for his annoyance quotient. But the intrusions of the World's Famous Supreme Team, not to mention the featured vocalist, are annoying nevertheless. And when "Song For Chango," which has existed since "before Jesus Christ was born," gets credited like almost all the other compositions to Malc and producer Trevor Horn, I wish he'd thought to mention which specific Africans contributed to which specific tracks. Culture may be collective, but (in this culture) wealth ain't.'

Sound familiar? Like *Percussions*, *Duck Rock* was neither without plaudits nor lawsuits.

*

Does the tune from Jane Birkin's 'Baby Alone In Babylone' sound naggingly familiar? If so, it's probably because it originally comes from Brahms. 'Bébé gai'? Franz Lizst. 'Lost Song'? From Edvard Grieg's *Peer Gynt*. Metaphorically stealing from dead people is something that all composers do, whether consciously or unconsciously. Johann Pachelbel's 'Canon In D Major' has turned up in everything from Aphrodite's Child's 'Rain And Tears' to France Gall's 'Toi que je veux', a staple baroque-pop progression, while the descending left-hand degression, known as the lament bass, can be found in hundreds of 1960s hits, including many by The Beatles: 'Michelle', 'Magical Mystery Tour', 'Girl', 'All You Need Is Love', 'Octopus's Garden', and so on.

Trying to figure out who did what when collaborating is a greyer area, and one where Gainsbourg usually came out 100 percent the composer. 'I provided and created the bedrock of all the albums we did together over the years,' says Alan Hawkshaw, 'and I'm talking about everybody: Isabelle Adjani, Catherine Deneuve, Jane Birkin, and him. We worked on a professional basis, and there were charges for arranging and conducting and all the rest of it—and playing, so at that time I considered it something we'd agreed on, and that was enough.'

As the star, Serge held all the cards. 'It was a question of Gainsbourg saying, *You need me to make this happen. If I don't use you then I'll just work with somebody else*,' says Jean-Claude Vannier. 'So basically there was a bit of a power-trip situation. And he wanted to be very famous—he loved to be famous.'

'In the 1990s, the French arrangers who worked with Gainsbourg went to SACEM, and there was a reckoning,' says Bertrand Burgalat. 'At that time I met the British arranger David Whitaker and put him back into work. None of them wanted to speak out about it because they didn't want to sound bitter, even the British arrangers like David.'

'Oh no, how could they do that?' protests Alan Parker, regarding arrangers clawing back credits. 'How could they prove it? I'm surprised SACEM accepted it. I wrote quite a bit on the last few albums of Serge's, but you don't contest it like that. I think that's awful.'

Burgalat says Gainsbourg used his reputation to call the shots, a dynamic between artist and arranger that wasn't unusual at the time. 'He was a great lyricist, he was a great musician, but he was also very lazy. He definitely had a talent for getting the right arrangers at the right moments to create these incredible works. But none of these guys wanted to say that.' When I mention to Burgalat that that was the way Gainsbourg and Goraguer fell out, he says, 'I think they all did eventually. This work of arranging was very frustrating.'

Jean-Claude Vannier is one of those arrangers who clawed back credits that were owed to him, even if he claims to bear no ill will for his relegation to the shadows as Gainsbourg took the limelight. 'I worked with Serge for three years and made *Melody Nelson* in that time. He said, *We are like Cole Porter—I am Cole, you are Porter*. I didn't want this arrangement with him any longer, so I went away and did my own separate things.' Vannier claims not to care that he doesn't get the credit he deserves, even when he made a track as dazzling as 'La Horse' and it was Serge's name on the label and up on the screen as the credits rolled. 'It's not important, it's not something I worry about,' he says dismissively. 'I didn't go to the cinema, and I didn't see Gainsbourg's name on the screen, so it makes no odds to me. I write music and then I move on.'

Alan Hawkshaw wasn't one of the arrangers who went to SACEM in order to recoup earnings and receive credits. 'In retrospect, perhaps I should have done what all the rest of the boys did and claimed a piece of all those albums.'

4

SCREEN

ANNA (1967)

[With my face, in pictures, I get to play all
the traitors and bastards.*]

Winning the Eurovision Song Contest in 1965 was the breakthrough Serge
Gainsbourg had been waiting for. It didn't make him famous as a singer—it
was France Gall who won with 'Poupée de cire, poupée de son', after all—but
it elevated him to a new, special place in the pantheon of songwriters available
for hire. Overnight, he was the toast of the French music industry.

The French had actually passed on 'Poupée de cire …', which is how he
and Gall and conductor Alain Goraguer came to be representing Luxembourg
under the tutelage of the TV producers Maritie and Gilbert Carpentier.
Maritie and Gilbert were a televisual power couple in France and French-
speaking regions who remained indomitable in their field for the four decades
before they retired. At the time, they produced up to six shows a week for
Radio Luxembourg, and Gainsbourg had been writing songs regularly for
their shows.

'Poupée de cire, poupée de son' won the tenth edition of the Eurovision,
and stylistically it was in contrast to all of the previous victors up to that
point. At about 155bpm, it is a song that could reasonably be described as
'upbeat', as opposed to all the big, showy ballads that went before it—and it

---

* 'Moi, avec ma gueule, au cinéma, je joue les traîtres les salauds.' Serge Gainsbourg, *Pensées
provocs et autres volutes* (Librairie Générale Française, 2007)

[90]

dragged the final kicking and screaming into the 60s, modernising the contest by sheer force of its brilliance. It would influence what was to come, right down to the lyrical content and studied cookiness of Sandy Shaw's 'Puppet On A String', a winner for the UK two years later. What's more, the fact it was so successful really annoyed the French, who'd gone with crooner Guy Mardel in a yachting-club blazer, singing the word *jamais* over and over again over a pedestrian waltz. ('N'avoue jamais' came in a respectable third place.)

In classic Gainsbourg style, the song borrows liberally from Beethoven, reinterpreting a section from the German composer's 'Piano Sonata No.1', while the lyrics provide a meta analysis of the modern performer—a mannequin who we project our fantasies upon, trapped forever in her own songs. 'My records are a mirror in which everyone can see me,' she sings. 'I am everywhere at once, broken into a thousand voices.'* There is a sense that, as a doll, everything she does is for an external master controlling her destiny and even using her for his own ends—a svengali or bunraku figure. 'Sometimes when I'm alone I sigh,' she sings. 'I ask myself, What good is it? / Singing about love without reason / Without knowing anything about boys.'†

The second part of the English title 'Puppet Of Sound' is often translated as 'Puppet Of Sawdust'; this double meaning undermines idealised dreams of stardom further, and is a knowing nod to Igor Stravinsky's ballet *Petrushka*, about the loves and jealousies of three puppets. There's a sense that the singer is stuffed and shaped and made to order, and that it wouldn't really matter who was delivering the lines. Glamour is turned on its head, and once stardom is attained, the Sisyphean drudgery starts all over again.

This meta awareness is everywhere now, but to be part of the pizzazz would have been an enviable position in 1965, with few thinking about the smoke and mirrors of show business, and fewer still engendered with feelings of cynicism and contempt for the entertainment machine. It's a song that was years ahead

---

* 'Mes disques sont un miroir dans lequel chacun peut me voir / Je suis partout à la fois brisée en mille éclats de voix.'

† 'Seule parfois, je soupire / Je me dis à quoi bon / Chanter ainsi l'amour sans raison / Sans rien connaître des garçons.'

of its time and of a quality that isn't necessarily requisite in most Eurovision entries. 'If you read the words, they're really desperate,' says Jane Birkin. 'Of course it's a jolly tune, but the words are miserable. Wonderful words. He said with the hit he had with Eurovision, he turned his vest inside out and the interior was made of mink. And it's true, his fortunes changed from then on.'

Years later, in 2008, Sebastien Tellier entered one of the all-time great songs into the Eurovision Song Contest—by my reckoning at least—and certainly one with some of the most unexpected chord changes. Appearing stage right in Belgrade in a golf cart, accompanied by five bearded women, he performed 'Divine', taken from his then recently released album *Sexuality*. 'At the time, I didn't think about it when I was asked to do Eurovision,' says Tellier, 'I immediately said yes. But later, when I had doubts about the relevance of my participation in this show, I thought of Gainsbourg, and that reassured me. He is an essential figure for all French musicians. He's like a father, and we use him as the benchmark. And I often think of him. His music and the artistic point of view that emerges from it—together they form an absolute in French culture. A form of perfection!' 'Divine' came nineteenth.

Serge was back in the saddle, and in onomatopoeic overdrive, for Eurovision 1967, two years after he won it, this time writing Monaco's entry, Minouche Barelli's 'Boum-Badaboum', which came fifth. Another entry he wrote, 'White And Black Blues', performed by France's Joëlle Ursull, came second in 1990. It had originally been called 'Black Lolita Blues', but Joëlle had turned it down as she thought it was insulting. Second place was nowhere for Serge, though. 'He was mortified when he didn't win,' says Birkin. 'He rang me up, crying. I said it's crap nowadays anyway, what do you care about that? And he said, When I go into a competition, I must win it. And it's true, he did win it. So to come second was shameful for him.'

Another song by Gainsbourg, 'Comme un boomerang', was turned down by a French Eurovision panel for being too provocative, though it would take on a strange, high-yielding afterlife. The French chanteuse Dani had been due to represent France in the UK in 1974, but the country withdrew from the contest as a mark of respect to president Georges Pompidou, who'd died of a heart attack the previous week. Dani was asked to take part in Eurovision the following year, and she requested to do a specially penned song by Gainsbourg, ten years after he'd won it with Luxembourg. The panel asked for amendments to be made to the text because it was deemed too racy. Dani refused, and France entered Nicole Rieu's syrupy torch song 'Et bonjour à toi l'artiste' instead. (It came fourth.)

'Years later, Dani told me Gainsbourg had written a song for her for the Eurovision Song Contest and it didn't get through,' a dapper Étienne Daho tells me, sitting in a big airy room at the French Institute in South Kensington. Daho is a huge pop star in France, a kind of gallic David Byrne, who has duetted with everyone from Marianne Faithfull to Jeanne Moreau, Saint Etienne and Charlotte Gainsbourg, and produced records for Birkin, Lou Doillon, and many more. 'This song was sitting on the shelf in the record company, picking up dust. It's very strange because Serge usually had a very good memory, but he didn't remember that song for some reason. He didn't give it to Catherine Devenue or Jane Birkin or Charlotte or the other actresses that he worked with in the 80s. He was usually very adept at recycling what he'd done before—ideas or puns—but he forgot about that song. And then, when I heard it, I immediately knew it was a good song. I produced it for Dani and she said, I want you to sing it with me. I said, It's not a duet, it's not right. So I told her, I'll sing it, and then you'll realise very soon it's not a duet. And so I did one vocal, and the engineer was switching between her voice and mine, and I realised it was quite good, actually.' Daho laughs. 'She has a very low voice, a man's voice—she's our French Marianne Faithfull—and it was too high for me, so it was a gender switch, which was very interesting and confusing for people at the same time. And so the song was a massive hit.'

Dani and Daho enjoyed the sixth best-selling song of the year in 2001 in France; Gainsbourg's version, which he'd recorded for Dani as a guide, was released ten years later, to mark the twentieth anniversary of his death, and became the fortieth best-selling single of that year. It was also covered by Chilly Gonzales, Feist, and Dani herself, for the *Monsieur Gainsbourg Revisited* tribute album that came out in 2006.

Eurovision did wonders for Gainsbourg's profile, and he in turn remained loyal to Maritie and Gilbert Carpentier, writing review songs and sketches and anything else they might require, mostly for Saturday-night entertainment shows. 'That's why he never refused to do a TV show with Maritie and Gilbert,' says Birkin. 'He wrote songs for nothing for those shows every Saturday night because Gilbert was the head of Radio Luxembourg. That's why he was so faithful until their death and his, to write numbers that were so clever and so witty, just for a Saturday night.'

His relationship with the Carpentiers began properly in 1963, when he was asked to write bespoke songs for *The Sacha Show*—a job that he turned out to be fast and effective at. Many of these songs written for light-entertainment programmes over the years were never registered at SACEM. Ina.fr is littered with songs by Gainsbourg, often performed by other artists that never found a home beyond one televisual outing. You can sometimes find them on YouTube, too, like 'Raccrochez c'est une horreur', a throwaway sketch song he and Jane performed together during the 70s. Birkin recalls it fondly when she suddenly remembers it. As she plays it to me on her phone, her eyes moisten at the memories, and I can't help feeling I'm slightly intruding upon the moment. 'When you re-see them again, they were so funny,' she says, laughing with tears rolling down her cheeks. 'He rings up and says, *Ello ma poupee*, and I say, *Raccrochez c'est une horreur!*'

TV became an alternative universe where Gainsbourg was writing throwaway ditties like 'Raccrochez c'est une horreur' for revue shows for the weekend, a situation that we have little cultural understanding of in Britain. Can you imagine Bruce Springsteen penning songs for *The Partridge Family*, or Lou Reed moonlighting writing songs for *Sesame Street* (even if he did start out on Tin Pan Alley)? In France, though, it meant Gainsbourg maintained a kind of household fame even when his own records were tanking. Birkin too became far more recognisable to the French public thanks to the medium of TV. 'Incredibly, he'd write these songs just before the shows, sort of for a joke,' she says. 'Whether it was for Sylvie Vartan or me, he'd write a song that he wouldn't even deposit at SACEM. He'd just write it and we'd go out and do it on the night. So if I'm well known in France it's because of the songs Serge would write for Saturday nights. It was television that made me well-known here.'

The Gainsbourgs didn't go out to gigs during the 70s. They frequented comedy nights instead. Serge Gainsbourg's own sense of stage fright may have been alienating enough that he didn't want to watch anyone else doing what he felt he should be doing, or he may have regarded live comedy as more a part of his own *milieu* at that time. Birkin was big box office as a comedy actress, and Serge was good friends with the comedian Michel Gérard Joseph Colucci, better known by his stage name Colouche, a madcap and profane hell-raiser who died in a motorcycle crash aged just forty-one.

'It's funny that you mention Colouche,' says Bertrand Burgalat. 'I've never really seen the two names associated, but both of them were playing with social taboos, and in a way that cheapened the discourse. In the 70s, there were still these administrations we'd elected: Giscard and Pompidou, which was the world of my parents. And society was still voting right wing at the elections but, culturally, '68 had had an impact. So on television there was a game with censorship and provocation, and Colouche and Gainsbourg were surfing that, in a way. They had a similar role in society—they were in the same market. When you see the French television of the 60s and 70s, it's incredible because people are inhibited by the language they can use, but in another way there was a freedom, because everyone was playing with censorship, and as a result they were doing things that you wouldn't be able to get away with today. So it was censorship, but it could easily be subverted.'

There's a clip recorded at the latter end of the 70s for a Carpentier show featuring Gainsbourg, Johnny Hallyday, and Gérard Depardieu dressed up as bikers singing a reggae version of 'Harley Davidson'. The sketch descends into farce as it wears on, with Hallyday and Depardieu wrestling Gainsbourg and tickling him. It's a fairly low-quality TV encounter between three giants of their respective professions, but despite a lack of direction, all three appear to be enjoying themselves, and one suspects this kind of sketch passed as a reasonable excuse for entertainment at the time.

'Things were so simple in the way they interacted with other artists of their generation,' says Charlotte Gainsbourg, remembering the entertainment scene she experienced as a child first hand. 'Of course, my parents were not mainstream. Claude François was a huge success at that time, and they absolutely were not at the same level of popularity. But on those shows they all shared in something that was very unpretentious. Everyone had fun disguising themselves and taking part in the comedy, and it was so normal to participate. I mean, today in France, we're not able to do that. There's too much competitiveness. People are unable to look at each other in the same way and share in the same things. I always felt that it was such a great time, to be able to have fun in such an honest and spontaneous way.'

Charlotte recalls *Le gala de l'union des artistes*, a circus show involving stars from film and television that became something of an institution where anyone who was anyone got involved. 'It was a charity event that all artists did, and they had to rehearse and do circus shows. My mother did it maybe three or four times—it was quite a bit of work, but everybody played that game, and in such a charming way when you look at it now. I think that degree of popularity and playing around and having fun was not contrary to their work—it was completely different, it was something else.'

In 1973, Birkin took to the high wire for a death-defying stunt in a big top. 'She must be oblivious, I think,' quipped Gainsbourg at the time. 'It's curious because in everyday life she collides with the furniture.'* Although with hindsight it appears that Gainsbourg and Birkin were living double lives, making transgressive as well as progressive records on the one hand—records that weren't selling in the main—while also writing and performing cheesy songs for mainstream Saturday-night television, these seemingly disparate worlds wouldn't have been at odds with French audiences. France has a smaller ecosystem of stars than in the UK, meaning appearances on chat shows would be more regular, for starters.

'France is a place where, if you make a strong enough splash at the

---

* 'Elle doit être inconsciente je pense. C'est curieux dans la vie elle se heurte à tous les meubles.'

beginning of your career, then you have tenure. It's a tenure-based thing,' says Chilly Gonzales, who then asks me if I know who Guesch Patti is. I confess ignorance. 'Guesch Patti had this one hit in 1987 called "Etienne", and she still gets on talk shows from literally having one hit. It's quite nice in a way. It's the opposite of the English approach, where you have your moment in the sun and then everyone forgets about you. If this were France then Menswear would still be on every talk show.'

'If someone is very cool, like Gainsbourg, then it's absolutely his right to participate in all the shows he wants to, even if they're cheesy,' says Vincent Palmer of the French punk-rock trio Bijou. 'The important thing for an artist is to enter people's lives. Then people can then pick and choose what they want from the artist.'

Growing up in the UK in the 80s, there was a cultural apartheid between musicians who considered themselves artists and the brash, working men's club-based comedy that gripped the mainstream. You'd never see David Bowie on *The Little & Large Show*, although he did do *Kenny Everett* once. Even comedy itself was bifurcated between a new school of more credible alternative comedians (*The Young Ones*) and the old guard (Jim Davidson). These worlds were supposed to be separate from one another; alternative comedy and mainstream comedy shows appealed to different demographics of age and class with little overlap. In the UK, Gainsbourg would have had to have chosen his audience, but in France, he was free to maintain a very public persona and play the media, while making more challenging records that at the time had more of a niche market.

His biggest headache had nothing to do with credibility. Bertrand Burgalat says the source of Gainsbourg's main frustrations were closer to home. 'I think what was depressing him more than anything else was the success of Birkin. He would often mention that in interviews, including in front of her, saying, She's more famous than me now. At the beginning, she was a trophy, an accessory, and suddenly her records and her films were doing a lot better.'

It's true that Gainsbourg and Birkin worked on a lot of films together, and it's also true that Gainsbourg usually played second fiddle. Critics complained that it was impossible to watch a movie with Jane Birkin in it without hearing a Gainsbourg soundtrack. The pair became largely inextricable when they were an item—an arrangement that irritated studios and sometimes viewers too. But perhaps most difficult of all for Gainsbourg to take was the fact Birkin was the star.

'She did really well after they met,' says Dr. Leila Wimmer, a Film and Television Studies lecturer at the London Metropolitan University. 'She said herself with John Barry that she was the perfect bland housewife.' (Or, as *Newsweek* put it at the time, 'John Barry with his E-type Jaguar and his E-type wife.') 'With Gainsbourg, she didn't want to repeat that, so, after she got the part in *La Piscine*, she got other offers, and she was glad she wasn't going to be in that situation again.' Birkin remembers that before she landed further parts after *Slogan*, the film she and Serge met on, she'd considered going back to England—a course of action that brought out the drama in Serge. 'He was terribly sentimental,' she says. 'When I said I was leaving to go back to England, after *Slogan*, he sat in front of a candle all night crying. But in a very good light, somehow. But they were real tears, because I said I didn't want to be in France if I didn't have any movies or reasons to be there. I didn't want it to be like when I was with John Barry, where I was waiting around and being a bore. And so he cried for real.'

'Gainsbourg was hanging around the set on *La Piscine*,' says Leila Wimmer. 'He used to follow her when she made all of her films after *Slogan*. I also want to emphasise that those films she made were major box-office hits. She was always in the news with him or after him or without him. Even today, she's all over France because her second collection of diaries is coming out.* She's on the cover of *Les Inrocks*, and she's all over the TV and the talk of the town. She had her own career, and she's an icon, a sex symbol, a respected actress—she's part of the cultural heritage of France.'

The Birkin Bag arrived in 1983 to consolidate her image in her own right, though she was already a recognised fashion trailblazer in 1974 with

---

* *Post-scriptum: Le journal intime de Jane Birkin 1982–2013* (Fayard, 2019)

her androgynous white-T-shirt-and-jeans combo with an idiosyncratic wicker basket, a look beloved by the French for its naturalness and originality. In the 1970s, Birkin was box-office gold for the kinds of comedies Goldie Hawn was making in the US at the same time, and then in 1988, according to Wimmer, she made the symbolic leap from comedy actress to serious *comédienne* thanks to Agnès Varda turning the camera on her for *Jane B. par Agnès V*, a docudrama that blurred the lines between fact and fiction. Gainsbourg makes an appearance in that film, shuffling in apologetically and already looking for all the world like a spectre. His skin is puffy and sallow, probably as a result of liver problems. He looks less like an ex-lover of Jane's and more like an ailing grandfather.

*

I'm all set to meet Anna Karina in a Belle Époque brasserie on the Boulevard Saint-Germain at 2pm on a surprisingly warm April afternoon, and, with an hour to go, my partner suddenly receives a call from the American Hospital telling her she has to go immediately for a blood test (to cut a long story short: she's absolutely fine). The only problem is that we have our son with us. Anyone who has spent time in Paris with an infant will know it's not the most child-friendly city to get around, so I take baby Jean to meet Auntie Anna while Claire scales steep stairs on the metro system *sans bébé*.

Passing the Green Gallant as we cross the Pont Neuf, I attempt to explain to a boy a month short of two years old that we are about to meet French film-star royalty. I'm not sure how much a child his age understands, but he says 'Wow!' several times in an adorable way. 'But you must behave,' I tell him. 'No,' is his swift and troubling reply. Jean also decides he doesn't want to get back into his baby stroller, so I carry him onto the Boulevard Saint Germain, and soon I'm sweating and dishevelled from carrying a two-stone toddler and pushing a pram in a hurry. As we roll up to the elegant restaurant, a nineteenth-century former patisserie called Vagenende, Karina is sitting outside, smoking a cigarette. Glistening and holding a chunky baby, I introduce myself. 'I'll be in in a minute,' she scowls.

I'm ushered to a table in the left wing of the establishment by the maître d', and Jean and I settle into our chairs, waiting. Karina eventually sits down and pours herself some wine from a chiller bucket. I give Jean some water, and he sits there quietly as I lift the glass to his mouth. Over the next thirty minutes he'll rest serenely in his chair looking up at Karina intently, seemingly digesting every word. I'm on tenterhooks for much of that time, waiting for him to play up, but he never does. By the time Claire arrives and takes him away again, Karina has warmed to him, and sees the funny side of the fact a writer has brought a toddler along to an interview—something that had never happened to her in her long illustrious career as an actress and singer. Eight months later, Karina dies of cancer. I feel honoured that, as young as he is, Jean got to meet a *nouvelle vague* icon for half an hour.

I'm there to talk to her about Gainsbourg, and more specifically about *Anna*, the 1967 musical about an advertising executive who falls in love with a girl, or the image of a girl, throwing up a number of possibilities and quandaries that are as popular with modern audiences as they were back then. The ad man, played by Jean-Claude Brialy, spends the film trying to find the girl, played by Karina, who just happens to be right under his nose without him realising. As well as bringing my son to the interview, there's been another hiccup, too. In the weeks leading up to our meeting I've not been able to track down a stream or DVD of the film (something I've rectified since). Karina mocks me about this throughout: 'Ah, you didn't see it? You can get it on the internet, I'm sure. It's called *Anna*! With two *n*s.' As someone who prides himself on being prepared most of the time where interviews are concerned, it's a mildly mortifying predicament, but we press on nevertheless.

Serge Gainsbourg wrote *Anna*, his first screenplay, alongside Jean-Loup Dabadie; he made the soundtrack in collaboration with the estimable Michel Colombier, and the picture itself with director Pierre Koralnik. If the new wave wasn't coming to Serge, then Serge would come to the new wave. 'Serge and Pierre came to my house in 1966, because at that time I lived close to the Odeon. And so they came and they said, Do you want to do a musical? I said, Yes, I've always wanted to do a musical! I love it, I love it!' Karina wasn't sure for certain if the film had been written with her in mind. 'Maybe it was because it was called *Anna* and they couldn't be bothered to find someone with another name?' she said, laughing.

Koralnik, who I speak to later via phone to Switzerland, where he's lived since the 70s, confirms they had her in mind all along. 'I knew that she had a great voice and that she could sing very well, so it was easy to work with her. I didn't know if she would accept or not, but that was my first idea. I thought there was a chance because she was just leaving Jean-Luc Godard at the time. She was kind enough to accept it.'

The producer Michèle Arnaud, who Serge had known since the days of the Milord l'Arsouille, had brought Koralnik and Gainsbourg together. 'One day I got a call from Michèle,' says Koralnik. 'She asked if I could put Serge up in my apartment for a short while, because he wanted to leave his wife. She was pursuing him all over Paris, and he needed refuge somewhere. So I said okay, and he came and he stayed for a year and we worked together on the musical.'

They'd met briefly once before, on the set of a film in Switzerland—the wonderfully odd *L'inconnu de Shandigor*, in which Serge tinkles the still-unreleased 'Bye Bye Mr. Spy' on an imposing organ. 'I knew he could do better, or different,' says Koralnik. 'I liked his work very much, and I knew he could do more interesting things. And he took some pleasure in writing something different from the usual three-minute pop songs for singers.' The team who started out at the Milord brought France its first full-length colour film made for television, which also unusually got a small cinema release thanks to some wheeling and dealing from its charming director.

Anna, first broadcast on TV in January 1967, is full of visual surprises. And Marianne Faithfull is in it as well. When I met her in 2014, for *Fact* magazine, she scotched the rumour that Gainsbourg had asked her to sing 'Je t'aime' with him. 'No, I'm one of the few women he didn't offer it to, thankfully. God! No, we were really, really good friends but he never wanted to fuck me, which is very good, I think. He offered it to everyone else, fucked them, and then decided they weren't quite right. And then he found Jane.' Unbeknown to me at the time, Faithfull's manager, François Ravard, who escorted her to her chair in the garden of an elegant brasserie, had been a great drinking partner of Serge's and produced his last film, 1990's *Stan The Flasher*. Ravard and the actor Claude Berri, who played the titular role, both harboured apprehensions about a movie about a sad suicidal sex case, but they went through with it out of respect for their great friend. In for a penny, Serge's pal Jacques Wolfsohn gallantly goes down with the sinking flick too.

'Having Marianne in the film was a contractual obligation,' says Pierre. 'I was lucky to have her, but it was an obligation to put someone who already has distribution and wanted to be known in France, so they proposed Marianne Faithfull. I was very grateful to have her. I thought she was beautiful.' Faithfull's inclusion was a happy accident, even if she is a bit of a spare part in the picture.

Pierre was less fortunate when he followed up, in 1970, with *Cannabis*, a crime thriller starring Serge in a flamboyant football commentator's coat, with Jane Birkin as the love interest. The melting pot of backers meant an actor had to be present from each country that had invested: Curd Jürgens from Germany, Gabriele Ferzetti from Italy, and England's Paul *'Just Good Friends'* Nicholas. While they're all fine actors in their own right, the language problems disturbed the rhythm of the picture, according to Koralnik. He and Gainsbourg had also intended to do a proper sequel to *Anna*, with Karina in the starring role, and a script had been written while they were in retreat in the South of France, but production problems scuppered it.

Back to *Anna*, where things were running far more smoothly. The production passed quickly, with few complications—a turn of events Karina had been unused to with her unpredictable husband, and then ex-husband, Jean-Luc Godard, for seven feature films. 'We started to work, and Serge was a wonderful guy at that time,' said Karina. 'He was very specific about things. Very professional. So we worked very hard, because some of the songs were very challenging. We spent three weeks on it, but I was used to it. *Vivre sa vie* was three weeks. *Bande à part* took five weeks, maybe not even that. The longest was the first one, *Le petit soldat* …, but that's got nothing to do with Gainsbourg!'

Fascinating nonetheless. Karina regaled me with great tales about working with Fassbinder ('he was involved with a butcher at the time, and I had to sleep in the garden because they were always screaming'); growing up dirt poor in Denmark and coming to Paris penniless ('I never cut meat with a knife until I was eighteen'); and making the movie *Man On Horseback* with Volker Schlöndorff in Eastern Europe when the Russian tanks rolled in ('I came back to France in May '68, after being in Czechoslovakia, and I wondered what all the fuss was about'). She was refreshingly blunt: 'When he was on TV sometimes, with all the lines I'd say, Serge, what are you saying? My God! But Gainsbarre was a sweet person, too—he just wasn't very elegantly dressed, and sometimes he'd say *Fuck you.*'

The soundtrack to *Anna* is a fine effort from all concerned—even actor Jean-Claude Brialy, who'd had little experience of singing up to that point. Michel Colombier brings a gentle, moody atmosphere to 'Ne dis rien' that works as a motif throughout the film. Serge brings ambitious French nineteenth-century conceptual ideas from one of his favourite authors on 'C'est la cristallisation comme dit Stendhal'. And Anna Karina gives a zesty performance for the irrepressible 'Roller Girl'. But the standout moment is 'Sous le soleil exactement', a song so beautiful and elegant that it sounds as perfect when Karina performs it as it does when Serge performs it.

Karina could really sing, unlike a lot of the women who performed his chansons, and her rendition is a masterclass of dynamics and power when needed, soaring in the chorus before it all drops out again and the timpani tumble back in. It's rare to hear a Gainsbourg composition treated in such a way, and a surprise, too, if you're at first familiar with his sleepy-eyed version. Karina tried it his way, up close to the mic and breathy, then decided to do it her own way. Serge's is more a sultry, dishevelled Sunday morning in the sack as sunlight pours through the skylight kind of vibe.

'Looking back now, I remember how difficult it was to get him to work,' says Pierre Koralnik. 'I tried to discipline him and make him work in the daytime, but he always wanted to go out and we were partying somewhere every night. And then I'd have to bring him back because he was so drunk, and then wake him up in the morning like I was his nanny. It continued with Jane.

Then I had to do the same but with both of them! I had to take them back to their place and then try to organise the next day of work. I was like an acrobat trying to do everything. When I think back to that time, it was easy, but as a young man I did a lot of running around after Serge.'

Karina got the run-around too when she needed a song for her directorial debut, *Vivre ensemble*, in 1973. 'I finished the film, and of course I gave Gainsbourg a call. I needed to mix in a song, and he said he'd do it. And then he called me two weeks later, because I was still in the cutting room, and he said, I can't do it because I'm making an album with Jane Birkin, but I'll give you another song.'

That song was 'La noyée', a beautiful waltz that he'd written with Yves Montand in mind, although it had proved a little too spicy, lyrically, for the crooner. Meaning 'The Drowned Girl' in English, Gainsbourg's affection for the Pre-Raphaelites would have likely manifested in this song, in reference to Sir John Everett Millais's *Ophelia* painting that currently resides in the Tate Britain; he may also have been referencing Brecht's 'Vom ertrunkenen Mädchen' (from the play *Baal*), which has the same titular meaning in German. 'I say yeah, I listened to the song, it's okay, I'll take this song with the music,' Karina recalled. She swiftly recorded it but then, as she mixed it, Gainsbourg suddenly remembered it was under license to the New York publishing company Soultown Music, as he'd been humming it in scenes in the movie *Romance Of A Horse Thief* in 1971. Karina's production didn't have the kind of capital to free it from the American publishers, so she called Colombier in a panic as a last resort. Colombier, who was conducting an orchestra in Austria that evening, put her in touch with his pal Claude Engel. The musician obliged and saved the day, he and Karina writing and recording a song together for *Vivre ensemble*, no thanks at all to Serge.

As beautiful as 'La noyée' is, Gainsbourg never released a version in his lifetime. He considered it unsuitable for his voice, and it is unusually melodious for one of his songs from the 70s. Many years later, the future first lady of France, Carla Bruni, would record what would become a well-known version. Gainsbourg did perform it once on TV, in 1972, with Jean-Claude

Vannier at the piano, though Vannier dismisses it as a 'Richard Strauss rip-off', barely distinguishable from a passage in the opera *Chevalier à la rose*, not that that would normally deter Serge.

Vannier brought his mastery to many of Gainsbourg's soundtracks, doing the heavy lifting on music that lives long in the memory, like the mesmeric 'La Horse' or the opening sequence of *Les chemins de Katmandou*.* He began with Robert Benayoun's enjoyably pretentious, surrealist telekinesis thriller *Paris n'existe pas*, and then he properly got his teeth into *Slogan*, with the gorgeous incidental music 'Evelyne' and the ornate and luxurious 'La chanson de Slogan', which not only brought the trinity of Gainsbourg, Vannier, Birkin together for the first time but was also Jane's vocal debut. What a luminous symphonic flatbed to commence your pop career upon!

The story of Serge and Jane's romance and how they first met has been covered extensively elsewhere, including in Véronique Mortaigne's 2019 book *Je t'aime: The Legendary Love Story Of Jane Birkin And Serge Gainsbourg*, so I don't want to spend too much time on it. It's a tale often repeated verbatim by Birkin: the pair meet on Pierre Grimblat's *Slogan*; Grimblat casts her after he spots her in a Chelsea cafe (she happens to be on the way to the audition), despite the fact she can't speak any French. He's looked all over Europe for a girl who is 'naive and a vixen', based on his own perceptions of a lost love— Francois Truffaut had encouraged him to write about his former romance in order to exorcise the pain, and *Slogan* is the result. Jane *is* the girl, he decides, and the leading man is put out that Marisa Berenson doesn't get the part.

Birkin goes to Paris for a screen test with Serge Gainsbourg, who she reads with, and who is unspeakably arrogant; Jane still can't speak a word of French and calls him Serge Bourguignon by mistake, much to his annoyance.† She wins the part, and the first week of filming proves to be a frosty one between the leading actors. Grimblat then sets up a Friday-night summit for the three

---

* The master tapes of *Les chemins de Katmandou* had been thought lost forever, but they were discovered in an old suitcase by the daughter of Vannier's former copyist in 2015.
† Serge Bourguignon is a well-known director in France who won the Best Foreign Film Academy Award in 1962 for *Les dimanches de Ville d'Avray*.

of them at Maxim's, to iron out their differences, and cunningly doesn't show up. Serge and Jane finally hit it off, and as part of the détente they go dancing at a transvestite bar, and she soon realises he's not arrogant at all, just sensitive. They head to Jane's hotel, where Serge passes out. They live happily ever after for the next eleven years …

There's a break in filming during the making of *Slogan*, and rather than hang around in Paris with nothing to do, Jane Birkin gets a part in *La Piscine* alongside Alain Delon. The director Jacques Deray is in need of someone to fill the role quickly, and Grimblat recommends her. There are two versions of *La Piscine*, which was shot in both French and English with the same cast.

Raechel Leigh Carter, who publishes an excellent fanzine, *My Chérie Jane*, and formed the tribute band Baby Birkin in the late 90s, suggests that while Jane has memories of being unable to speak any French, her actual grasp of the language may have been better than she remembers. 'I think she exaggerates quite a lot when she says she couldn't speak a word of French. She'd been to French finishing school, and I think she could speak some French. It probably was ropey, but I don't believe she couldn't speak a word of French at all.'

The movie that Serge and Jane met on is perhaps the highlight of the couple's chequered filmography together, and the documentation of their love affair in its infancy brings a pleasurable sparkle to the film. Grimblat had also been an award-winning ad man himself, and the way the movie is cut with some of the techniques he would have employed at his previous job gives the picture a splice-happy contemporaneity. In fact, Grimblat was up for an award in Venice for a Renault advert he'd made as head of ideas at Publicis when *Slogan* was being made. Given that nobody really knew what he looked like, being an advert director and not Alfred Hitchcock, he took a film crew and photographers along to the ceremony on the off chance that he had won. Instructed to sit in the front row—a good sign that he was in it to win it— he sent Serge to sit there instead and found a seat in the fourteenth row to watch from. And, sure enough, Gainsbourg had to get up onstage and collect Grimblat's award, pretending to be the director. 'So the actual scene in the film where Serge wins an award was shot for real,' says Raechel. 'You can see it in

Serge's eyes that he looks absolutely terrified, because he thinks he's going to get found out.'

The part was written specifically for Serge, a great drinking mate of Grimblat—who claimed nobody else could have played the part. Serge didn't get to be the leading man often, and he was more interested in taking smaller parts so he could be with Jane, and also so that he could travel. He went up the Himalayas on location with Birkin for *Les chemins de Katmandou*, and, before he met her, he went to Columbia for *Estouffade à la Caraïbe* in a film with Jean Seberg, and to Hong Kong for *L'inconnue de Hong Kong* with Dalida.

With soundtracking, he no doubt had more of a sense of why he was there, and with some great arrangers he created memorable music that has in most cases outlasted the films: firstly with Alain Goraguer (*L'eau à la bouche*), then with Michel Colombier (*Manon 70*; *Le Pacha*), then with Vannier, and later with Jean-Pierre Sabar (*Madame Claude*; *Goodbye Emmanuelle*). But Gainsbourg's film career is a patchy affair made up mostly of films that are not easily available. These are not movies you'll find streaming on Netflix or brought together in tandem for the BFI Player or the Criterion Collection. These are films one has to track down, sometimes for quite a lot of money and few discernible benefits. Gainsbourg wasn't a bad actor, it's just that some of the films he found himself in were of a disposable quality.

Take, for instance, two Italian-produced films shot with the director Gianfranco Parolini in the early 60s: *Sampson* and *The Fury Of Hercules*. Though the villainous characters he plays are different from each other (at least in name), the costumes and even the cast are largely the same for two Brad Harris vehicles with the same modus operandi: flash Brad's enormous muscles at every opportunity. Both films were largely panned, but Serge won some of the few plaudits for his portrayal of Warkalla in *Sampson*, while his turn as Menistus in *The Fury Of Hercules* is one as dastardly and camp as Edmund in the first series of *Blackadder*.

He's a menacing presence on screen, at least in a pantomime sense, but these films were two rare examples where he got to do more than just play the pianist (see *Mr. Freedom*, *Strip-Tease*, *L'inconnu de Shandigor*, *L'inconnue de*

Hong Kong …). He also managed to get typecast as an advertising executive, playing similar roles in three films (*Anna, Paris n'existe pas, Slogan*), a curious case of life imitating art. As we'll see later, Gainsbourg didn't just moonlight making ads, he embraced making them with élan, and his turns as a publicist may have planted a subliminal seed in the minds of agencies. As a bit-part actor and Birkin's on-set foil, he took bizarre roles, including a police inspector in the 1973 Scottish gothic horror *Seven Deaths In The Cat's Eye*, for which he was hilariously dubbed over by a Scottish actor.

Gainsbourg's experience working in film taught him one thing: he wanted to be a director. He got the chance in 1976 with *Je t'aime moi non plus*, a picture the producers may not have envisaged, given the titular association with the 1969 hit of the same name. *Je t'aime* the movie is a queer fantasy in which the beautiful homosexual icon Joe Dallesandro finds himself attracted to 'Johnny' (played by Jane), a short-haired tomboy working behind a bar in a one-horse town that's magically transported to rural France from somewhere in Middle America. A small posse of homosexual characters ride into town in a Mack Truck (there's not much character development in most cases), in an opening sequence not entirely unlike Sam Peckinpah's *Convoy*, which would hit cinemas two years later. The eighteen-wheeling machismo of *Convoy* captured the zeitgeist, whereas the more sexually ambiguous *Je t'aime moi non plus* received derision in the main.

In a revealing strip for *Lui* magazine featuring Jane as she is often seen in the film, i.e. *au naturel*, Serge contributed a succinct editorial to accompany the spread: 'In *Je t'aime moi non plus* alongside Joe Dallessandro, Jane gave me her all. Look at her now in little white tennis socks and short hair as she is in this film, bent over the radio listening to the reviews, or over the jukebox as it spits the "Ballade de Johnny-Jane", the leitmotif of my latest film.'*

The chintzy piano instrumental for 'Ballade de Johnny-Jane', made with

* 'Dans *Je t'aime moi non plus*, aux côtés de Joe Dallesandro, Jane m'a donné le meilleur d'elle-même. Et regardez-là maintenant, tennis, socquettes blanches et cheveux courts, telle qu'elle est dans ce film, se pencher sur le poste de radio pour écouter les critiques, et devant ce juke-box qui crache 'La ballade de Johnny-Jane', leitmotiv de mon dernier film.'

Jean-Pierre Sabar (or sometimes Sabard, if the mood took him), became a mainstay on French TV and must have made Gainsbourg a small fortune just through incidental use alone. The soundtrack for the picture was a much bigger hit than the film itself. While the knives were out, one voice of reason on the radio, François Truffaut, was effusive with praise. The hero of French cinema, who'd already had an indirect influence on Serge's and Jane's lives after encouraging Pierre Grimblat to write a screenplay about his experiences, admired *Je t'aime moi non plus* greatly for both its story and its cinematography—and who could fail not to be moved by Willy Kurant's beautiful camerawork and the rich verdure of the *mise en scène*?

Perhaps some antipathy came from the fact it wasn't a particularly erotic picture, despite the promise of lots of sex and nudity. Krassy and Johnny don't exactly hit it off sexually at first, and it's only when she suggests to him that she's a boy that he's able to penetrate her from behind, which precipitates lots of screaming in agony rather than ecstasy. 'When you think about it,' says Raechel Leigh Carter, 'imagine the disappointment for people who knew the saucy couple from the 45rpm are going to be getting it on, and then they see a gay man and a girl with short hair saying "you can take me from behind" and then screaming and screaming. It's not exactly a turn-on.'

Andrew Birkin was on set during the filming, and he even had a small part. 'It got cut out,' he says, laughing, 'probably because of my performance. Serge was rather apologetic about it, and I've still got the album somewhere, which he signed to *the beautiful motorcyclist* or whatever. I liked the film a lot, actually—I thought it was very original and had a point of view unlike most movies. There's something very distinctive about it and something unique.' Was there anger that the critics had been unkind? 'I know that he and Jane and I were very disappointed with the fact the film was dismissed in England. We weren't angry, that's too strong a word. It was only showing in one cinema as far as I was aware, and in a rather seedy Soho cinema at that.'

Raechel Leigh Carter says a film like *Je t'aime moi non plus* is exactly the kind of thing that would have been screened in Soho at the time: 'I would have loved to have been old enough to have been around Soho in the 60s and 70s, because back then that was where you saw Arthouse films. We don't have any diversity with cinema these days because people will only put on films that they think will make money. Back then they would put on loads of different films throughout the week and those cinemas would get enough of the dirty-mac brigade in to make it pay. I don't know why they expected *Je t'aime* to be showing anywhere else, considering the subject matter.'

Je t'aime moi non plus is a much better film than it's been credited for—a homegrown love letter to America in the style of one of Wim Wenders's travelogues, with some very progressive ideas about homosexuality at that time as well. There are awkward moments, naturally, and many involve Gérard Depardieu's character—a horse-riding peasant who threatens one of the gay characters with the girth of his enormous penis. But otherwise it's risqué auteurism, which perhaps would have been better appreciated had Gainsbourg taken fewer risks, and that would have been a shame. Also, the picture benefits from its focus on Jane, whereas the films after *Je t'aime moi non plus* would tip the scales into wilful self-indulgence. Given the logistics required to get a film off the ground, and how expensive they are to make, it's the one art form where the old cliché about making it for yourself ('and if anyone else likes it, it'll be a bonus') doesn't apply.

'His films were not very good, I'm sorry to say,' was Anna Karina's honest and damning verdict. 'But you can't be good at everything!'

5 AESTHETICS

BONNIE & CLYDE (1968)

LA PACHA (1968)

INITIALS B.B. (1968)

> Dandyism is behaviour on the brink
> of suicide. It's an attitude of choice, a
> constant game where you escape reality.*

On Paris's Rive Gauche, a few hundred metres from the River Seine, is a conundrum that has confounded for nearly three decades. The interior of 5 bis rue de Verneuil remains largely as it was the night Gainsbourg died of a heart attack in 1991. Inside is part sarcophagus, part cabinet of curiosities, full of the dandy provocateur's gathered treasures. If it sounds like a museum in the making, then its bijou dimensions and its inaccessibility mean that nobody quite knows what to do with it.

'With the museum not really happening, I realised I couldn't rent it, I couldn't sell it, I couldn't do anything else with it, so it's been a struggle,' admits Charlotte Gainsbourg, who's been in discussion with various authorities and has been allied with one or two benefactors over the years. 'Now I'm not alone

---

* 'Le dandysme est un comportement au bord du suicide, C'est le choix d'une attitude, un jeu constant pour échapper à la réalité.' Serge Gainsbourg, *Pensées provocs et autres volutes* (Librairie Générale Française, 2007)

on the project,' she says, sounding hopeful, 'and that's quite reassuring. I think something will happen. I don't think it will happen soon.'

Plans to open up 5 bis Rue de Verneuil to the public look to finally be in place, and in early 2020 Jane Birkin told *Paris Match* that they were aiming to do so for the thirtieth anniversary of Gainsbourg's death, though with the France going into lockdown soon after and the ongoing challenges of Covid-19, it was impossible to say whether or not that might happen as this book went to press.

Chez Gainsbourg is French pop's very own *Marie Celeste*, a relic of glorious artifice that invokes the spirit of fin-de-siècle decadence as seen through the eyes of a raffish 60s musician. He once admitted that he was unsure if it was 'a sitting-room, a music room, a brothel, a museum?' The flat is situated on a working street where the neighbours include Juliette Gréco. The tags and murals on *le mur Gainsbourg* at the front of the apartment constantly evolve according to the whims of his fans, and the graffiti itself has become a tourist attraction, a colourful, aerosoled splurge on an otherwise bourgeois street. But inside things are different. Or, rather, things are largely as they were.

'Often I talk to musicians and people I work with, and it's always very special when I offer to open the house,' says Charlotte. 'It's very intimate. It's a little embarrassing, but it's such a wonderful place. It's very surreal now. Well, maybe not surreal, but sort of stopped in time.'

'The house is still alive,' says the photographer Tony Frank, who took some of the most recognisable pictures of Gainsbourg over a twenty-year period, including famous shots in the courtyard of the building. 'I told Charlotte, it's too small to turn into a museum. There are so many little objects that people would break.' Frank was invited back in 2017 to shoot pictures of the items within, which were then published in a book named after the famous address.* The house now belongs to Charlotte alone; she bought out Serge's other children, Lulu, Paul, and Natacha, shortly after their father died.

---

* Tony Frank, Jean-Pierre Prioul, *Gainsbourg, 5bis rue de Verneuil* (EPA, 2017)

'Everything is the way he wanted it. It was very precise,' Charlotte adds. 'There are many, many objects, specifically on the table. There's a big coffee table with the home phone, and then tonnes of objects that had not only a specific spot, but also orientation, and it would mean you would have to put the lady figurine or the little man in exactly the right spot or my father would see it. Everything had a place. As children we were able to play, of course—we had a playroom, but the sitting room was always a place you could come into but you couldn't stay. It was very contained, but very beautiful in that way too. To me, those memories are so precious. But it's a weird thing to try to explain. Nowadays it seems a little unreal.'

'So, to have two children in that house …,' says Birkin, expressing exasperation as if she were still there. 'We weren't allowed into his salon, we weren't allowed to touch the piano … and so we stayed in the kitchen and the children's room. I wanted to get a room over the road and build a tunnel to get there, or a bridge, just to have a room of my own.' Jane had to make do with a small boudoir ('I could go and *boud* when I was cross'). After she left, it was filled with mildly terrifying vintage dolls and became Bambou's *chambre des poupées*. 'And Serge used to come in and complain about the mess,' says Jane, 'and I would get into such a rage because I was happy in a mess. But it used to drive him barmy. So everything with him was artistic.'

Gainsbourg's fastidiousness bordered on the maniacal. Birkin admits that living in Rue de Verneuil was 'a nightmare' at times, though it had its upsides: 'It was exquisite to be able to give him presents because he used to put them in a place and he'd say, From now on, nobody will touch it. It was rather wonderful to be able to give him something and to know it would fit into that little palace of his. And so I used to buy him bronzed rats from Japan or medical things he'd put on his table, or tapestries for the wall. I gave him a little lead figure when he was making *Equateur*, and he put it on top of his little bibliothèque, which had syringes from the last war in mahogany.' She adds, 'But it was a museum. He told me there was such disorder in his head that if he looked down and there was anything out of place, he'd go mad.'

The house at 5 bis Rue de Verneuil was a dominion of organised disorder, random yet meticulous, 'So you never knew how to do things right. He didn't want them dead straight, so they'd be slightly … like that,' Jane says, demonstrating by moving her coffee cup a few degrees to the left. 'And then, with the packets of cigarettes, when he'd finished with them, he'd turn them over. So there was a method to it. And he used to rush off and clean the ashtray after two or three cigarettes because he wanted everything to be frightfully clean.'

Gainsbourg was 'sweet' with Jane's dog, Nana, despite not really being a fan of dogs. 'He'd say, Has he finished drinking now? and I'd say yes, and he'd rush off to the kitchen to get a little mop to clean around the bowl, an exquisite Chinese work of art that he'd given this bulldog to drink out of.' Would he likely be considered obsessive-compulsive today? 'Probably, yes,' says Jane. 'Or like someone who has a museum.'

Charlotte scoffs at the idea that her father was OCD: 'No, not at all! He was just very obsessed with aesthetics but not in a nervous way at all. Not the way we imagine OCD. It was something he chose. He just decided to be that way and taught us everything about aesthetics, so he shared his vision with all of us. And it was obvious we would be the same, and we would think the same way.' Was he inspired by J.K. Huysmans's *Against Nature*? 'Yeah, that's one of the books he told me to read, and I'm actually reading it again right now. The character in that book, Des Esseintes, was a great influence.'

Against Nature, or À rebours in French, was a cornerstone of the decadent movement, famously quoted at the trial of Oscar Wilde as a source for *A Picture Of Dorian Gray*. It was written by the French civil servant Joris-Karl Huysmans and published in 1884. The British poet and critic Arthur Symons called the novel 'elaborately and deliberately perverse'. It concerns the main (and almost only) character, Des Esseintes, his meticulous scenery, lethargy, and his abhorrence for anything natural. It's a roman-à-clef wherein the hero doesn't do very much at all, preferring to idle away the days in a laudanum haze, imagining adventures rather than partaking in them, arguing that travel narrows the mind. The *I* character in *Withnail & I*, played by Paul McGann, carries the book around in his pocket in the film, and its creator, Bruce Robinson, has been of the opinion that À rebours is one of the funniest books ever written, although one suspects Huysmans wasn't playing it for laughs.

'It pleased some young men in various countries to call themselves Decadents, with all the thrill of unsatisfied virtue masquerading as uncomprehended vice,' wrote Symons in 1899. Despite the supercilious tone, it's a reasonable assessment of the conflicted nostalgia of the Decadence. There's a cloying for art's halcyon days, and a very modernistic embrace of hedonism and decay, the paradox at the heart of the movement. Aside from a love of Baudelaire, Des Esseintes's tomes are mostly written in Latin and hanker for the classical decadence. Gainsbourg's reading habits were more concerned with the French *fin-de-siècle* reboot.

Like Des Esseintes (or Huysmans), Serge had a proclivity for beautiful, very expensive, first-edition books, which adorn the shelves of his bibliothèque in Rue de Verneuil. Biographical subjects within his bookcases include Chopin, Velázquez, Rembrandt, Van Eyck, Max Ernst, and Francis Bacon; there's poetry by Rimbaud and Baudelaire, works by Montaigne and Benjamin Constant, *A Journal Of The Plague Year* and *Robinson Crusoe* by Daniel Defoe, and works about surrealism by André Breton and Maurice Nadeau. More contemporarily, *NovöVision* by the neo-Symbolist French music journalist Yves Adrien, which was highly influential among latter-day aesthetes when it was published in 1980, sits among the shelves. But in order of preference, he went on record to say that Huysmans was no.1.*

'Serge Gainsbourg owned an original edition of À rebours with the pages worn from being read and re-read so much,' writes Franck Maubert in *Gainsbourg À rebours* (the title part-inspired by Huysmans). 'It was his bible, his blueprint and his secret reference. He could recite passages by heart to anyone who would care to listen.'† Another biographer, Bertrand Dicale, goes

---

* 'Par ordre préférentiel, À rebours de Huysmans, Histoire de Surréalism, Daniel Defoe wr la Journal de l'année de la peste, Benjamin Constant, Montaigne, Rimbaud bien sûr, Baudelaire.' Tony Frank, Jean-Pierre Prioul, *Gainsbourg, 5bis rue de Verneuil* (EPA, 2017)

† Franck Maubert, *Gainsbourg à rebours* (Fayard, 2013)

even further in his 2009 book *Gainsbourg en dix leçons* regarding the influence it had on his apartment: 'It is quite clear that the interior of the Rue de Verneuil house-museum, designed by Serge Gainsbourg with a maniacal passion, is like one of Des Esseintes's dreams: surgical tools, police badges, precious boxes, a tarantula … it's a snob's junkyard of arbitrary delights.'

Marie-Dominique Lelièvre, who had a poke around the place before writing her 1994 biography, describes it as the house of a single man and egotist who subjected his partners and his children to its inhospitable environment: 'Gainsbourg's favourite chair is stiff like an orthopedic prosthesis … the furniture is rigid and severe: military furniture. It is forbidden for anybody except Serge Gainsbourg to sit there. He lives in a despotic tension, not allowing himself to relax.'*

There's a table festooned in police medals, handcuffs, bullet cartridges, and a book opened to the pages of a Browning revolver. Serge owned about 250 pieces in all, a tribute to the Gendarmes who'd provide him with company toward the end of his life. 'He was really friendly with the police,' says Alan Parker. 'I remember a couple of times when we went to Paris and I stayed around the corner from his house in a little hotel. We had drinks at his place and I went out for dinner, and when we came back there were local police hanging out there, and there were always bunches of roses at his gates. Other times we went out and he was absolutely out of it, and he'd be slumped down in the street somewhere. A policeman came along one time and said, *Ah, Serge!* He picked him up and took him back to his apartment. He was so loved by everybody.'

'The police were the only people who'd listen to him when he went down there at 4am,' says Birkin. 'He'd turn up with a bottle of champagne and they'd listen to his anecdotes and his Jewish jokes. Then he could tootle back. He wasn't responsible for them, and they weren't responsible for him. Who

---

* Le siège favori de Gainsbourg est raide comme une prothèse orthopédique … Ce meuble est rigide, sévère: du mobilier militaire. L'étiquette interdit à quiconque, hormis Serge Gainsbourg, d'y siéger. Il vit dans une crispation despotique, ne s'autorisant pas de détente.' Marie-Dominique Lelièvre, *Gainsbourg sans filtre* (J'ai Lu, 1994)

else could he call on at four in the morning? We had all bought answering machines, so we didn't have to listen because we had to get up for work. He liked their badges and he liked them to put the siren on, like a sheriff. He really was like a child. Such a strange mixture, and for him, who had to wear the Star of David on his chest during the war as well.'

Across the room from the law-enforcement paraphernalia is a table decorated with vinyl 45s by forty-five women he wrote chansons for: Françoise Hardy, Nana Mouskouri, Anna Karina, and the rest. 'He was so happy to be famous, because he had a long wait,' says Tony Frank. 'After that, he was very happy. He did a lot of records for different women—Catherine Deneuve, Isabelle Adjani, Jeanne Moreau, Vanessa Paradis, and so on—and he put the record covers all on a table because he was very happy and proud. Also, when there were articles in the newspapers, he framed the headlines up on the wall: "Je t'aime moi non plus" was used as a headline a lot.'

Arbitrary objects dotted around the *maison-musée* include an engraved glass liquor decanter hidden in a nineteenth-century bronze pumpkin; a nineteenth-century globe-mounted tarantula on brass wire by the Maison Deyrolle, specialists in taxidermy and pedagogical charts; a fetching nineteenth-century Écorché—a skinless, life-size figure; an original Rouget de Lisle parchment of 'La Marseillaise', with a portrait by the national anthem writer's friend Jacques-Philippe Voiart framed next to it. Furthermore, photographs of Marilyn Monroe can be found around the house and lining the dark first-floor hallway, including a picture of her in the morgue—a comment perhaps on the transience of beauty and a reminder of his own mortality.

The security at Rue de Verneuil was upped many fold in 1988 after Serge returned from rehearsing with his band in New York, ahead of a week of shows at Le Zénith in Paris, to find an intruder had broken in through a skylight and had made himself at home, soaking in Serge's low-slung tub after escaping from a mental institution. Jewel-encrusted bars decorated with ornate designs were mounted on the gates like it was the Élysée Palace. After he died, firefighters struggled to break their way in as he lay there, entombed on the floor with all his objects around him like an ancient Egyptian king. The shell of 5 bis had become a dark sarcophagus that had turned in on itself with the death of its famous propriétaire.

Artworks still within the walls of Rue de Verneuil include Paul Klee's 1913 etching *Schlimme Botschaft von den Sternen* (*Bad Message From The Stars*) and Claude Lalanne's steel sculpture *L'homme à tête de chou*, both of which became names of albums. There are many other pictures: some seem significant, others random. There's a picture of Georges Brassens, who he admired; there's Édith Piaf, who he admired less, although he would sing 'Mon Légionnaire' on his final album; a photograph with Mitterrand, whose politics he didn't share, and one with Jane Seberg in the 1967 movie *Estouffade à la Caraïbe* (*The Looters*).

Gainsbourg bought the property outright in 1968 with the thirty million francs he made from France Gall's 'Poupée de cire, poupée de son'. He'd already acquired the deeds when he met Birkin, soon-to-be mother of Charlotte, who helped him with some of the specifics, but he chose the place with Brigitte Bardot after his father noticed the property in the paper and told him he had to go and view it right away. Serge returned for a second visit in the morning with B.B. and expressed his desire to buy it there and then. The street had brought him luck in '63, and now he was standing at the threshold with France's original Sex-Kitten. Good news from the stars. 'Bardot is the sun, Gainsbourg, a black asteroid,' writes Lelièvre.* Serge remained in his digs at the Cité des Artistes campus and sought about decking the halls in bitumen black and lining them with his collected curiosities. It would be many months before he could move in, and by then he was with Birkin. 'Everything you put against something black is immediately precious,' says Jane. 'It makes it beautiful. And he had chandeliers everywhere, and little lights. He used to blow up at me because I would forget to turn the lights off on the staircase. It was because he had to go off getting lightbulbs all the time. You needed a lot of lights, and it was a bit like being in an art gallery.'

---

* 'Bardot est un soleil, Serge Gainsbourg un astre noir.' Marie-Dominique Lelièvre, *Gainsbourg sans filtre* (J'ai Lu, 1994)

Sam Lévin's life-size portrait of Bardot, which adorned his Cité des Artistes residence, would greet visitors as they entered the Rue de Verneuil apartment—at least once Birkin moved out in 1980! Bambou must have been very understanding to allow him to keep it there—another part of the narrative stood in its rightful place like all the bottles and cans and syringes and figurines. And Brigitte's name—or at least her initials—adorn his 1968 studio album *Initials B.B.* Even after the breakup he'd been keen to absorb her into his art and make it a part of his mythology, sometimes indiscreetly. After all, B.B. represented a calling card that could open up markets in other places. In *Gainsbourg à rebours*, Maubert recounts a time when a bedraggled, drunken Serge asked someone he'd just met, 'Vous connaissez Brigitte Bardot?' When they nodded in the affirmative, he retorted, 'I fucked Brigitte Bardot.' Another time, Alan Parker was needling him to find out more about Brigitte and asked him what she was really like. 'She loved it over the bonnet of the car and she screamed her head off,' he replied.

*

The year 1968 might look like it was a productive one, with two studio albums and a soundtrack for *La pacha*, but closer inspection highlights duplicates and a number of re-releases to cash in on Gainsbourg's appearance as Brigitte Bardot's foil on *Le show Bardot*. *Bonnie & Clyde* is credited as a studio album, but more than anything it's a random compilation of his career over the last six years, featuring six different arrangers and two Bardot recordings of Bourgeois and Rivière songs that had nothing to do with Serge. *Initials B.B.* features Gainsbourg recordings going back as far as 1965, with Arthur Greenslade at the Philips studio in Marble Arch: 'Marilu', 'Docteur Jekyll et Monsieur Hyde', 'Qui est "in" qui est "out"', and 'Shu Ba Du Ba Loo Ba' were all from a three-year-old EP. The newest track, 'Bonnie & Clyde', appears on both albums, as do the slightly older 'Comic Strip' and 'Docteur Jekyll et Monsieur Hyde'.

Seen merely in terms of success, 'Bonnie & Clyde' could be regarded as the poor relation to 'Je t'aime … moi non plus'. If these songs were written together in the space of one night, as Gainsbourg claimed, then 'Je t'aime' reaped all the headlines and the infamy and the money while 'Bonnie & Clyde' slipped into the shadows; the cooler, edgier twin, beloved of all true Gainsbourg heads. 'Bonnie & Clyde' sounds exotic and otherworldly even now, and it contains a hauntological loop augmented by the intrepid strings of arranger Michel Colombier, making it both remarkably contemporary-sounding and forever trapped in a moment too. The strings are repeated with obstinate regularity to represent the sense of a couple on the run, while the hiccupping voice at the end of each phrase that could be a yodelling woman or even a Brazilian *cuica* drum is actually the voice of Colombier himself.

And then on top is Gainsbourg and Bardot's nonchalant sing-speak, reciting Bonnie Parker's poem 'The Trail's End', translated into French by Serge, about the exploits of her and her lover, Clyde Barrow, and the inevitability of the oncoming quietus. Gainsbourg had written the song after going to see an early press screening of the film. It seemed perfect fodder for *Le show Bardot*, but a rights row nearly broke out when somebody at Warner Bros. objected to its inclusion in the show. As luck would have it, Bardot's pal Warren Beatty spotted the very dossier on Jack Warner's desk in Hollywood and helped to get it waved through.

The origin of the repetitive loop in the song almost certainly came from the arranger, Colombier, who had previously been working with the *musique concrète* pioneer Pierre Henry on an experimental ballet, *Messe pour le temps présent*, that they performed at the Festival d'Avignon in 1967 and again in '68, with Colombier charged with the instrumental *mise en scène* while Henry took care of the electroacoustic composition on top. An album, *Les jerks électroniques de la messe pour le temps présent et musiques concrètes de Pierre Henry pour Maurice Béjart*, also came out, featuring avant-garde synthesizer noise layered over a more conventional rock production, with primitive loops of various samples, such as the sound of cash registers, clattering throughout the recordings.

Gainsbourg would have been open to the idea of looping sounds, and he proved to be way ahead of the game with an extraordinary performance at Le

[120]

Gala de l'Union des Artistes in 1966. Footage survives of Serge stalking the stage and playing short riffs on various instruments, with the notes then being magically looped, presumably by musicians hidden from view. With cigarillo in mouth, he starts with the bass guitar, then moves on to the drums, which the footage suggests he'd never played them before in his life. Once the groove is in place, he moves on to the guitar and adds some chords and a line over the top, and then finally ends up at the piano, where he demonstrates his jazz hands. It's not a tight performance, but it does demonstrate Gainsbourg was thinking about the possibilities of looping many years before acts like Jamie Liddell, tUnE-yArDs, and Andrew Bird were building their live acts around looper pedals.

Other songs from this same era recorded with Colombier utilise looped rhythms and as such have a curious contemporaneity. 'Requiem pour un con' and 'Contact' by Brigitte Bardot are both built on the repetitive grooves of percussive bongos played by session musicians. 'I have a soft spot for the Bardot stuff,' says Dom Thomas, a founding director of vintage vinyl label Finders Keepers, and creator of Mancunian fantasy band Whyte Horses. 'It's like house music but from forty years earlier. The production is incredible. He's basically sampling his own instruments, which is very clever and ahead of its time. It's really forward-thinking. Absolutely genius. And it's like nothing from that era.'

A clip of 'Requiem pour un con' taken from the movie *La pacha* shows Serge coming nose to nose with legendary French actor Jean Gabin at the top of some stairs, and then face to face through a recording studio screen as the musician stands at the mic with plumes of smoke billowing from his lungs. He'd met the legendary French actor on the set of *Le jardinier d'Argenteuil* in '66, a film in which he had a small part, and he'd been recommended to director George Lautner by Gabin, who took a liking to Serge. Gainsbourg would go on to soundtrack Gabin's 1970 movie *La horse* with Vannier too. Jean Gabin had made many films beloved of the French people: *Pépé le Moko*, *La grande illusion*, *La bête humaine*, *Le plaisir* ... A gritty, working-class hero he may have been, but most of his glories were pre-war. By the time he came to make *La pacha* and *La horse*, he'd insisted on banning scenes that required any vigour, such as walking up stairs, for fear they might bring on a heart attack.

The title of 'Requiem pour un con' features a rude word in French which wouldn't have been in use in the media too much in 1968. 'Con' can apparently mean something fairly innocuous like 'idiot', and it can also mean something far more offensive like 'cunt'—it just depends how you say it. According to *Le Gainsbook*, the rhythm track started out as a leitmotif intended to pop up throughout the film, played by the percussionist Jacky Rault, which was then extended with large congas and shakers and then a full track by Serge, which would be released as a single. The vocal line plunders Antonín Dvořák's *New World Symphony*, which wouldn't be the only time he lifted a memorable musical phrase from No.9 in 1968.

The sci-fi-inspired number 'Contact' with Bardot uses Afro-Cuban-based percussion but feels analogous to a techno track, an homage to Vadim's *Barbarella*, which was in cinemas at the time. Bardot repeats the titular word at the end of each verse with a futuristic echo on her voice. 'Contact' anticipates the tropes of electronic dance music decades before its time. New York's Silver Apples, who released their eponymous debut in 1968 and the follow-up, *Contact* (no relation), in 1969, could be said to be doing something similar, but these visionaries were rare. 'Contact' by Bardot is built on a metronomic pulse and a recycled bass line, and, because this is 1968, each phrase begins with a twanging sitar. The eagle-eared will notice that it's actually the same twanging as on 'Harley Davidson', also recorded with Bardot around the same time, suggesting Serge was so voracious for montage that he'd begun to eat himself.

'A thing that bothers me is that when someone becomes so iconic, like Gainsbourg, they become all things to all people,' says Chilly Gonzales, warming to his theme. 'Sometimes I would see French musicians using Gainsbourg as an excuse to not do the work. I would hear musicians get too satisfied too quickly and not write additional sections. And they would hold up Gainsbourg as a model and I'd say, He's the exception, he was the one guy who's allowed to do loops. Okay, bring me "Requiem pour un con" and

I'll let you have a loop, but this is not "Requiem pour un con". We all know Gainsbourg's nonchalance is studied; musically, it's something you have to work very hard at to become. *Gainsbourg didn't give a shit about how he looked, how he sang, about having songs with very many parts, so therefore I have a license to be a lazy singer, a lazy songwriter, I don't have to care how I look, I can be gross, I can be a bit of a dick, and all because Lord Gainsbourg was doing it.* That was frustrating to me. This is often the case where someone becomes so iconic that you can see what you want in them. It happened to Jesus, right?'

Gonzales goes on to say that he was continually frustrated to hear this name invoked to justify lowered standards by French artists. I mention that Bertrand Burgalat and Mick Harvey had been surprised when they started analysing Gainsbourg's work to find he rarely wrote middle eights. 'He often didn't write a chorus either. In a way, he was anticipating hip-hop—he was a master at it, what can I say,' he adds. 'I remember when Sebastien Tellier's *Sexuality* came out, and I was really frustrated because I thought thirty seconds of every song sounded really amazing, and then they would just stay the same. And I was really surprised when I mentioned it to him and he used Gainsbourg as an example. He said, I'm trying to write songs that don't have storytelling in them. Well, okay, but you can also make a film with no plot, a cake with no taste, you can also have sex without an orgasm …'

I ask Tellier about this via email. He replies, 'For the loops, personally, it was much more the DJ culture at the end of the 90s that gave me the desire than the first Serge Gainsbourg loops. But when you come across a perfect chord suite, why change it? The sample and loop culture taught me the beauty of repetition. It helps the artist to hypnotise his audience. It turns over again and again like an obsession.'

As well as looping rhythms, Gainsbourg became adept at recycling material and moving it around if it didn't get used. 'Bloody Jack' on *Initials B.B.* had been sung on TV by the dancer Zizi Jeanmaire in 1967, not long after France Gall had rejected it. It's often thought that Gall had stopped working with Gainsbourg after the ignominy of 'Les Sucettes', but he provided her with two great songs, 'Teeny Weeny Boppie' and 'Néfertiti', which sat alongside classics like 'Bébé Requin', written by Joe Dassin, on her criminally underrated *1968* album.* 'Teeny Weeny Boppie' in particular—which was offered to Gall after she'd rejected 'Bloody Jack'—owes a large debt to Carla Thomas and Otis Redding's 'Ooh Carla, Ooh Otis' duet, and it hitches a ride on the psychedelia bandwagon too.

'Teenie Weenie Boppie took LSD! It's so clichéd! Part of the charm of all that is that it's completely touristic,' says Bertrand Burgalat, laughing. 'Serge does psychedelic music, but there's no psychedelic band doing music like it. It's soundtrack music and completely idealised. When you listen to Soft Machine in the mid-60s and what Gainsbourg is doing, Gainsbourg sounds more psychedelic, but it's psychedelia from a scene from *The Persuaders!* where Roger Moore and Tony Curtis go down to the nightclub and start dancing.'

'Teenie Weenie Boppie' got the full simulated Stax treatment by David Whitaker, and the talented British arranger also helped realise 'Comic Strip', a song that is onomatopoeia in excelsis. Fresh listeners to Gainsbourg are often stunned by the kaleidoscopic madness of 'Comic Strip', with a Scopitone video to accompany it. The 16mm jukebox promo for 'Comic Strip', with vintage hues that make it look like an animated Polaroid, has outlived the dubious business practices of a company who invented a kind of French psychedelic proto-MTV for the 1960s.

'There was this one album we did where he wanted to do Dvořák,' says Alan Hawkshaw. 'So we did quite a large portion of the *New World Symphony*, which I played on the keyboards.' 'Initials B.B.' is unmistakably predicated on a triumphant phrase from what must have been Serge's favourite symphony at the time. There's some footage that can be found on YouTube where the constituent parts of 'Initials B.B.' come together, from Serge's piano in his lodgings at the Cité des Artistes to the recording studio in London. At the start of the film, he's sitting at a piano conversing in pidgin English with arranger Arthur Greenslade; by the end, he's channelling the enthusiasm of a puppy.

---

* In case you're wondering, 'Bébé Requin' has nothing to do with the ubiquitous and infernal children's song 'Baby Shark'.

'He knew what he wanted,' says drummer Dougie Wright. 'He couldn't put it down on paper or anything. That's why he had Arthur Greenslade there to write things down. But he certainly knew what he wanted from the musicians.' Like most of the session musicians, Dougie had time for Serge, which wasn't always the case with artists they were working for. 'He was a character. He wasn't a prima donna by any means. He was a strange character, but he was easy to work with, and he was a lot of fun actually.' As the old black-and-white footage unfolds and the strings unfurl, you witness an abundant joy take hold of Serge's face. It's a rare glimpse into the process relatively early on where he's clearly far from jaded.

'Initials B.B.' is the perfect embodiment of Serge at his late-60s zenith, tearing a strip from the classics with London's finest session musicians under the inspired direction of Greenslade, full of literary references (Edgar Allan Poe's 'The Raven'; Louis Pauwels's *L'amour monstre*, recommended to him by Bardot) interwoven with raw, heartbroken testimony. There's gentle self-mockery, too, with the comedically bathetic image of him sitting moping in a London pub. It's juxtaposed with the unreachable and exotic sounding Almería, where Brigitte goes to film at the end of their relationship. And then there's a mention of Guerlain perfume ('she wears nothing except a little essence of Guerlain in her hair'*), which anticipates his foray into advertising in the 70s. Perhaps inevitably, 'Initials B.B.' was used for a Shalimar ad in 2011, and, not to be outdone, Miss Dior got Sophia Coppola and Natalie Portman together the same year and used 'Je t'aime … moi non plus' to flog their *eau de toilette*. Where many artists might have feigned annoyance while counting the cash, Serge would have undoubtedly been delighted, and he probably would have bought himself another expensive watch with the proceeds.

*

'When I first met Gainsbourg, he was very, very chic, very elegant, very polite. A very sweet person, basically,' said Anna Karina. 'He was very dandy-like.

---

* 'Elle ne porte rien d'autre qu'un peu d'essence de Guerlain.'

Very well-dressed, polished shoes, a tie. He was not Gainsbarre yet.' Which begs the question, can a dandy remain a dandy when they start to take less care in their appearance? Franck Maubert thinks so, taking the words of Jules Barbey d'Aurevilly, in an essay on Beau Brummel, as his creed: 'You can still be a dandy in a crumpled garment.'*

As well as a penchant for Carnaby Street-inspired Ranoma suits, Serge developed a taste for expensive watches, once he could afford them—a habit that he maintained from his days as *prince de la mode* to whiskery *roi du denim-double*. According to the Milan-based magazine *Italian Watch Spotter*, whose judgment I defer to, Gainsbourg wore a Cartier Ronde in the 70s, which he replaced with an Omega Speedmaster toward the end of the decade, at least when he wasn't wearing his Rolex Daytona. The mid-80s saw him sporting a Rolex Submariner with the classic date and Oyster bracelet. He could also be seen from time to time with a Breitling Navitimer on his wrist, as well as a platinum Breitling bracelet that the company made especially for him. He also liked to give watches as presents, like the one he gave his best friend, Jacques Wolfsohn.[†] It is now in the possession of Jonny Trunk of Trunk Records.

'I'm quite into watches,' says Jonny, enthusiastically. Trunk met Wolfsohn's son on the off chance, and they struck up a conversation about the Omega SEAmaster 100 Wolfsohn Jr. was wearing. 'I went around to this guy's house and he laid out these watches and there was this big Cartier Gérald Genta at the end, a highly complex kind of watch, and there were only about twenty made. Basically it did everything: it told you the day, the date, when it was a leap year, and it had a minute repeater which basically chimes every quarter of an hour if you want it to. I said, What was your dad doing with this? He said, My dad was a music publisher, and this is a watch Serge Gainsbourg gave to him for publishing some of his records.' The fact it was a gift from Serge

---

* 'On peut être dandy avec un vêtement chiffonné.' Barbey d'Aurevilly, *Du dandysme et de George Brummel* (1845)

† Jacques Wolfsohn was the founder of Disque Vogue who set Francoise Hardy and Jacques Dutronc on their way.

to Wolfsohn, and not worn by Serge himself, meant the timepiece would be worth less. 'Very 80s,' adds Trunk. 'Worth about twenty grand and hideous, a product of its time.'

Serge switched from 60s bespoke suits to 70s denim, as was the fashion, and he received something of a makeover from his style-icon partner. 'I found his shoes at Repetto,' says Birkin. 'I knew that he'd got very fragile angles and flat feet. And he had such soft skin; I knew that it would hurt him to wear shoes, with his toes and delicate little ankles and feet. So I found him this pair of shoes, and after that he said he'd wear nothing else. I rang Repetto and I told them his shoe size—which was forty-two or something—and they were like little gloves, which I knew wouldn't hurt him. And I always thought socks were a bit mediocre, so he looked lovely when he had his little ankles bare.' When the Revolutionaries drummer Sly Dunbar met Serge a few years later, in the late 70s, he remembered passing comment on Serge's footwear. 'He was a real nice person. He wore those Repetto kind of shoes, right? I said, I like your shoes. He bought me four pairs!'

Jane Birkin's influence helped to bring out Serge's feminine side: 'He had no hair on his skin, so it was particularly pretty to buy him bracelets. So I found this place that had second-hand jewellery from Russian princesses. I'd buy him diamonds that he'd put around his very white wrists and around his neck. Then they were stolen when he was slaughtered one New Year. And he said, *I've been deplumed!* They'd taken all of his jewellery, and so I bought him a sapphire one. He was a pleasure to dress because everything looked so good on him.' In the Chelsea market he found himself a pinstriped jacket. 'You could tell it was a woman's jacket because it was shaped around the bosoms. He wore it over a khaki shirt and his jeans, and the whole thing created a style that people have copied.' Birkin also preferred that he maintained stubble, 'because otherwise he looked too shiny when he used to shave. It made him look too young.'

His sartorial image remained largely the same until his death, save the trademark dark shades of Gainsbarre, the evil alter ego of his own alter ego. Gainsbourg was the sensitive dandy with the lyrical dexterity and wit;

Gainsbarre was almost heroically monstrous, a scruffy construct he could project all of his alcoholic-driven bad behaviour onto, a vessel for outrage and mischief who he could point at and say, 'It wasn't me.'

'It is forbidden to put on a mask,' he once said. 'I think I've been putting on a mask and wearing it for the last twenty years, and I can no longer remove it, it sticks to my skin.'* A big fan of Oscar Wilde, Serge may have been thinking about one of his quotes: 'Man is least himself when he talks in his own person. Give him a mask, and he will tell you the truth.' In *The Aesthetics Of Self-Invention*, Shelton Waldrep says that Wilde fashioned a complex system of personae 'fuelled by an erotics of opportunity—a desire to become socially respectable, professionally serious, and to have both a marriage and an existence in the demimonde of London'. Gainsbourg's fashioning of a complex system of personae wasn't designed to hide anything, it was used to expose everything, so that we could see him from every angle, like a work of living cubist ingenuity.

---

* 'C'est une défense de mettre un masque. Moi je crois que j'ai mis un masque et que je le porte depuis vingt ans, je n'arrive plus à le retirer, il me colle à la peau.' Serge Gainsbourg, *Pensées provocs et autres volutes* (Librairie Générale Française, 2007)

6

MUSES

JANE BIRKIN / SERGE GAINSBOURG (1969)

> I have three platinum rings on my ring finger. Three rings for three Bs: Bardot, Birkin, Bambou ...*

There can be few hills in Britain that are scaled with as much enthusiasm as Peppard Road in Berkshire. I leave Reading Station just after 10am and take a forty-minute trek up a steep incline to the BBC Written Archives Centre in leafy Caversham. It's the hottest day of the year, but even a sweaty back will not deter me. The archives hold records that look older than the building that contains them, a quaint converted schoolhouse in an anonymous suburb. Records start from 1922, and we're specifically concerned with 1969, the year 'Je t'aime … moi non plus' topped the British charts and created a scandal, and Serge Gainsbourg and Jane Birkin became Europe's most notorious couple for a short while.

The BBC's archive supervisor, Kate O'Brien, isn't at the centre to meet me when I arrive—she's on holiday, though she leaves around ten pink folders piled high on a desk waiting to be perused. There's a decade or so of research material laid out before me, which includes minutes from meetings, memorandums, and a whole miscellany of papers relating to the running of the Popular Music Department, mostly during the 1960s. You sense that even by 1969, the BBC was still reeling from The Beatles and the sexual revolution.

---

* 'J'ai trois bagues en platine à l'annulaire. Trois bagues pour trois B: Bardot, Birkin, Bambou.'
Serge Gainsbourg, *Pensées provocs et autres volutes* (Librairie Générale Française, 2007)

Radio 1 was just a few years old, a concession to changing times by grey-suited, painfully polite, Oxbridge-educated bureaucratics talking in their received pronunciation while collectively still trying to get their heads around working-class-driven culture. Was it this equivocation that let in conniving monsters like Jimmy Savile, who was never anyone's idea of a hipster?

Points arising at a meeting for Radio 1 and 2 on December 30 1968 show the Corporation was already having trouble with its star DJ. Savile 'did a retrospective of Number Ones of '68 in spite of express directions that we should leave this to Alan Freeman,' says the memo regarding his show *Savile's Travels*. 'This is particularly regrettable in view of the position of their transmissions!' A year before this act of recalcitrant individualism, Radio 1 was still having teething problems, and its controller, Robin Scott,* was tired of receiving complaints about one of its DJs overplaying Engelbert Humperdinck records. He wrote, 'I would not expect Jimmy Young to be plugging a new Jimi Hendrix record but equally I am opposed to the present practice of playing the same pop records day after day, particularly when it becomes an irritant. I suspect that a number of listeners turn off their set when "The Last Waltz" is being played once again. When after heavy plugging of the record a BBC recording is included (or Jimmy singing "The Last Waltz" himself) this makes things even worse.'

A draft memo from 1963 laid out the five main types of song that were banned from any airplay on BBC national radio. Advertising, inadvertent or not, was strictly interdict, forcing The Kinks to swiftly re-record 'Lola' without the words 'Coca-Cola' to get it played on the radio—hypothetically, 'Ford Mustang' wouldn't have been played either, for obvious reasons, not that Radio 1 would have entertained it anyway. Filth was also out: 'Smut, suggestiveness, offensive words, [bad] taste in general' reads the missive, which would have meant much of Gainsbourg's back catalogue was forbidden; 'Sacrilege, blasphemy, vulgarisation and cheapening of religious feeling': 'Ecce homo' or 'Je t'aime … moi non plus', which Pope John XXIII branded 'blasphemous'; nothing political or concerning current affairs ('La jambe de bois (Friedland)';

---

* Not to be confused with Robin Scott of M fame.

'Le sable et la soldat'); and adaptations of the classics—the most nonsensical of these restrictions—which would have nobbled 'Docteur Jekyll et Monsieur Hyde', and might have meant no 'Chatterton' either. Thomas Chatterton was the eighteenth-century Romantic poet who ended it all at the tender age of seventeen and was immortalised by the Pre-Raphaelite Henry Wallis in the melodramatic oil painting *The Death of Chatterton*. Perhaps just being a tragic literary figure wasn't enough to get a song outlawed, but Gainsbourg reeling off a list of great figures who'd ended themselves, from Nietzsche to Van Gogh, would have surely excluded it anyway.

With this all in mind, the BBC would have surely had conniptions over the content of Jane Birkin and Serge Gainsbourg's erotically charged 'Je t'aime … moi non plus', a record featuring orgasmic simulation and lyrics about coming and going between the loins (or the kidneys, if taken literally). So it is with sadness that I have to report, having traversed a mountainous slope with temperatures pushing 40 °C, that there's nothing in the BBC archive to let us know how the Corporation dealt with this troublesome single. It had two chart runs in 1969, going to no.2 in the summer, and then no.1 a few months later with a different distributor—the Northern Irish label Major Minor Records, which had a deal with Decca—after Philips subsidiary Fontana got cold feet amid the controversy. It finally went to no.1 on October 5 1969, a full three months after it first slipped into the charts at no.50, becoming the first foreign-language song to make it to no.1 in the UK, and the first banned song as well. 'Things were usually saved for posterity,' says the man at reception whose name I forget to take as I'm leaving to go home. He adds, 'if they didn't think the documents to be historically important then they would be destroyed.'

Not of historical importance? 'Je t'aime … moi non plus'? A song banned by the BBC and attacked by the Vatican? A 45 that was too hot for *Top Of The Pops* was not of historical significance? A chanson that had to be switched with 'Love At First Sight', the instrumental version, *sans souffle*, by some Bournemouth-based chancers called Sounds Nice? The Beeb was firefighting against an unprecedented blaze, so the fact the internal memos no longer survive is disappointing above anything else.

Curiously, a month before 'Je t'aime' charted, another song entered the UK charts that also got the BBC into a moral panic: Max Romeo's 'Wet Dream'. The ska number peaked at no.10, and, during its headache-inducing run, managed to hang around the charts for nigh on half a year—an inconvenience for the BBC, as presenters weren't allowed to say its name on air. The upholders of decency at the Corporation must have thought they'd got lucky when 'Wet Dream', clinging to the lower reaches of the Top 50 for three weeks, appeared to be falling out of the chart altogether. Only the next week it climbed thirteen places to no.32, putting it within range of *Top Of The Pops*. Then, nearly a month later, on the July 16, it suddenly leapt up the chart again, this time to no.21.

This surprise advancement, presumably impelled by word of mouth and schoolboy tittering, was addressed at the departmental meeting on July 15, with instructions circulated with immediate effect. The head of pop music issued the following advice on how to handle this particular hot potato: 'Obviously it will not be dropped from a verbal list of best selling records, but it will not be played under any circumstances. Compères should not say on the air that we are not playing this record. Inevitably there will be press enquiries—any which reach you should be referred immediately to the Press Office. We are concerned at the difficulty many of the [sic] must face every week in deciding whether something is permissible—the invariable rule is "consult" (usually the relevant Chief Producer). Check: The song in question is called "Wet Dream".'

One wonders why the directives regarding 'Wet Dream' survived, but everything about 'Je t'aime' was destroyed. Could a disdainful view of French pop music at the time, as well as the British superiority complex, have played their parts? 'I don't think there's anything conspiratorial going on there,' says music writer Rob Chapman in an email. 'I've seen banned record files going back to WW2, and what you see by the late 60s is that the Beeb has pretty much given up trying to be censorial about everything other than overtly sexual or political stuff. Like everything else at the Beeb (keeping some shows and wiping others for instance), it's harsh bureaucratic decisions in the name of expediency.'

I also asked for a statement from Kate O'Brien at the BBC Written Archives Centre, who said this: 'With regards to your question about the files that aren't retained for inclusion in the archive, in general, once a file becomes non-business current, they are stored for a period of time and then appraised in accordance with the corporate retention schedule at the time. At that point some will be destroyed, some will be put back in storage to be appraised again at a later date, and some will be accessioned into the archive. Broadly, those that are kept are either of business importance and/or potential historical/cultural interest.'

The *NME* first reported on the song in August 1969, with writer Richard Green adopting the groovy, alliterative, sexist patter of the times: 'One of the most pleasant interviews this year—if not ever—was going round to Jane's house in Chelsea to see one of the dolliest dishes on the scene. She really is as attractive as her pictures make out and she's got a personality to match.' Once the cringe-inducing drooling is dispensed with, Green finally gets his pencil out and asks Birkin if she thinks the track is immoral. 'There's nothing unnatural about what's on the record, is there?' replies Jane. 'And when you read the poem that the song comes from, it's really very moral. I don't think people are offended by it.'

'I must agree,' says Richard. 'It's certainly a lot milder than Max Romeo's current hit, and the tune is pretty. There is, though, going to be controversy surrounding it for a long time and it would be a pity if it spoiled the record's chances.'

*

'The deep-breathing girl, Jane Birkin, gets the boys breathless with her panting contributions to the lovely tune and deep-voiced singing of Serge Gainsbourg in "Je t'aime … moi non plus", their big single hit which is on this LP,' wrote another unnamed scribe at the *NME* in September 1969, in a review of the *Jane Birkin/Serge Gainsbourg* album. 'The remaining ten tracks feature the soft, purry, baritone singing of Serge in six songs, and the other four are Miss Birkin's who sounds very interesting singing about "Orang-outan", "18–39", "Jane B" (with a bit of Chopin) and "Le canari est sur la balcon". All in French and the sexier for it. The backing music is terrific.'

Birkin will forever be tied in the imagination to 'Je t'aime … moi non plus', especially in the country she was born in. She often tells the story of a British taxi driver who asks her what she does, and when she says she used to sing with a French guy and he hears the words 'Je t'aime', he pulls the cab over and starts spitting, 'Fucking "Je t'aime"? I fucking 'ad five children listening to that fucking song.' She adds, 'I said that on the BBC quite recently and was banned again for that anecdote.' Another charming chap, this time from the gutter press, asked her if she was 'doing any more dirty songs?' shortly after Gainsbourg died—a question so insensitive that she went back to France enraged and requested every famous French person she could think of write a few words about him: 'From Chirac to Saint-Laurent, Godard to Bardot … all the people the English can't say they don't know. Every single person I could think of wrote two lines in their own writing of who Serge was to them so I could say, That's who he was.'

That fucking song represents something different to different people all over the world. For Isabelle Adjani, who was a schoolgirl when it came out (and who hid the single from her parents), it was 'transgressive … but also sweet'. The late Australian INXS singer Michael Hutchence remembered the song from his childhood, which would be the cue for him and his brother to go to bed when it arrived on the family hi-fi. He says, courtesy of a posthumous voiceover from the documentary *Mystify*, 'My parents used to have some good parties occasionally and they'd play a lot of soul music. There'd always be this period of the night when they'd put on this record by Serge Gainsbourg called "Je t'aime". That would be the signal for the kids to go! We'd say, Oh, no, not this song. We had no idea what it meant. But I do remember it being a very evocative atmosphere and the sexuality being very strong. It impressed me that a piece of music could have such an impact on a room.'

Another artist whose favourite Gainsbourg song is 'Je t'aime … moi non plus' is the seminal French disco playboy Cerrone, who more than likely got the idea from his fellow countryman to overlay 'Love In C Minor' with the sound of panting. 'Yeah, "Je t'aime … moi non plus" is my favourite Gainsbourg song,' he tells me over the phone from Paris, 'because of the atmosphere, the ambience … the guy was absolutely unique!' Marc Cerrone may have also been indirectly influenced by Gainsbourg in his first band, Kongas, who mixed rock music with African rhythms. I wonder also if Gainsbourg was inspired by Cerrone's work on his 1978 Eurotrash hit 'Sea, Sex And Sun', or even 1981's four-on-the-floor banger 'Le physique et le figuré'? 'No! Serge was more of an influencer than an artist to be influenced,' he says, modestly, adding, 'The period of time was very open and perfect for all provocateurs, something we could not do today.'

'Je t'aime … moi non plus' may have been sexually provocative, but it also held mystery for Anglo Saxons, especially as most had no idea what was being sung about—meaning much had to be left to the imagination. 'I know certain people close to Princess Margaret who think it's about sodomy,' Serge told *Rock & Folk* in 1971, almost certainly meaning Lord Snowdon, who was a pal of his, and who photographed the cover shot of *Aux armes et cætera* in the desert. '[It's] a fact which made them very happy,' he added. 'Perhaps that's the reason why I got to no.1 in England.' Not knowing what it was about exactly, and it being suggestive of an act that had only recently been decriminalised, would have stoked and augmented the inferiority complex the British have about the French being more sensual and better-versed in the ways of carnality, deviant or otherwise. Gainsbourg represented a sexual shaman, then, who'd hypnotised the beautiful, errant English girl into unspeakable acts. Listeners might also have felt that, while he was a dirty Frenchman, there'd also be an underlying apprehension that he might know about things that they didn't.

It wasn't just the English who had strange notions about the sexual mores of their near neighbours. The French had developed a peculiar fixation with *les petites Anglaises* as the 60s got into their swing. According to Dr. Leila Wimmer, the 1954 comedy farce *Les carnets du Major Thompson*, known in the English-speaking world as *The French, They Are A Funny Race*, had enforced longstanding stereotypes of English women having long teeth and big feet. Then the cultural explosion of Carnaby Street, The Beatles and the Stones, and the *mini-jupe* warped perceptions about the English, leading to a theory that British girls were permissive and sexually available—an idea that culminated in the 1976 comedy *À nous les petites Anglaises* (*Let's Get Those English Girls*).

'The film was a box-office hit, although I'm not sure you'd find it easily now,' says Wimmer. 'This new idea of Englishness taps into the wearing of the mini-skirt, which was obviously designed by Marie Quant and worn in London and was very, very short. So I guess that's where this impression that women were loose came from. Young English women acquired a reputation for being anything but shy in sexual matters.'

Birkin herself may have benefitted from the fantasy that English girls were suddenly emancipated libertines. 'She said herself, *There are millions of dolly birds in London, but I was lucky, I was the first one to come to France,*' says Wimmer. 'She's attached to modernity, to pop, to Swinging London.' Birkin being herself also proved to be a breath of fresh air across *La Manche*. 'She'd already become a fashion icon even before the Birkin bag; that look of hers, which was androgynous in a white T-shirt, jeans, carrying a basket—that was completely new. Fashion with her was very natural and I think that's what appealed to the French because it was so different.'

Gainsbourg is said to have offered 'Je t'aime' to various female singers, but fantasies about *les petites Anglaises* aligned when he chanced upon Jane. The song wasn't written for her, of course—it was originally inspired by Bardot, though it made Jane famous all around the world. 'So people who are now probably *retraité* [retired] remember that record,' says Birkin, who has been living in Paris for over fifty years and is so used to speaking French all day that she peppers her sentences with French words. She still retains her cut-glass English accent, though. 'When I go to South America or the antique shops in Buenos Aires, they come out with these LPs with "Je t'aime" on it for me to sign so they can get more money from flogging them. Even in Hong Kong I'm known because of that song, so I'd be most ungrateful not to appreciate it. I know when I die that'll be the song they play. They might for Bardot, too.'

While Jane sounds genuine, the associations Bardot might have enjoyed with the song were stymied by her own hand. She begged Serge not to release it out of respect for her husband at the time, Gunther Sachs. One suspects Serge knew he had a hit on his hands, and one can only imagine the disappointment he must have felt when she forbade him to release it. Whether it would have been such a big hit with Bardot, despite her huge celebrity, is a moot point. Her delivery is more forceful than Jane's and may have represented too much of a threat, particularly to male listeners, back in 1968, when it was first recorded.

'Birkin is younger, she projects a young femininity, a bit more vulnerable,' says Wimmer. 'Bardot on the other hand is predatory. I don't mean that in a nasty way, but she was in control. She was a major star … really big. She didn't hide anything, she picked who she wanted to be with, which at the time wasn't done. When she was pregnant she admitted she didn't want to be a mother and left the son with his dad. In that sense she's much more masculine. The fact she didn't have a motherly instinct: that was shocking.'

The apparent origin of the song, according to Serge, came from a lover's tiff with Bardot, which took place during their brief, candescent affair. Gainsbourg had disappointed her in some way, probably having had too much to drink. Giving Serge a chance to make amends for his bad behaviour, Bardot called up the next day and demanded that he write her the most beautiful song he could imagine. He dutifully went off and wrote two songs in one night: 'Bonnie & Clyde' and 'Je t'aime … moi non plus'. Or did he? In another version of events, from Serge himself, he says he actually wrote 'Bonnie & Clyde' and 'Harley Davidson' in one night, and then wrote 'Je t'aime' on a separate occasion, back at Brigitte's place. 'Bonnie & Clyde' and 'Je t'aime … moi non plus' have been conflated together, probably because of misreporting that then got repeated over and over. Writing 'Bonnie & Clyde' and 'Harley Davidson' as a pair would make more sense. Furthermore, the creation myth of 'Je t'aime … moi non plus' eschews a crucial factor: it already existed, at least in an embryonic state, as a soundtrack instrumental.

It's quite possible that Gainsbourg wrote the words for 'Je t'aime … moi non plus' that night, but the generation of the song is more fitful and metamorphic. Filmmaker Édouard Luntz, the director of the 1966 movie *Les cœurs verts*, must have surely smiled to himself when he heard this story, given that the song had first been recorded as the incidental instrumental 'Scène de bal' in a film about a young gang of Nanterre-based grifters. The swaggery rock'n'roll intro of the later single isn't there, and the song itself is stripped back with a simple guitar line carrying the tune, but it's unmistakably 'Je t'aime'.

The Bardot version, recorded at Studio Barclay on Avenue Hoch with the arranger Michel Colombier, is slower and weightier than the one recorded with Birkin, with an echoey production style, quavering violins, and Barbot's passionate, rasping alto. 'She sings it in the most womanly way,' Birkin tells me. As an admirer of Colombier's work, having heard the Birkin version first (like most people), for me the Gainsbourg/Bardot recording misses the snap of the Arthur Greenslade rendition, where the instrumentation often falls out completely, adding to the erotic tension.

That snap was provided by Dougie Wright and Dave Richmond, and the latter has vague memories of the recording of 'Je t'aime'. 'We did it at Philips, and we then went to hear the playback. You often went to a playback with the first song to see what sort of balance you were getting. And we could hear all these noises in the cans, and then we looked on the right-hand side of Philips going up the corridor and there was Serge and Jane sitting on a settee, laughing at us looking at them. They were very happy. That image sticks in my mind particularly.'

Bardot certainly adored Gainsbourg—and the song, too—and came to regret not having released their version. There's an account of the pair parting from one another from her flat at 71 Rue Avenue Doumer, where they spontaneously sliced their fingers open and shared in a lover's blood pact. Bardot smeared 'Je t'aime' on the mirror; Gainsbourg 'moi non plus'. It was the end of the relationship, which they both probably realised. Bardot flew off to Almería to film *Shalako* with Sean Connery, and, according to the biographer Barnett Singer, was disappointed by Connery's baldness and incomprehensible Scottish burr.* What's more, she was stranded in the middle of nowhere and unable to call Serge by phone, and apparently felt suicidal. The weeks away from each other did their damage to a union that had plenty against it from the start, and both parties moved on … eventually.

Incidentally, Lucien Ginsburg also entered into a 'gyspy marriage' blood pact with his first wife on the day they divorced in 1957, according to a

---

* Barnett Singer, *Brigitte Bardot: A Biography* (McFarland, 2010)

chapter in Lise Levitsky's exposé *Lise et Lulu* entitled 'Le Pacte'. They drank champagne and found a hotel and made a vow that entitled Serge to booty call Lise whenever he liked—an arrangement that apparently continued sporadically throughout the rest of his life, and involved sexual baptisms of new abodes and romantic walks through the Bois de Boulogne, holding hands, which would have been a brazen kind of assignation when he was the most famous man in France.

'There's a desperation to "Je t'aime",' says Birkin. 'Because he wrote it for Bardot, when he says *moi non plus* [me neither], you get the feeling it's because he doesn't really believe her. That it won't go anywhere. So, contrary to what everyone thought, because of the heavy breathing, and I know that it goes down as a love song and of course it's an erotic song … but it's also about somebody who doesn't believe things are going to last. How right he was.' The Bardot version remained unreleased for two decades and became mythical in the process. It had been played on the radio only once, on *Europe 1*, having 'leaked' out from the studio it was recorded in. Soon after the lunchtime spin, Sachs started threatening lawsuits. With no internet to disseminate it, it became an apocryphal part of French pop lore. Photographer Tony Frank tells me mischievously, 'When I went to his house once, he said, *Quick, Jane's out*, and he took this record out from another record cover. It was "Je t'aime … moi non plus" with Bardot.'

In 1986, Bardot asked Gainsbourg if she could release it to raise funds for La Fondation Brigitte Bardot, set up to provide protection for animals. Birkin: 'Serge phoned me, and he said, I've got very bad news for you, I've had Brigitte on the phone and she wants to bring out "Je t'aime" because of her animals. I said to Serge, Of course she does and of course she should. And so it did come out so she could have the money for her animals. It's bad luck to come out second because everyone remembers the first one. And because it was an octave higher, and it having that choirboy thing to it perhaps added a certain frisson.'

The release demystified the legend, and it didn't perform in the way that Bardot would have hoped. She and Gainsbourg did rekindle a friendship in his final years thanks to the release, though. In 1989, Gainsbourg, recovering from an operation, dined with her at Bazoches, and sank a bottle of 1970 champagne as they talked. 'Alcohol, moral distress, and the loneliness of his soul were reflected in his physical body,' Bardot wrote in the foreword to the book *Over The Rainbow*.* Serge pulled out his chequebook and gave two hundred thousand francs to Bardot's foundation there and then.

The reclusive Bardot was unavailable for comment, though some of her words from *Over The Rainbow* are worth reproducing here, if only to convey the depth of her affection that has endured throughout the years. Written in 2006, the book reads very much like a declaration of love tinged with regrets about what might have been: 'Ultimately nobody really understood the depths and the multiplicity of this fragile, tender and impertinent—even insolent— man,' she writes. 'I've had an extraordinary opportunity to meet a man so different from the others, who has put his genius, his talent, his availability, his tenderness, his sweetness, his admiration, in the service of the love we shared for a time. Alas, but it was a devouring passion that burned us. ... Serge, like all Russians, carried with him the magnificence of a prince, an inborn class, a complete contempt for mediocrity, an ecstasy for aesthetics, in search of the sublime, a certain quest for perfection.'†

*

'Bardot—a curvaceous blonde with a kittenish grin—wasn't merely a muse: she was also a trendsetter,' wrote *Time* magazine in 2012. Bardot is often seen as too spirited to qualify as a muse, which does beg the question: what are the

---

* 'L'alcool, la détresse morale, la solitude de son âme se répercutent aussi sur son physique.' Brigitte Bardot, foreword to Alain Wodrascka's *Serge Gainsbourg: Over The Rainbow* (Didier Carpentier, 2006)

† 'Finalement personne n'a vraiment cerné la profondeur et la multiplicité de ce caractère si fort et si fragile, si tendre et si impertinent voire insolent, si vulnérable. ... J'ai eu la chance extraordinaire de rencontrer un homme différent des autres, qui a mis son génie, son talent, sa disponibilité, sa tendresse, sa douceur, son admiration, au service de l'amour que nous avons partagé pendant peu de temps, hélas, mais qui fut une passion dévorante qui nous brûla. ... Serge portait en lui, comme tous les Russes, la magnificence d'un prince, une classe innée, un mépris total pour la médiocrité, une extase de l'esthétisme, la recherche du sublime, une certaine quête de la perfection.'

prerequisites? Gainsbourg wrote beautiful songs at her behest, and, as the passive inspiration for those songs, surely she is a muse by definition, no matter how ballsy she might be. The *OED* defines a muse as 'a person or personified force who is the source of inspiration for a creative artist'. In Simone de Beauvoir's essay 'Brigitte Bardot and the Lolita Syndrome' from 1959, she calls Bardot 'France's erotic hoyden' and suggests that a woman with a sexual appetite that only men were traditionally supposed to possess was a new phenomenon entirely at that time—the opposite of submissive and pliable.

Germaine Greer, on the other hand, has said the man is merely an arty amanuensis transcribing the muse's sensuality like a vessel: 'A muse is anything but a paid model. The muse in her purest aspect is the feminine part of the male artist, with which he must have intercourse if he is to bring into being a new work. She is the anima to his animus, the yin to his yang, except that, in a reversal of gender roles, she penetrates or inspires him and he gestates and brings forth from the womb of the mind.'*

The concept of the muse emerged from classical Greek mythology, an idea that has been kicking around for six millennia. In 1994's *Les Muses*, the French philosopher Jean-Luc Nancy argued that Christian iconography had pushed the artist-muse relationship to the margins up until the nineteenth century, when it made a spectacular comeback. Now, the muse is under threat from modern thinking. The idea of an objectifiable waif hanging around submissively in order for a man to make great art does seem questionable seen through contemporary optics.

'What are the life skills appropriate to an artist's muse?' asked Fiona Sturges in a July 2019 article for the *Guardian*, responding to the Nick Broomfield documentary *Leonard And Marianne: Words Of Love*, about the relationship between Leonard Cohen and his muse, Marianne Ihlen. 'Hotness is a given; and sexual availability, while not compulsory, has generally been appreciated. The ability to keep a house tidy is a plus, as is being supportive of the artist at all times, even if he—and it is nearly always he—is being an arsehole. It helps,

---

* Germaine Greer, 'The role of the artist's muse', the *Guardian*, June 2 2008

of course, to be mysterious; if one is to be endlessly gazed at, it's best not to give everything away at once. As for a life, and a career of one's own, well, history has shown that such things are rarely tolerated.'*

This dynamic of powerful, creative male and inert but beautiful female is the most clichéd version of the muse: the Pre-Raphaelites and Elizabeth Siddal; Alphonse Mucha and Sarah Bernhardt; Josef von Sternberg and Marlene Dietrich; Miles Davis and Frances Taylor; Jean-Luc Godard and Anna Karina (although she said she was more 'amusing than muse'), and so on. Charlotte Gainsbourg has a thing or two to say about the idea of the muse, not only as the child of a relationship featuring a famous songwriter and muse, but also as a muse herself for three of Lars Von Trier's most notorious pictures. 'Yeah, I wish it had lasted longer,' she admits. 'I think it's a beautiful idea, and of course it's very flattering to be someone else's muse.'

Charlotte sees the relationship between her parents as more creatively symbiotic than is often credited. 'She was more than just a muse. I think she inspired him, but she also moved him. She also harmed him in a way where he went away and wrote some of the most beautiful songs for her because of that hurt. She wasn't just a muse. The word muse implies something only physical. I guess it was much more profound than that.'

I wonder if the relationships between artists and their muses have always been more symbiotic, but history, only concerned with men, forgot to record the full female contribution. Recent analysis of manuscripts from the original music scores of Johan Sebastian Bach suggest his wife Anna Magdalena was more than just a copyist for her famous husband, a scenario that has surely been duplicated throughout the centuries in countless different ways. While this may be the case, Charlotte makes the reasonable point that not all muses are women. 'I was thinking of Joe Dallesandro just now,' she says, 'and of course he was a muse for Warhol and other people, too, so it's not only a feminine/masculine thing, and it's not just an objective thing, because you

* Fiona Sturges, 'Was Leonard Cohen's Marianne the last artist's muse? Let's hope so', the *Guardian*, July 23 2019

imagine someone being like a piece of clay where you mould them for your purpose. I don't believe that. I'd love to have a muse myself—to be that attracted to and inspired by someone. It's definitely not only women.'

'I work with people who bring things out in me,' says Chilly Gonzales, citing Feist, Jarvis Cocker, and the Canadian superstar Drake. 'I like to have the feeling that someone is curating me, because I am more of an idea generator and I'm quite flexible and enjoy having constraints put on me. When I worked with Jarvis, despite the fact I don't fancy him, I still feel that he brings out something in me that wouldn't normally be there, and I have a fascination watching him do his part of the work.'

In 2006, Gonzales produced a Birkin album, *Fictions*, which featured guest musicians like Johnny Marr and Mocky, and songs by Kate Bush, Tom Waits, Dominique A, and Rufus Wainwright.* Unusually, there were no Gainsbourg compositions. 'Jane relied upon us and also some people at the label which in a way might seem quite passive,' he says, 'but there were also moments where she would express comfort or discomfort, sometimes indirectly. So it's not as simple as saying one is passive and one is active in any working relationship. I think it's an outdated view that might also carry a lot of sexism in it and a lot of old school projections onto genius figures. The great man theory is still alive and well if people are saying that Bardot wasn't his muse.'

If Birkin was Gainsbourg's muse on the album named after her, then curiously many of the songs are about, or inspired by, other women, not just 'Je t'aime … moi non plus'. 'L'anamour' was written with Françoise Hardy in mind before he recorded it himself; Likewise 'Sous le soleil exactement' was for Anna Karina; the jaunty 'Elisa' is about his and Jane's age difference, but appears to bear the name of his first wife; 'Les Sucettes' is a naughty little number given to an unsuspecting France Gall; and 'Orang-outan'—one of the most irritating songs in the Gainsbourg songbook—is about Jane's toy monkey.

---

* When I interviewed Johnny Marr for *Huck* magazine in 2019, he said how much he enjoyed the experience of working on the album with Birkin. 'She wrote me such a beautiful handwritten letter that I carried around in my luggage for years.'

'Jane B' is clearly about Jane Birkin, though the 'assassin's knife' at the end of the song takes them into the realms of grizzly fiction. 'Jane B' is carried by a delicious clattering groove underpinned by Chopin's prelude 28. '"Jane B" is just wonderful,' says Racheal Leigh-Carter. 'Who wouldn't want to sing for a man who did something like that for them? The song is about her and it's not. If it was really it would be pretty sad because he murders her off at the end, but you know, it's got her name on it, it's definitely for her, it's describing her, the colour of her eyes and where she comes from. He puts his life into his work.'

Maybe even more wonderful is 'Manon', first written and recorded in 1968, for the film *Manon 70*, and believed to be inspired by an early infatuation with Catherine Deneuve in the titular role. 'Manon' was too passionate for the director, Jean Aurel, who insisted on using the Colombier-arranged instrumental for the film, without Serge's guttural, sexy monologue. If history remembers the moment Dylan went electric at the Newport Folk Festival, then Gainsbourg experts pinpoint 'Manon' as the moment Serge embraces *sprechgesang* and finds the confidence to mutter the words and let the orchestration carry the tune. Rather than feel rejected by Aurel, this is the moment where he realises the power that his voice has augmented by strings. The drama is ramped up yet further with the orchestration by Alan Greenslade on the *Jane Birkin/Serge Gainsbourg* album. The results are dizzying.

'"Manon" is just insane,' enthuses Mike Patton. 'It's him growling with a full orchestra. Wow.' Patton had wanted to cover it on the *Great Jewish Music: Serge Gainsbourg* tribute album in 1997, but he was told to record 'Ford Mustang' instead. The compilation also features a rendition of 'Black Trombone' by Tom Waits's guitarist Marc Ribot, and 'La chanson de Slogan' by Blonde Redhead. The latter band's lead singer, Kazu Makino, also opts for 'Manon' as her favourite Gainsbourg song: 'The intro is everything you could ask for from music. "Manon" gives me an upside-down feeling whenever I hear it.'

Kazu is speaking on the phone from the island of Elba, where she'd set up a temporary home, and where she wrote her excellent solo album, *Adult Baby*. She adds, 'He really speaks to me the way he's so true to himself. A lot of artists are great, but he really sticks out as somebody who's so honest. What fascinates

TONY FRANK was Serge Gainsbourg's go-to photographer from the mid-1960s to the mid-1980s and has the most extensive catalogue of Gainsbourg-related images in existence. The photos shown here are just a small selection from his archive.

From the start: Gainsbourg smoking, Paris, with additional shading by Serge himself (1968); Frank's contact sheet from the *Salut les copains* 'wedding' photos, with Jane Birkin in crochet vintage dress, London (1971); *une soirée chez Régine* with Birkin (1968); donning a German army uniform for the *Rock Around The Bunker* cover that never was (1975); Caroline 'Bambou' Paulus and Gainsbourg holding their baby son, Lulu (1986); at the video shoot for *Lemon Incest* with daughter Charlotte Gainsbourg (1984); and enter Gainsbarre, as Serge returns to live performance with the punk-power trio Bijou (1978). *All images © Tony Frank.*

me is the way he was so down on himself, it seemed like he was always putting himself down. In a way it breaks my heart, but it makes me love him even more because he was so humble.' Humble and yet extremely arrogant at times, I suggest. 'It must be hard to love a person like that, I'm sure,' she says. 'When there are so many characters in one body. When you end up falling in love with a person like that, I'm sure it's quite the journey. Sometimes you love him, sometimes you don't even recognise him.'

*

In 2019, the Tate Modern in London put on an exhibition of photographer and painter Dora Maar—the largest retrospective of her pictures and sculpture ever held in the UK. Maar died in 1997, and her best work was undertaken during the 1930s as a member of a Parisian coterie of surrealists and visual artists including Man Ray and Paul Éluard, Brassaï and Henri Cartier-Bresson. This is not unusual in and of itself, but Maar's name is usually mentioned in conjunction with another artist: she was famously the mistress of Pablo Picasso, the *Weeping Woman* of the famous 1937 painting.

Maar was part of the Spanish master's life during a period that was both creatively and personally intense for both of them. Theirs was a tempestuous relationship that overlapped with his time with former lover Marie-Therese Walter—the mother of Maya Widmaier-Picasso—and then Francoise Gilot, who he met in 1943, and with whom he had two children, Claude and Paloma. Maar, who was born the year Picasso unveiled *Les Demoiselles d'Avignon* in 1907, was devastated he had replaced her with a woman forty years his junior (Gilet was born in 1921). 'No other woman impacted the art of Picasso more than Dora Maar,' writes Vérane Tasseau in an essay called 'Experimentation And Transgression'.*

Maar is remembered as one of Picasso's muses, though she was clearly as engaging as she was enchanting. Her experiments in photomontage and

---

* Vérane Tasseau, 'Experimentation And Transgression', from Katharina Beisiegel (et al), *Picasso: The Artist And His Muses* (Black Dog Publishing, 2016)

her mastery of chiaroscuro inspired Picasso as much as her beauty. Through him, she began to paint; through her, he learnt new techniques in etching and engraving, using aquatint on paper and copper plates etched in dry point. She photographed the successive stages of his anti-war masterpiece *Guernica*, and Picasso referred to the pictures to help him with his processes—a far more *quid pro quo* scenario than the one usually imagined between an artist and muse.

'I mean, he really was like a Picasso,' says Jane Birkin about Serge. 'He didn't just have one period, he had many periods. He had a period after "La Javanaise" at the very beginning, so perhaps that was his blue period, and then he had a pink period where he did *Initials B.B.* and "Je t'aime … moi non plus", *Melody Nelson* and *L'homme à tête de chou*, and then he had a sort of cubist or surrealist period where he changed his name from Gainsbourg to Gainsbarre and he pranced around doing shocking things, because that's what he needed as well. He needed to surprise people.'

In 2008, Birkin released *Enfants d'hiver* (*Winter Children*), the first album where she had a hand in writing all the songs. The title track was written with Canadian singer/songwriter Hawksley Workman, 'Madame' with Franck Eulry, and 'Période bleue' with decorated *chanson Française* merchant Alain Souchon. 'Période bleue' is heartfelt and moving, written in homage to the man she never really got over, full of evocative images of them staying at her place in Brittany or him dutifully looking after her dog. In death, perhaps, Serge becomes her muse, helping her to put into words some of her long-held tristesse.

The American singer Mark Lanegan had songs written for him to sing by Scottish musician Isobel Campbell, and became a male muse of sorts. Together, they drew a number of comparisons to Birkin and Gainsbourg in the music press, though the folky, kitschy style was closer to the template set by Nancy Sinatra and Lee Hazlewood, slightly earlier than Serge and Jane. Glen Campbell and Bobby Gentry also recorded an album around the same time as *Nancy & Lee*, and how aware of each other these couples were is open to debate, but it looks more like synchronicity than any studied counterfeiting. The ingénue with a soupçon of vampishness in partnership with an older, deep-voiced man exuding a mix of erudition and brutish machismo has become a mainstay in pop music, despite it being a fairly complex dynamic. It's an intriguing juxtaposition that captures the imagination, often with an added frisson of *are they or aren't they doing it?*

'The Nancy & Lee comparison can't help but occur to you,' says the gravelly-voiced singer over the phone from his home in Los Angeles, 'but I have to say that Isobel's voice is so unique, and there's nobody like her at all. And, also, there's a lot of guys with deep, rough voices like me, but the combination was hyperreal in a way. It was way more beauty and the beast than a lot of them. Glen Campbell and Bobby Gentry it was not!'

As for having songs written for him, Lanegan says it was a huge honour. 'I was a big fan of her music beforehand, and especially the solo record which she'd done before she jumped from Belle & Sebastian.* It was the first time I had had a woman writing songs for me to sing, and it was an amazing gift. I loved singing her songs so much.' Lanegan might have become a muse for Campbell over three albums, but she'd wanted Tom Waits to record with her originally; she approached Lanegan when Waits failed to respond—to great effect, I must add. The parameters of what a muse actually is are unclear, and they change from relationship to relationship. Given this ambiguity, it's a wonder the concept has lasted as long as it has.

*

As well as their shape-shifting genius and their celebrated (and not so celebrated) periods, Picasso and Gainsbourg also shared a striking similarity in the duration of their relationships. In most cases, both men stayed with their partners on average for ten years, with a little overlap here and there. Picasso lived longer than Gainsbourg and had six long-term relationships, and only his final partnership with Jacqueline Roque exceeded the customary decade. Gainsbourg, who lived thirty years fewer than the Spanish painter, had four important relationships that involved cohabitation, and these all fell within a similar timeframe.

'The love affairs of Serge Gainsbourg have something mechanical about

---

* 1999's *The Green Fields Of Foreverland*, recorded as The Gentle Waves.

them,' writes Marie-Dominique Lelièvre in *Gainsbourg sans filtre*, suggesting there's an identical programme where the partner is recruited between the ages of twenty and thirty and each relationship lasts around ten years.* His relationship with his first wife, Elizabeth Levitsky, lasted from 1947 to 1957 (they married in 1951); his second wife, Francoise Pancrazzi, was on the scene from 1958 to 1966 (they married in '64). Gainsbourg met Birkin in 1968, on the set of *Slogan*, and they separated in 1980, although they never married, despite what many assumed to be the case. Part of the disinformation comes from a photograph of Jane in a white crochet wedding dress and Serge in a dapper suit, a smoking gun if ever there was one. Except Tony Frank remembers the origin of those pictures: 'I was in London to do some work for *Salut les copains*, and the magazine said, Can you ask them to do a picture as if they were married? At the time, *Salut les copains* was doing this regular feature with couples who could be married but weren't. A few years ago, Jane asked me, What was that picture, I don't remember it? I didn't remember it either, but then I figured it out when I found another picture of Michel Polnareff and the French singer Dani (who'd later duet with Étienne Daho) dressed with flowers in her hair and all in white. And so Serge and Jane got dressed up in Jane's flat in Chelsea, and then we took the picture in front of a door and another down in Hyde Park. That's the story behind those pictures.'

Finally, there's Caroline von Paulis, who was with Gainsbourg until his death in 1991, although there's some debate about when they actually met and started their relationship. The official line is 1981, though the initial altercation on the dance floor of the Élysées-Matignon, when she called him an 'old cunt', was in 1978, when Bambou was heavily ensconced in the Parisian punk scene.†

Like Picasso's partners, each gets younger, with a thirty-three-year age gap between his first partner and his last. Perhaps more significantly, these partners reflect their times in ways that might suggest Gainsbourg not only chose them as mates but also as fashion accessories. 'Lise' Levitsky fits the idealised fuller

---

* 'La conduite amoureuse de Serge Gainsbourg quelque chose de mécanique.'
† Paulus apparently called him a 'vieux con'.

body shape of the 1940s; Jane Birkin the fashionable gamine of the 1970s. 'Similar to the items that he adds to his collection, women are the centrepieces of his luxury,' says Lelièvre. 'Every new Gainsbourg girl generates a new Gainsbourg.'* Lelièvre also claims there are pornographic pictures stashed away at Rue de Verneuil featuring more fulsome models who don't conform to the public-facing 'frail, fine, rare, decorative' Gainsbourg girl.

Levitsky was of Russian descent, which would have pleased Serge's parents, and their relationship came off the back of an unrequited obsession he had with the niece of Leo Tolstoy's who, he says, drove him mad and was the catalyst for his misogynistic streak. When his and Lise's relationship was faltering, he admitted to Michèle Arnaud that Lise's body shape no longer fitted his requirements. *Pied-noir* heiress Françoise Pancrazzi reared two of Serge's children (Natacha and Paul) and kept him in a style he became accustomed to during the 60s, providing him with expensive watches and displaying a stultifying jealous streak; Pancrazzi apparently ruined the couple's wedding day when a fan called him to wish him well. 'You had to see Gainsbourg chased by this panther ready to massacre everybody,' said Juliette Gréco.[†]

Britannique Birkin was a part of the Swinging London cynosure and fitted the image of *les petites Anglaises*. And Bambou, who brought some Eurasian exoticism to Gainsbourg's palette, had one child by him—Lulu—who, like his mother, was unavailable for comment for this book. Paulus received her nickname from Gainsbourg in reference to her blackened panda-like eyes, a result of her addiction to heroin. She brought a certain danger into his life, just as his own malevolent alter ego, Gainsbarre, began to emerge. 'With Birkin, Gainsbourg hobnobs with Alain Chamfort,' says Lelièvre. 'Bambou on the other hand reveals Sid Vicious to him.'[‡]

---

* 'Semblables aux objets qu'il collecte, les femmes sont les pièces maîtresses son luxe. ... Chaque Gainsbourg girl neuve engendre un nouveau Gainsbourg.'
† 'Il fallait voir Gainsbourg poursuivi par cette panthère prête à massacrer tout le monde.' *Paris Match*, March 1 2016
‡ 'Serge fréquentait Alain Chamfort grâce a Birkin, Bambou lui révèle Sid Vicious.'

7

POSTMODERNISM

HISTOIRE DE MELODY NELSON (1971)

> [I am the New Wave. By New Wave I mean
> the avant-garde of chanson.*]

The journey of *Histoire de Melody Nelson* has been a curious one, and one that has proved to be more serendipitous than the final journey of Melody herself (her plane crashes, brought down by hoodoo of the Cargo Cult of Melanesia). Largely ignored when it was released, it became a cult concern after Gainsbourg's death, and has stealthily crept into the pantheon of canonical works in the *Anglosphere*—often feted in Top 100 lists now, it's a name that rolls off the tongue whenever a conversation about French music arises.

'In England, it's very well respected, and many British composers and musicians often choose it as one of their favourites from anybody French,' says the album's arranger, Jean-Claude Vannier. A record that would have been considered *recherché* even a decade ago could now be regarded as a *passé* choice in a list of favourite records in these fickle times.

When I spoke to Rose Elinor Dougall for a 'Baker's Dozen' feature for the *Quietus* in 2017, *Histoire de Melody Nelson* was one of the albums she chose.† Quite right too. 'I must have first heard this when I was seventeen or eighteen,' she said. 'Most of the years I've listened to it, I haven't exactly

---

* 'La nouvelle vague, je dirai d'abord que c'est moi. Nouvelle vague veut dire qui est a l'avant-garde de la chanson.' Gilles Verlant, *Gainsbourg* (Albin Michel, 2001)

† For a Baker's Dozen, artists are asked to name their favourite thirteen albums, as you might already have gathered.

understood what it's about, but you don't need to because it's laid out: this brooding, sexual, dark situation. It's so perfect with the concept and the music so perfectly linked together—it really does express what's intended in such a seamless way.'

It got me thinking about other artists who chose it along the way for a Baker's Dozen, and while it probably wouldn't challenge *Low*, *Trans Europe Express*, or *Unknown Pleasures*, regularity-wise, in the *Quietus*'s annals, a quick search of the site reveals a fine list of disparate acts paying homage, from arch Slovenian industrial heavyweights Laibach to Welsh indie musician Cate Le Bon. Laibach's Ivan Novak calls the album's closing track 'Cargo Culte' an eight-minute masterpiece worthy of The Velvet Underground, while the fact it was in French alerted the Eastern Europeans that great pop music could be made outside of the USA or the UK.

'It's one of the most perfect pieces of music ever made,' said Le Bon. 'When I started going out with my partner ten or eleven years ago, he was obsessed with this record and would play it over and over. Initially it was all *this is so cool and Serge is so sexy*, and the overall sound is amazing for such a short record. But then you realise that it is so minimal in a way; aside from the orchestration there is a juxtaposition of a really simple instrumentation and then these wild, beautiful string arrangements which is just incredible.'

Other admirers include Marianne Faithfull, who knew Serge well, and who performed 'Hier ou demain' for *Anna*: 'He was brilliant, and very strange in some ways, and I had a feeling that he really knew what he was doing. He knew he was laying down a new thing and a whole new register of music.' And Geoff Barrow from Portishead, who was clearly influenced by the album, which many have suggested was a precursor to the Bristol Sound: 'The players totally vibe with each other using dynamics of playing—something very hard to hear in modern production of popular music.' Then there's über-producer and Killing Joke bassist Youth: 'The bass lines turn me on. This has great vision and creates an amazing atmosphere that teleports me instantly to another imaginary time and place'.

'I think that album's great because it's perfect, but I'm bored with how everyone celebrates that one in a trendy, Hoxton-y way,' says Baxter Dury, on the phone from Hammersmith. '*Histore de Melody Nelson* is in my top ten favourite records ever,' says grunge star turned existential blues singer Mark Lanegan. LA-based French singer and actress Soko is also a big fan of the album and considers the one minute, fifty second 'Ah! Melody' the closest thing she can think of to musical perfection: 'It's so good, the arrangements are my favourite arrangements of any song in the whole entire world. I play it all the time. I'm always saying, *I want that bass sound. I want that drum sound. These trumpets are amazing.* Everything is incredible. The whole arrangement of the song is exquisite.'

David Holmes is another artist who attempted to emulate the sound of the record, specifically the first and the last track, when he made his *Let's Get Killed* record in 1997. '"Don't Die Just Yet" is an amalgamation of both "Melody" and "Cargo Culte",' he says over the phone from Belfast. 'You can't really say it was a sample—it was more of a tribute. I gave it a different title to work within the narrative of *Let's Get Killed*, but one hundred percent of the publishing went to Serge. We didn't try to cream any writer's credit or anything like that. That album just blew my mind.'

Charlotte Gainsbourg and Jane Weaver passed up *Melody Nelson* for other Gainsbourg albums (*L'homme à tête de chou* and the *Cannabis* OST, respectively) when choosing their Baker's Dozen selections, because they both felt it would have been too obvious a choice. In Charlotte's case, she's present in the famous cover shot, albeit deliberately hidden from view. The pet monkey Jane Birkin is holding conceals the fact she's four months pregnant with Charlotte. Jane's freckles were drawn on by Serge, and the red hair was a wig he bought from a hairdresser on the way to Tony Frank's studio as an afterthought.

'Usually, when I used to take the shot for a record cover for somebody and it was their first record, I asked to listen to it to hear what the style was,' says photographer Tony Frank. 'But I'd worked with Serge for a while, and with *Melody Nelson* I was almost completely in the dark. I went to the studio, and because I knew Jane was going to be wearing some blue jeans, I put a blue background behind her. Jane was pregnant, so she was a little bit tired and weak, and while I was putting the lights up she was saying, *Where is Serge? Where is Serge?* because it was late. He finally showed up and he opened up his suitcase— he always had an attaché case full of money and cartons of Gitanes—and he brought out a wig and put it on his head. There's a picture—the only one I have—of him with the wig on. He was late because he went to the hairdresser's to buy the wig for Melody Nelson, and we didn't know that. Jane was a bit more relaxed then. She saw him and he put the wig on to make her laugh.'

Frank says he took fourteen or fifteen pictures ('I think maybe now you would do five times more than that. In those days, you took less. It was enough.') Gainsbourg gave some direction from behind the camera, and the photographer learned more about the concept of the record as he was shooting. 'He was close to me and he would say to her, Put your head down a bit more. She's supposed to look like a girl of fifteen, and to be afraid, because the man with the Rolls-Royce just ran her over on her bicycle. We took a few pictures of her without the wig on, too.' A few days later, Tony went around to Serge's to take pictures of him in his courtyard for the inlay. 'It's interesting because I did three or four rolls, I said some funny things and he was laughing, *Stop stop stop* … the only shot he used was of his profile, looking down. That's the one he chose and I don't know why. I didn't ask him and I can't now.'

Gainsbourg took inspiration for Melody from Vladimir Nabokov in the first place. He says he learnt about an 'almost inhuman aesthetic coolness' from Huysmans, and 'coldness' from Nabokov. '*Lolita* hit me right in the face,' he told the writer Noël Simsolo in 1982.* The singer had apparently longed to set Humbert Humbert's 'Wanted' poem to music—an itch he nearly scratched with 'Jane B': 'Hair: brown. Lips: scarlet. Age: five thousand three hundred days' becomes 'Yeux bleus. Cheveux châtains … Âge: entre vingt et vingt et un.' Setting a Chopin prelude over some atmospheric organ and cascading toms, 'Jane B' was a great example of him taking various sources and making them hip while making them his own. He had hoped one of his songs on

---

* 'Lolita, je l'ai pris en plein gueule.'

No.4 would feature the verses from the book, too, but with Kubrick shooting the film adaptation at the same time, Nabokov refused permission. That didn't stop Gainsbourg taking Nabakov's blueprint and creating a number of facsimiles of *Lolita* with a slight variation each time, an inspiration that remained at the core of his work for the rest of his career (see also: *L'homme à tête de chou* and *You're Under Arrest*).

The name Melody Nelson came to him in 1968, soon after he met Birkin and discovered her middle name was Mallory. He inscribed his leather-bound book of lyrics, *Chansons cruelles*, with the words, 'It is only missing the "Chanson de Mallory" that I will write for you and also "Histoire de Mélodie [sic] Nelson".'* *Histoire de Melody Nelson* would take form slowly and arrive finally in 1971, a mini magnum opus of just twenty-eight minutes that was a testament to their love affair, right down to the tummy bump concealed by Jane's childhood cuddly toy. But Serge was already telling people about the concept of his next album back in 1969, including Jean-Claude Vannier, who he first worked with on Robert Benayoum's surrealist movie *Paris n'existe pas*.

Jean-Claude Vannier comes to meet me at Place des Vosges in the Marais, a well-to-do seventeenth-century square a stone's throw from his flat. The *arrangeur des arrangeurs* is not a celebrity in France, although he does hold enough sway in the local neighbourhood to get us a table with a red-and-white checked cloth next to the thoroughfare without dining. It's a mistake many a tourist makes, assuming they can sit and drink coffee when there's a knife and fork on the table, provoking the ire of pissed-off garçons all over Paris. Jean-Claude wafts over in a beige coat that looks several sizes too large for him, a shock of grey hair bobbling in the wind—details that may enforce stereotypes about mad geniuses.

When I'd emailed Vannier and arranged a rendezvous for March 2 2019, it had slipped my mind that it would be the anniversary of Gainsbourg's death, twenty-eight years on. As he takes his seat I immediately apologise for the

---

* 'Il y manque ici la 'Chanson de Mallory que j'écrirai pour toi, également Histoire de Mélodie Nelson,' according to the extensive sleeve notes of the 2011 box set released by Mercury France.

insensitive timing of our rendezvous. 'It's my birthday too,' he complains. 'Gainsbourg died on my birthday.' I wish him many happy returns and apologise again, this time for getting him out of his flat on his birthday. His website states that he was born on March 4, so whether this is a factual inaccuracy or he's having a laugh it's hard to say, though he seems genuine enough. 'Calamitous timing,' I say, and his face portrays an expression that somehow conveys the irritation that Gainsbourg, even in death, had managed to upstage him. At least that's my interpretation, though it could just be the look of a notoriously grumpy septuagenarian.

Jean-Claude Vannier was born on either the 2nd or 4th of March during a bomb scare in Bécon-les-Bruyères in 1943. His profile has mostly remained subterranean since, and he's watched the careers of those whose music he enhanced explode like supernovas: Françoise Hardy, Brigitte Fontaine, Barbara, Dalida, Claude François, Johnny Hallyday, and so on. Vannier took up the piano in his teens, teaching himself to alleviate the ennui of Courbevoie, a nondescript suburb of West Paris where, that one bomb scare aside, not much happens. I certainly got that sense of a nowhere suburb just that little bit too far from the centre of Paris when I stayed there in the summer of 2018. The writer Emmanuel Bove backs up this assertion, describing it as 'a place without history, where nothing ever happens, cruelly devoid of great criminal or evil character, and one that you could cross without even noticing'.

Jean-Claude was posted to North Africa at the age of eighteen after signing a contract he claims he hadn't read properly, landing a job working as a pianist at the Art Deco imperialist outpost, Hôtel Aletty, in Algiers. While he was ambivalent about the place, arriving toward the conclusion of the Algerian Revolution, the sounds he heard there opened his ears to endless possibilities. 'When I was eighteen I went to Algeria, although I didn't want to,' he tells me. 'The Hôtel Aletty is a very famous hotel you'll see in old movies about Algeria. It was a big place with a full orchestra and dancing girls. I was the only blond-haired man on the Kazbah.' Much has been said about Vannier's apparent use of Algerian music, though that's largely a misapprehension, according to the man himself: 'I liked the Algerian cabaret, but my music is not really influenced by Arab music. It's more influenced by Indian music and Nordic music. I like eastern music and Indian and Greek music. I wouldn't say I was especially indebted to Algerian music; I love it, but it hasn't really influenced me.'

Where the wild symphonic soundscapes for *Histoire de Melody Nelson* came from is irrelevant, given that they are unmistakably Vannier. It's easy to forget he didn't actually produce *Histoire de Melody Nelson*—that job fell to Jean-Claude Desmarty, but like with Arthur Greenslade on Gainsbourg's previous records, it's difficult to see where the arranger's job ends and the producer's begins. Vannier is sketchy about the processes of their interaction when I ask him, or perhaps the question is lost in translation. Desmarty brings the array of studio effects becoming fashionable at the time, such as phasing and reverb, but otherwise it is swathed in Vannier's motifs: the busy, swooping strings and the acres of space made to accommodate them.

Desmarty was instrumental in hooking Vannier and Gainsbourg up in 1969, via a mutual association with Claude Nougaro. Vannier flew to London to meet Serge with the prospect of working on *Paris n'existe pas*, but not before missing a flight and then throwing up on the replacement flight, thanks to some heavy drinking the night before. Sweating profusely and white as a sheet when he arrived, Gainsbourg identified in him a kindred spirit. In actuality, they couldn't have been more different in temperament and outlook. Vannier stayed at the Cadogan Hotel when he first arrived in London, a deliberate choice: 'It was run down at the time, and very cheap. And I loved that hotel as it was the last place that Oscar Wilde was in before going to jail. I love Oscar Wilde.'

Vannier comes from the tradition of French pop where an arranger is drafted in to do much of the work from a structural and instrumental perspective, and sometimes with the melody too. In many cases, arrangers would write much of, or all of, the music without getting a credit for it (see: the soundtrack to *La horse*). There is usually a producer in the studio, too, like with the British or American setup, though they're not lionised like the Phil Spectors and Joe Meeks and Quincy Joneses of the Anglophonic world. Matt Robin from Forward Music tells me, 'The French industry was much smaller and very much geared toward mainstream pop, which we called *variété*. In the

70s, it would always be the same musicians recording for everybody, so they'd just record in the same pop style. The A&R wouldn't think too much about producers. They'd just get the musicians in and decide what style they wanted with the artist: Bossa nova is trendy? Let's do a bossa. Disco is hip? Let's do a disco one ...'

'I don't know how it works with other arrangers in other countries,' says Vannier, 'but when a label or a singer asked me to do some arranging, I would do the whole job: conception, style, writing, arrangements, orchestration, choice of the musicians, conducting all of the recordings, the orchestra, the solo voice, the mixes, and everything else, freely, without anyone at my side. Usually, the artist and the label only discovered the finished song and the arrangement after I'd recorded it. In my opinion, the true composer should write all of the music and not ask for help from an arranger, like someone who needs crutches.'

Although lyrically Vannier had no input on *Melody Nelson*, his father did help provide the 'spirit of ecstasy' that propels 'Melody'. 'We discussed the lyrics, and Serge didn't know what car to use. I don't know anything about cars but my father knew them very well, and he sent us a list of all the Rolls-Royces and we chose the Silver Ghost from the list.' Clearly flush at the time, Serge bought himself a Silver Ghost and never got around to learning to drive it, famously using it as an ashtray.

From the opening track, the rhythm is often paired back to make way for the narrative, increasing at times to help the story along. Jean-Claude Vannier is the nemesis of drummers. 'I don't like the hi-hat,' he states. 'The noise is awful. I've never liked it. Drummers need them because it decompresses the sound. They can't tap on their thighs because it hurts too much.' Ironically, or even deliberately, one of Vannier's few writing credits on the original *Melody Nelson* was for 'En Melody', an instrumental featuring a violin solo from Jean-Luc Ponty and a side helping of grunting from Birkin, deluged with fast, funky paradiddles and plenty of cymbal-smacking sibilance. You suspect Serge might have been having a laugh.

Vannier was unable to overrule the percussive middle on the Gainsbourg composition 'La fille qui fait tchic ti tchic', performed by the actress Michele Mercier, a track that the percussive title lends itself to. Mercier was best known for playing the title role in the 1964 movie *Angélique, Marquise des Anges*, and she also appeared in Truffaut's *Tirez sur le pianiste* from 1960. 'La fille qui fait tchic ti tchic' shimmies along as the harpsichord descends, supported by Vannier's trademark swoops. While Jean-Claude and I disagree on its artistic merits, Mercier played an inadvertent role in inspiring one of the album's musical highlights.

'"La fille qui fait tchic ti tchic" is a really awful song,' he states, blunty, 'and it was sung by Michele Mercier, who was an awful actress.' During the recording sessions, Vannier remembers Mercier and a friend of hers, who was the boss of a radio station, inviting them to a high-class house of ill repute. 'I couldn't say this before, but we went to a bordello,' he says, laughing. 'It's pretty vulgar, but Coco Chanel and Édith Piaf had been to this place. And we went in and I saw all of the presenters on the TV channels and all of these government ministers on the first floor. We just had a drink there. It was a funny place. And the decor included the sculptures of "nègres portant des flambeaux" described by Serge in "L'hotel particulier". That was all inspired by this place. It's closed now so you can't go there.'

There are arrangements that could have only come from Vannier on 'L'hotel particulier', swooping in like sidewinders, with a slightly wonky left-handed piano break that lands so stylishly that it gives you goose-bumps. The album's narrator, meanwhile, takes Melody into a brothel to have his wicked way with her, and it's a scenario that Serge and Jane chose to enact in real life when they first met. In Birkin's *Munkey Diaries*, she recounts finding a grubby hotel in Pigalle, and the comedy of errors that follows.

On the night in question, the pair sink a couple of cognacs each in the strip club next door to the venue for Dutch courage. When they arrive, the receptionist interrogates Jane about her age. Jane can't help thinking about the prostitutes in the other rooms as they climb the stairs, or the state of the chamber where they intend to carry out a prostitute fantasy of Jane's: 'The room is disgusting, a gloomy grey, with an invasive bright light just above the bed, and a pathetic, dusty, pink and green plastic bouquet of flowers. Lucien puts the bouquet in front of the bare bulb to try to soften the light … "Play the prostitute," he says, so I removed my black stockings and my garter belt. I'm horrified to see there's nothing in the room except the double bed, not even a TV, aside from a very dirty sink with a dripping tap.'* As they're getting into character, Jane surveys the bed and wonders if there are ticks. Suddenly there's a banging and they hear a voice shouting, 'Open the door!'

'Go away! I paid my seven francs,' shouts Serge, angrily. Footsteps trail away, and they resume their foreplay … noisily. It's a scene they would go on to recreate in the movie *Je t'aime moi non plus* six years later. Suddenly the footsteps return. 'Open the door!' comes a voice from outside. In panic, the couple get up from the bed and stand behind the door to see if they can see who's there through the peephole. The door bursts open, landing on them.

Four men enter, and Jane immediately thinks she's about to be raped. 'You okay, little one?' asks the ringleader of the intrusion. Jane, in shock, replies in the affirmative. She's told to put her clothes back on, and the proprietor comes clean. A murder took place the week before just across the hall. The man is terrified it will happen again, given that the reputation he's built up over a number of years has been tarnished by the death of a young prostitute. They'd heard screaming, panicked, and kicked the door in.

'We're probably the only couple in love with each other who ever passed through their doors,' Jane writes, 'and thrown out for being in the throes of passion. We ran across the street to the taxi rank, and went back to our chic hotel where everything is permitted.'

*

---

* 'T'imagines pas la chambre, dégueu, d'un gris lugubre, une lumière brillante juste au-dessus du lit et un pathétique bouquin rose et vert en plastique couvert de poussière et emballé dan un filet. Lucien a calé le bouquet contre l'ampoule nue pour adoucir la lumière. … "Joue la prostituée," il a dit. Alors j'ai retiré mes bas nous et mon porte-jarretelle. J'étais horrifiée de voir qu'il n'y avait vraiment rien dans la pièce à part le lit double et un bidet, même pas une télé ou quoi que ce soit, il était posé contre le mur, pas était très sale et le robinet gouttait.' Jane Birkin, *Munkey Diaries (1957–1982)* (Fayard, 2018)

'*La nouvelle vague, c'est moi,*' declared Gainsbourg, like the Louis XIV of pop, on a TV programme back in 1963. At the time, he was promoting his stripped-back jazz album *Gainsbourg Confidentiel*, which remained largely confidential, given that nobody really bought it. Of course, this being Gainsbourg, he declared his genius to presenter Denise Glaser with an almost inaudible diffidence, and not in the bombastic way you might expect from the Sun King.

Gainsbourg saw himself as the songwriter of his generation, full of insights and originality—which he certainly was, but he also needed others to achieve his ambitions. If Gainsbourg was a genius then a certain fraction of that genius was the ability to find the right people to work with at the right time. It's a knack the greats have—David Bowie, twentieth-century Madonna, Miles Davis—and includes an innate sixth sense that anticipates a change in the weather and instinctively knows when to freshen up personnel and when to stick with what's already working. In Bowie's case, he famously broke up the band at the height of Ziggy-mania, a canny stroke. Gainsbourg didn't always get it right (see: *Mauvais nouvelles des etoiles*), but he had a habit of anticipating what would be coming around the corner, and he sometimes helped dictate the way the wind was blowing too. Cutting something short when there appears to be a winning formula in place is not without its risks, and record companies hate it: jump too late and you risk being branded a bandwagon jumper; jump too early and you easily confound your hard won audience. Gainsbourg was definitely too early with *Melody Nelson*. About thirty years too early.

The twentieth century is packed with singular innovators in pop, but a cursory glance at the inner sleeve will indicate contributions from other players that may catch your eye. How much credit they're given is rarely commensurate to the toil these giants behind the scene put in. Brian Eno has a term for it, *scenius*, which 'stands for the intelligence and the intuition of a whole cultural scene. It is the communal form of the concept of the genius'.[*] Scenius can include management, musicians, marketeers, and the milkman. To make all of those work to your advantage all of the time takes great skill

---

[*] Louise Gray, *The Wire* (August 2008)

and cunning, and, in Serge's case, it helped that he had a very savvy manager in Philippe Lerichomme.

Bass player John Kumnick, who went by the Spice Girls-like John K in the 80s, played with Bowie and Madonna and Serge Gainsbourg as well: 'I don't know if they all reinvented themselves but they all put themselves in new situations and surrounded themselves with new people, giving them new perspectives in their creativity, in their writing or with their personas. In that way Serge was the same.'

Most of the musicians on *Melody Nelson* weren't credited on the sleeve, which has turned the hunt for the purveyors of scenius into a mystery that has lasted half a century, creating confusion over who actually did play on the record. Much more on that later.

Another artist who didn't get his dues for a long time, but did get his name on the sleeve, is Vannier. 'It's so tough for him,' lamented Jean-Benoît Dunckel, when I interviewed his band, Air, in 2011. 'He gave so much to *Melody Nelson* and all the credit went to Serge Gainsbourg,' added his partner, Nicolas Godin. A decade on from that interview and Vannier is beginning to get the kind of attention he deserves for his significant contribution to that record in particular. Vannier's own instrumental work has also been reappraised thanks to the sterling work of Andy Votel, who re-released Vannier's debut solo album, *L'enfant assassin des mouches*, in 2005, launching the Stockportian's Finders Keepers label in the process. Since then, a whole generation has started to seek out the covert partners—and not just Vannier— who for decades remained in the shadows, only acknowledged by the nerdiest of fans: Michel Legrand, Michel Colombier, François de Roubaix, André Popp, David Whitaker, and so on. 'What's good is now everyone knows that Serge Gainsbourg had great arrangers,' David Sztanke, the symphonic French pop visionary formerly known as Tahiti Boy, tells me. 'People have now started to get interested in those arrangements, sometimes even as much as they were interested in Gainsbourg in the first place.'

If Vannier didn't get his dues, it's fair to say *Melody Nelson* didn't either. Released in 1971, it didn't go gold until 1986, when it finally limped past the eighty thousand copies mark. 'Yes, Serge gave me the gold record and said, At last we've got it,' Jane Birkin remembers. 'It was years after, and I was no longer with him.'

'*Melody Nelson* wasn't a success at all at the time,' Vannier tells me. 'When we received the list of money from SACEM, sales were so small that it may as well have been spare change. There was nothing. We were looking at the royalties, and Serge had nothing, and he asked me to show him mine, and I had nothing either. *Melody Nelson* became famous after Serge died.' Was it too avant-garde for its time, I wonder? 'Avant-garde?' asks Vannier. 'Maybe. I don't know. I can't judge, I'm too close to it.' Isn't something that gets discovered after someone's death some thirty years after they made it avant-garde by definition? 'It's difficult today to say,' he reiterates. 'It's difficult to understand why. Maybe young people are more receptive to it now.'

Jean-Claude's confusion here is understandable. *Melody Nelson* certainly attempted things that had never been tried before, and, as is the cliché, pushed the envelope, but it's not avant-garde in the sense that it dispenses with structure or attempts to reinvent form like *L'enfant assassin des mouches* (Serge came up with the tracklisting and the title, which translates as *The Child-Killer Of Flies*). At the time of the latter's release it was considered so outré that Vannier's record company would only agree to press one hundred copies. Here was a record that became a myth and lived up to the promise when Votel rescued it twenty-five years later.

Originals now change hands for around five hundred euros on Discogs, while you can get your hands on a Finders Keepers version for about twenty quid. 'Andy emailed me and said he wanted to release this forgotten record,' Vannier told me when I interviewed him once before, for the *Stool Pigeon* in 2011. 'I thought a young man was having a laugh at my expense.' Full of skittish Vannier leitmotifs—fire engine sirens, glockenspiels, celestial choirs, industrial noise, arabesque strings—it also reverberates with sleazy funk, dirty bass, and some Bedouin drone-rock for good measure. It's like Alejandro Jodorowsky directing an episode of *Starsky & Hutch*.

'I often say that *L'enfant assassin des mouches* is my favourite LP of all time, because as a Desert Island Disc it has something for every mood—it's like the Swiss Army Knife of European progressive pop,' says Andy Votel. 'That's essentially what makes it the perfect Finders Keepers release—it ticks every box. An entire collection in one record, if you will. I first bought the album because it was rumoured to be the unofficial sequel to Gainsbourg's *Histoire de Melody Nelson*, and I wasn't disappointed. Many progressive-rock experts had warned me that it was terrible, but I had already learned that my taste had become the absolute opposite of the connoisseur's choice. There's an example of bad information.'

Vannier is clearly as confused by my question about *Melody Nelson* being avant-garde as he was when Suzelle Records held their noses having heard *L'enfant Assassin des mouches* in 1972. As an artist, he knows how to make great music, but he has little sense of what people will like or what they'll buy. Mike Patton, who worked with Vannier on the collaborative 2019 album *Corpse Flower*, says the latter's instinct for unusual arrangements is a rare and extraordinary gift. 'That's one of his shining talents,' he tells me over the phone from San Francisco. 'He's got the absolute technique and delicacy of a classical composer, and yet he's well versed in jazz and rock, and he likes to fuck shit up. And he does it in a really effortless way. It doesn't sound like cut and paste, it doesn't sound like postmodern bullshit, it's actually composed that way. It's with intent, and that's why he's really, really special. Not a lot of people can do that.'

Vannier's sense of sonic adventure is tempered to some degree on *Histoire de Melody Nelson* (a statement you'll probably agree with if you've heard *L'enfant assassin des mouches*). Both records are otherworldly on a first listen, but *Melody Nelson* entices you in where Vannier's solo record might repel you with its strangeness, at least to begin with. *L'enfant assassin des mouche* can rightfully be considered avant-garde, where *Melody Nelson* is, if anything, a retro-futurist patchwork where nineteenth-century symphonies get to coalesce with funk and psychedelia—an alternative reality where Serge brings high art and low art together in his own image. It's at once as recognisable as *art nouveau*, with all its flourishes and frills, and yet it's like nothing you've seen or heard before, enmeshing what the British called 'the modern style' with the psychedelic.

These days, hybridization rarely feels audacious like *Melody Nelson* does when you first hear it, but I experienced a similar rush of excitement recently when I heard J Dilla's *Donuts* for the first time. *Melody Nelson* and *Donuts* are two albums I somehow neglectfully managed to get into about a decade and a half after the artists who made them had died, but the 2006 record has provided me with some of the sensations that I first experienced listening to *Melody Nelson*—kind of a *shock of the new* and a sense of familiarity at the same time. *Donuts* is as exhilarating as it is playful, and it sounds like the future while also mining the past with Dadaist irreverence. This may also be because sampling is the most hauntological of art forms when it's well sourced and done intuitively and masterfully by someone like the Detroit savant, real name James Yancey.

At the other end of the scale is Jive Bunny & The Mixmasters offering a cynical exercise in nostalgia with reconstituted rock'n'roll records. *Retro* is aware of what it's up to with a side helping of irony; nostalgia drips with sentimentality and tells you the past was better. Go to eBay and spend too much money tracking down the records of De La Soul, whose material has been in limbo for decades thanks to legal wrangling over samples, and you'll likely experience a Proustian rush when you put them on, especially if you were a teenager when *3 Feet High And Rising* came out in 1989, like I was. It sounds as bright as its Day-Glo yellow cover, and it evokes a happier future in an alternative reality where George Clinton is president instead of Donald Trump. There's nothing nostalgic about Melody Nelson either despite its use of the music of the past.

You probably don't need me to tell you that The Beatles changed the pop landscape in 1967 with *Sgt Pepper's Lonely Hearts Club Band*, an album that appeared to universally resonate (and wasn't hurt by all the hype, either). Suddenly, France too had pop musicians who were less interested in writing expendable pop songs and more turned on by the idea that they were actual composers birthing weighty music free from the strictures of the style-cramping 45. Artists like Gérard Manset and William Sheller blurred the boundaries of classical and rock with epic releases in France, while progressive bands like Gong, Magma, Moving Gelatine Plates, Triangle, and Heldon redefined the boundaries of what was possible in the field of rock.

Manset in particular had a big hit in 1970 with the symphonic *La mort d'Orion*, a lush, rock-tinged libretto with spoken word that proved to be influential with French artists and surprisingly further afield too. 'Everyone knows Serge Gainsbourg and he's amazing, but actually the guy who had a big influence on my music, and the guy I idolised from France, is Manset,' says Mark Lanegan. The former Screaming Trees singer once wrote a piece for a magazine about his favourite obscure album—the aforementioned *La mort d'Orion*—and, years later, Manset approached him from his enforced seclusion to suggest a collaboration. As a mysterious figure who brushes off the media and one who has never played live despite a deep well of curiosity from his fans, it was an unusual occurrence that Manset should be seeking out somebody else.

'It was the *La mort d'Orion* record that grabbed me!' enthuses Lanegan. 'It's one of those little pieces, the most obscure records that you love. Somehow, he heard about this piece and he was doing a record where he was redoing a bunch of his songs and he asked me to do "Elégie funèbre" from the end of that record as a duet in French. So I did my part in French and I sent it to him and he wrote back: *I'm going to get this translated into English.*' Lanegan laughs demonically and clears his throat. 'Nothing sounds more ridiculous than an American with a country accent, which is what I have, singing or even speaking in French. Okay, Iggy got away with it, but otherwise ...'

Lanegan says hearing his voice against Manset's aged vocal, giving the track even more weight than the 1970 version, was one of the defining moments of his career. *La mort d'Orion* was revered as a cult work on its release, an album that was diametrically different to the three-minute yé-yé hits that had prevailed just a few years before. *Melody Nelson* stepped into this changed landscape, and it was made possible because Serge was considered bankable by his label after the success of 'Je t'aime ... moi non plus'. More ambitious projects required money, and there was a lot of it around in the early 70s in the music industry. A thirty-piece orchestra and a seventy-strong choir don't come cheaply, after all.

'Wasn't he doing interesting and deep albums because that was the fashion?' asks Bertrand Burgalat. 'I think when he was doing something like *Melody Nelson* he thought he was doing his own version of *Tommy*. He was disappointed by its lack of success, but he put himself in the market, and he had the habit of writing hits for other singers and then doing a more artistic *Rive Gauche* kind of thing on the side.'

Whether it was the fashion or not, Gainsbourg saw this album as his window of opportunity to join the immortals, and the disappointment of indifference upon its release must have been crushing. 'It's funny that *Melody Nelson* bombed,' says Mick Harvey. 'As I understand it, he had huge expectations and thought he'd written his masterpiece. I can really imagine what that would have done to him. *Well fuck it then, I'm just going to be this drunk guy, make trouble and get attention.* The best work you do, nobody gives a shit.'

'I got hold of an advance copy and gave it to somebody I knew at the BBC,' Andrew Birkin, brother of Jane, tells me. 'I thought it was wonderful, absolutely fabulous, and I still think it was Serge's masterpiece. It was to Serge what *Dark Side Of The Moon* is to Pink Floyd. Even though you can get distracted from different bits and pieces, like some of Vannier's lush orchestration, which I thought was a bit over the top; nevertheless, I think it's also what made it. I thought that it would do well in England and that it would be his breakthrough, which it certainly wasn't. But you can say, *Well what do you expect? Nobody can speak French over here?* No, the big disappointment was that it did so badly in France.'

Phonogram, the successor to Philips, must have felt confident it would pick up, having commissioned videos for all seven songs for a TV special with the Emmy Award-winning director Jean-Christophe Averty. Entitled simply *Melody*, it was shown on French TV on December 22 1971. Not even a Christmas audience watching in their millions gave the record, which had been out for eight months by that time, much of a boost. Was it too sinister and sexy? A confusing combination, perhaps. And was it too pretentious visually?

A black-clad Serge sits behind the wheel of a Rolls-Royce Silver Ghost and knocks Jane Birkin off her bike, which then leads to some hallucinatory gyrating with the work of a plethora of surrealists and proto-surrealists projected onto blue screens as they enter into intergenerational flagranti. The paintings of Salvador Dalí, Max Ernst, Félix Labisse, René Magritte, Paul Delvaux, and Douanier Rousseau are projected as *mise en scène* as Serge and Jane go to town with the chroma keying.

Here we have Serge as a kind of lusty curator, projecting the past masters of surrealism onto the walls with what was then futuristic technology, while the music amalgamates rock and funk with classical strings that deviate from time to time beyond the European scales viewers might be used to hearing. 'Valse de Melody' in particular could have time-hopped straight out of *la belle époque*, a simulacrum of a fantasy loosely inspired by Jean Sibelius's 'Valse Triste' from 1903. To add a nagging extra layer of familiarity, listeners may well have heard the instrumental version without realising it, as Serge had already used it for a Martini advert in 1970.

Jane and Serge themselves are playing versions of themselves, too; you know it and they know it. They're caricatures taken to logical fictional extremes: Jane plays the helpless waif; Serge prowls and looks directly to camera, raffish and predatory—if he wasn't singing, he'd be breaking the fourth wall, but because we know it's a story, perhaps he is breaking the fourth wall anyway. It's metafiction. The whole thing is achingly postmodern.

The Melody character is fifteen years old, and it's probably important to flag up some cultural differences at this point and mention that the legal age of consent in France is fifteen, and there are no statutory rape laws, meaning that if there wasn't 'violence, coercion, threat, or surprise' then the Serge character would be, no matter how icky, on the right side of the law. Serge was clearly playing with the boundaries of what was acceptable at the time—it might be legally okay, but does that make it okay? He could also cover his ass slightly with the fact that Jane Birkin was twenty-four at the time, but under today's scrutiny that detail would appear flimsy at best.

Internet-savvy twenty-first-century cultural consumers are used to styles and sounds from across the decades being woven together in a kind of audio-visual montage, but retro fads (30s music hall being referenced in 60s pop; the 50s craze that ran throughout the 70s) were a fairly new cultural phenomenon that came with a new pervasiveness of media. Gainsbourg's attempts to fuse together so many disparate elements of sound and vision from across the years in a multimedia event would have blown minds, but he also would have confused the hell out of a lot of viewers watching in 1971 who essentially voted with their feet.

*

'I loved the cozy atmosphere of London studios,' Jean-Claude Vannier told *Le Monde* in 2008. 'The carpets were spread out in the studio, so it looked like an apartment. The English musicians of the time were not wild rockers. They mixed their musical modernism with "high tea", a custom that I liked very much. The quality of the musicians did a lot for the record. The next year our bassist, Herbie Flowers, played on "Walk On The Wild Side".'*

Vannier conducted versions of *Histoire de Melody Nelson* and *L'enfant assassin des mouches* at the Barbican in 2006, with Jarvis Cocker, Mick Harvey, the Super Furry Animals' Gruff Rhys, and Badly Drawn Boy taking on the vocals, and then repeated the exercise in 2011, this time at the Hollywood Bowl with Beck, Mike Patton, Victoria Legrand from Beach House and Sean Lennon. The big names performed the songs, while the musicians from the record were in attendance to accompany them: Dougie Wright, Herbie Flowers, Vic Flick, and 'Big' Jim Sullivan. 'Herbie Flowers was a very violent man when he was out and about in the old days, but now he's like a little old English lady in his demeanour. Incredible,' Vannier says, before quickly adding, 'Anyway, he wasn't on the original record.'

---

* 'J'aimais l'ambiance cosy des studios londoniens. Les tapis s'étalaient dans le studio, cela lui donnait des airs d'appartement. Les musiciens anglais de l'époque n'étaient pas des rockers sauvages. Ils mêlaient leur modernisme à un côté "thé de 5 heures" que j'aimais beaucoup. La qualité des musiciens a fait beaucoup pour le disque. Quelque temps après, notre bassiste Herbie Flowers a joué dans "Walk On The Wild Side". Je viens! A n'importe quel prix.'

As previously mentioned, the mystery of which musicians actually played on *Melody Nelson* hasn't entirely been solved, though some more clarity arrived in 2011 courtesy of Tony Frank and an undeveloped roll of film. For the fortieth anniversary of the record, Frank was asked to sift through his photos for additional shots to use for a deluxe repackaged version, and, as he returned to the originals, he came across a spare roll that he took at the time that hadn't been fully developed. Tony had taken some shots down in the basement at Philips's Marble Arch studio but never developed them: 'I took these pictures of the rhythm section,' he says, 'and I took six or seven of Serge in the sound room, but it was so dark at that time, and I couldn't see anything in the negatives.' When the pictures were finally developed beyond the contact sheets he already had, they caused shock and consternation. Frank had captured the engine room at work, but the men in the photos weren't Dougie Wright or Herbie Flowers.

The word was out that somebody else was playing bass, and the other session musicians quickly identified Dave Richmond, with a fine pair of fashionable mutton chops, stood there in the studio. The other drummer has remained a mystery since the discovery, despite the best efforts of Andy Votel to identify who was behind the kit that day. Votel co-ordinated a campaign with the remaining session men to check their diaries. For the record, Dougie Wright did play on some of the sessions, alternating with the unknown drummer. 'I played on quite a bit, but I didn't do it all,' says Wright, over the phone. 'I'll be quite honest about that. It's doubtful whether everyone did it all, if the truth be known. You get a lot of musicians saying, *I was on that, I was on that, I was on that*, and you think, *Hang on a minute! This is getting silly, to the exclusion of the great players.*'

'I did virtually almost everything The Walker Brothers and Dusty Springfield did back then,' says Alan Parker. 'Take "No Regrets", for instance. The solo on that song was recorded at the Marquee studios on Wardour Street. I'm credited for it, and about eleven guitarists have claimed it was them.' As well as playing for Gainsbourg, Dougie Wright played with the John Barry Seven, and he met a teenage Jane Birkin when she was married to the bandleader. In the 60s beat boom, Wright was known as the Fourth Walker, such was his proximity to the band. 'Scott Walker knew what he wanted, and I think he indisputably had one of the best voices of the 1960s,' says Dougie, who I interviewed a few months before Walker's death in March 2019. 'I think I'm led to believe that he's gone very surrealistic over the years, and I don't subscribe to that sort of thing.'

With some session musicians claiming to have been on the record—or having played the Barbican or the Hollywood Bowl under the misapprehension that they were on the original—are these players being dishonest for a quick buck, or has a collective amnesia come over the British equivalent of the Wrecking Crew? Why, if they played on some of the greatest records of the 1960s and 1970s, do they not have any recollection of doing so? The fact of the matter is that most of them played on so many records by so many artists, week in, week out, for so many years, that the sessions bleed into each other in the memory banks. 'We weren't even necessarily told who it was we were playing for,' says Dave Richmond. 'The people who you were working for were incidental, really.'

'It's funny, people say the memory plays tricks on you, and it does, to an extent,' says Dougie Wright. 'The reason I remember the hit material I recorded was because it usually got played on *Jukebox Jury*. And *Jukebox Jury* usually made it a hit! I made a mental note of all that stuff I was on, and even today, when an introduction starts, I can remember it, and then usually where we recorded it, funnily enough.' Dougie remembers playing on 'Je t'aime … moi non plus', but *Melody Nelson* draws a blank. 'There was only one musician who actually had the time and savvy to write down every song title he recorded in the studios. Nobody else ever did that, we just put down the dates of the session. Unfortunately he's passed away now.'

Even though the musicians didn't write down separate tracks or artists in their diaries, the fact that they were in the Philips studio on the dates that correlated meant they'd played on the sessions. Big Jim Sullivan played on the early sessions—a fact Vannier can definitely vouch for. 'Yes, we recorded first in England with Big Jim. He was a very good guitarist who's dead now. I found the diary with the meetings of the rendezvous. It's all there in black and white. We played night and day. Jim Sullivan was completely booked up for months, so I remember we had to wait for him. We played several times with him and Alan Parker.'

'People have done various articles on me where they say I played on this or that,' says Parker. 'I say, Did I? The memory is unreliable. When you think, if I started when I was seventeen, that's about fifty-five years ago or something. Your memory does get a little bit detached from your brain.' (Three years later, Parker played the main line on 'Rebel Rebel' which is one he definitely remembers.)

'My great mentor, Andy Votel, must have made about a hundred calls to me checking my diaries,' says Dave Richmond. 'He's done a great service, has Andy Votel, and whatever he says is true. We double checked it in the diary. He was very precise.' Curiously, having been identified as the bassist forty years later, having been unaware he was on the record (and having missed out on the Barbican and Hollywood Bowl), it's Dave who now has the best memories of the sessions. The famous, much-sampled bass line on 'Melody', with the unmistakable bass vibrato at the beginning of the track, came from Richmond following what Parker was doing on guitar: 'I had Alan Parker in the cans, and I heard him doing this double-note slide thing on a session we did at Morgan Studios, and I said, How did you do that? So he showed me, and I started doing something similar on bass around that time. So, on "Melody", you probably notice a double-note glissando, and it's almost in unison but not quite. Of course I could hear Alan in my cans—he was doing a few things like that, so I thought I'd put some in. We were literally just improvising as we went along.'

Dave, who also plays that divine, chunky bass hook on '69 année érotique', remembers being given total freedom to experiment by Gainsbourg and Vannier: 'Very often, we were given these very rigid bass parts where the composer wants you to play it note for note. But I very rarely played anything exactly as it was written, and none of us did. You'd get a feel going and then you'd hear something in the drums or the guitar and you'd echo it or compliment it. It was just a thing that you did and you didn't even think about it.' Alan Parker on the other hand suggests that Vannier could be 'a little bit fragile and a little bit grumpy if we changed any of his arrangements'.

If Vannier remembers a genteel atmosphere where the session men would down tools to take high tea, Dave 'Champagne' Richmond paints a picture of bacchanalian fraternity, rolling from studio to studio and quaffing as they went. 'There must have been about twenty studios—we were just going from one to the other, and there'd be another set of guys there. It was a tremendous social time we had, there was quite a lot of drinking going on with certain members, including myself.' Was that where he got the 'Champagne' in his name from? 'Yes, that's right. Especially if we did Chappells, where there was a passage and opposite was Yates's Wine Lodge. The Champagne was about a pound and ten shillings in old money—£2 for a Moet, but their own champagne was cheaper. At that point we were probably getting about £15 or £20 per session, which was very good going in those days. We were getting three of those envelopes a day.'

The session players were usually paid a decent one-off fee, with cash handed straight over in a money bag: 'You declared it, but it came in little envelopes,' says Dave. 'They just dished out the cash. Martin Kershaw is reputed to have never opened one of those cash bags—he just used to throw them into a wardrobe. And after a few years he bought himself a flat in Marble Arch with twenty grand. A lot of money in those days.'

8
ROCK BOTTOM
VU DE L'EXTÉRIEUR (1973)

[Bullshit is the relaxation of intelligence.*]

'"Je suis venu te dire que je m'en vais" is my favourite song by him,' says Chilly Gonzales. 'I think lyrically it's less of the *goo-goo-goo ga-ga* style of Gainsbourg. It has a little of the wordplay flair with this whole *I came to tell you I'm going* idea. It has this little twist to it, but it just connects with me on a more emotional level.'

'I love it!' says Nicolas Godin, one half of Air, sitting across a table from me in Because Music's commodious London boardroom. The opening track on *Vu de l'extérieur* is incontestably one of Gainsbourg's best loved and prettiest songs. Much has been made of the debt of gratitude Air owed to *Melody Nelson* for their debut, *Moon Safari*, but less has been said about influences from elsewhere (or about them borrowing 'Le Talkie Walkie' for an album title!). 'I took a lot of influence from that song,' adds Godin, 'especially the guitar picking on "Cherry Blossom Girl". He's a very good composer.'

So what does he think of the rest of the album, *Vu de l'extérieur*? 'The album is terrible,' he retorts. 'Such a lazy bastard!'

*

---

* 'La connerie, c'est la décontraction de l'intelligence.' Serge Gainsbourg, *Pensées provocs et autres volutes* (Librairie Générale Française, 2007)

The year 1973 was a peculiar one for Serge Gainsbourg, his *annus horribilis*. After the disappointment of the reception *Melody Nelson* received, he appeared to be in the creative doldrums. The career of his partner, Jane Birkin, was beginning to eclipse his. He fell out with his preferred collaborator, Jean-Claude Vannier, effectively terminating their creative partnership. His fixation with the fundament began in earnest, and he even started to write a book about a man with incurable flatulence (his *anus horribilis* too, perhaps). And then, in May of '73, he suffered his first heart attack.

Di Doo Dah by Birkin had been released in February, and had brought Serge, Jane, and Jean-Claude into creative union one last time. The first album Gainsbourg wrote for Birkin as a solo artist is musically timorous to match her high-pitched, fragile, almost shard-like vocals, and it's decorated with then-fashionable country twangs, as well as Vannier's otherworldly strings—an unusual, intoxicating mix. Lyrically, there's an abundance of fantasy being played out in song. 'Help camionneur!' sees Jane hitchhiking in the hope of getting fucked by a big-boned truck driver; another has her docking at a port in Dakar to enjoy a gang bang with some local seamen. Serge is poking the listener and stoking prejudices and peccadillos, but if a song came out now called 'Banana Boat' about a stowaway seeking out sex with Senegalese sailors then there's a good chance there would be an outcry that the song was racist. Then there's 'Encore lui', a creepy story about her being followed around the streets of Paris by a man who ends up in her bed at the conclusion of the song. It's a playful album, but it's difficult not to feel Jane was being left exposed. Her vulnerability was no doubt part of the fantasy.

On the title track, Birkin ruminates on her tomboyishness and lack of endowment—an obsession from adolescence that Gainsbourg attempts to inhabit, though the show is stolen by Vannier's voluptuous, swirling symphonics above everything else. Some of these fantastical fixations—and most obviously the tomboy and the trucker tales—would find their way into the script of *Je t'aime moi non plus* three years later.

The back sleeve features a black-and-white Tony Frank contact sheet with some of the pictures of Jane crossed out with red pen—a trick that would be revisited in the future, with the sheet of photographs taken of Serge in the backyard at Rue de Verneuil—while the front cover, taken by the Russian French photographer Sam Lévin, references an earlier picture of Bardot crossing her arms across her *décolleté*—a picture that Gainsbourg pulled out of storage and displayed prominently at 5 bis after Jane moved out.

Raechel Leigh Carter isn't quite so sure that the Birkin cover is referencing Bardot: 'People make quite a lot of the similarities between those pictures, but Sam Lévin did lots of portraits. And, also, people like to insinuate that Serge somehow led Jane astray, that she didn't want to do these things, but she'd already done *Wonderwall* and *Blow Up*, and she'd already been scandalous in this country before she went there. In truth, they're two people who both think they're unattractive in one way or another—him because he thinks he's ugly, and her because she's self-conscious about her body. And he manages to convince her that she's so beautiful.'

In a peculiar case of life imitating art, or vice versa, Birkin starred in the Roger Vadim movie *Don Juan ou si Don Juan était une femme …* (*Don Juan, Or If Don Juan Was A Woman*), playing one of Brigitte Bardot's conquests. Bardot is a dead-eyed seducer taking dispassionate pleasure in the destruction she leaves behind her as men are lured against the rocks, enraptured by her beauty. The scenarios are done in flashback as she confesses everything to a hot priest (played by Mathieu Carrière) with the look of a young Brian Eno about him. Along the way, as if to illustrate Bardot's character's voracious sexual appetite, she ends up naked in bed with Birkin.

Don Juan is as lavish as many of Vadim's other pictures, though there's a paucity of eroticism. There's something mechanical about the whole thing, not that that's necessarily a bad thing—it carries some of the pathos of *Alfie*, but with a female in the role of the taciturn philanderer. And, yes, obviously she has sex with the priest.

It's very watchable, even if, due to a lack of availability in the UK, my copy is in French with Polish subtitles, causing some cognitive dissonance. There must have been moments of dissonance on set, too. Serge had a habit of following Birkin onto films, and one can only imagine the awkwardness this caused with his two great loves filming a scene naked and in bed together. *Don Juan* threw up connections that Vadim was the architect of: Gainsbourg and Bardot were former lovers, and Vadim and Bardot were ex-husband and wife working on their fifth film together. Bardot retired from acting shortly after filming the movie, which failed to set the box office alight. Whether any of these are connected, it's impossible to say.

The same year also saw Gainsbourg begin his sequence of singles factory-designed to raise attention. He'd done it once before with 'Je t'aime … moi non plus'; he just needed a variation on the same formula and *voila!*, success and piles of cash. Along came a number of packages trussed up with a huge proverbial bow saying, 'Look at me!', executed lyrically and musically irrespective of any artistic integrity. Most of them weren't terribly good, though 'La décadanse' is one of the better albumless singles he released in the 1970s. In a rare moment of understatement, his bid to shock was too subtle and too well thought through to penetrate the collective consciousness of the French record-buying public. The tacit penetration isn't penetrative enough.

'Gods forgive us our offences … the décadanse,' sings Serge, as he flips Birkin back to front, so his genitals nestle in the derriere region and they slow dance together facing the same direction. There's an inference that a sin against nature is taking place with some regularity in this union, but not explicit enough to get the press in a froth like 'Je t'aime … moi non plus'. Gainsbourg was also abundantly aware that dance crazes converted well into astronomical sales, but 'La décadanse', with all its allusions to *fin-de-siecle* miscreants and bum sex, was a little too clever to catch on. 'I thought, *How extraordinary to turn your partner around*,' says Jane Birkin. 'What an extraordinary idea, and why did nobody think of it before? He had so many original ideas. "La décadanse" was an extraordinary song to have written, and of course it was perverse.'

Gainsbourg recorded his follow up album to *Histoire de Melody Nelson* between March and May 1973 with many of the same crew of London session musicians. Alan Hawkshaw, who'd been given the new job of musical director, had to be very hands-on. Drinking and smoking more than ever before, Serge appeared to be leaving his health, and the music, up to the gods. Or, if he could get away with it, to the session men. The driven, enthusiastic Frenchman they'd encountered in '68 was now lackadaisical and creatively coasting just five years later.

'I don't recall Serge ever being truly sober, but he didn't act like a drunk either. He held his liquor well,' says Hawkshaw, on the phone from Florida. 'Serge was a chain-smoker and an alcoholic, so we adjusted and got used to that.' Hawkshaw used to wonder from time to time if the booze and cigarettes were keeping Serge going, and, if he should stop, he feared what might happen to him. 'We weren't drinkers at the same level as he was. I mean, we often went out with him and the whole band,' says the Hawk. 'He recorded at my studio in Hertfordshire toward the end, so we'd often go out for lunch. Serge was a very funny guy—he had a great sense of humour.'

Alan also describes Serge as having 'a heart of gold' in his book, *The Champ*, remembering a time the Frenchman joined a search party in the garden looking for Hawkshaw's daughter Kirsty's missing hamster, getting down on his hands and knees for an hour. His drinking prowess and love of Gitanes are also etched into the memory: 'Every morning he wanted a glass of Pernod, and this was after he'd already had some for breakfast. Then he'd have his cigarettes in the studio. And I remember going to the local Italian restaurant, and the way he got started was to have ten Sambuca drinks. He lit each one and polished them off one by one. This was before he'd eaten anything.'

Tony Frank remembers turning up in the morning on Serge's doorstep to do a shoot, and his client insisting that they go and buy some lemons first. 'So we went out for these lemons, and when we finally got back, he took two glasses out and poured vodka like *this* into a glass'—Tony indicates a measure of around three or four inches—'a tiny splash of tomato juice, a little Worcester Sauce, and lots of Tabasco. He cut the lemon in two.' He indicates one quick squeeze. 'That was why we went out! At that time, I used to drink a lot of alcohol, and also strong drinks with a kick, but I drank half a glass of what he'd poured, and tears were falling from my eyes. And he said, *Now we are awake.*'

Frank remembers best laid plans being thwarted frequently by the lure of the highlife: 'Sometimes he'd call me up and say, You must come over and we must talk about the pictures we're going to do. And I'd come over and we'd go to a restaurant for three hours: an aperitif, a big meal, another drink, and every time different wines and a Cognac or an Armagnac, and then we never did what we were supposed to do. We did it every time, and then we did the work when we had to do it. Like professionals.'

Tony wasn't needed for the *Vu de l'extérieur* album cover, a picture by rock photographer Jean d'Hugues of Serge surrounded by a collage of monkeys. Gainsbourg liked to claim that these primates were more attractive than him.

Hawkshaw's working relationship with Gainsbourg stretched back to the late 60s, when Arthur Greenslade was his arranger, and lasted until 1983 and Jane Birkin's album *Baby Alone In Babylone*, with Hawkshaw at the helm. Vannier had decided to leave Serge to his own devices in '73, so the singer took the plunge without a recognised arranger, promoting Hawkshaw out of necessity—a working relationship he clearly came to enjoy, as well as the *esprit de corps* with his preferred British session musicians.

Hawkshaw: 'He'd come over to London and booked a studio at Philips in Marble Arch with me, Dougie Wright, Brian Odgers, and Alan Parker, and to be honest he didn't have anything specific written. He was just pitching things, and we were more or less getting nowhere on the first session we did together. So I said to the boys, Look, go take five and I'll sit with Serge and try to write out some parts so we at least have a route map. That's how he and I ended up working together. I sat down with him and was able to squeeze out of him the feel, the meters, the keys, and I finished up virtually sketching out the basic parts, which we then rushed in and copied in the office, and I gave it to all of the boys. They're typical seasoned session musicians, so we could improvise, as long as we had a key to play in and a basic idea of what the feel was, and then we could come up with all sorts of things. Serge liked that way of working for a while.'

Alan thought little more about that first session but, months later, Serge called him up and booked him as musical director. Gainsbourg would usually insist on working with the same musicians—Parker, Wright, and Odgers—but frequently he wouldn't be clear about what he wanted. 'Bless his heart, Serge,' says Parker. 'Luckily, he always booked the guys who were understanding, and he didn't have any hard nuts, if you know what I mean. He came in with songs half-finished, he'd sit down and hum something and expect you to pick it up from there.'

Hawkshaw remembers sitting around at Rue de Verneuil with sessions booked and no material. They would knock together songs with Alan sitting at the piano, suggesting styles and rhythmic metre, scribbling chord structures there on the spot. Serge drank all the time and worked when he had to: 'He was always in a steady state of alcoholism. He wasn't one to be rushed, but we as session men were. Often, we could get a bit impatient with him. In those days, all the musicians were hard to get hold of—everybody was unbelievably busy. If Serge wanted studio time, he had to be very specific.'

Their working methods sound as chaotic as *Vu de l'exterieur* sounds as a record. This, after all, is an album where two songs, including the title track, break down before their natural conclusions. Then there are tracks like 'Hippopodame' and 'Panpan cucul', where his voice breaks into an audible laugh as he's reciting the lyrics. There's a sense that these will have to do, and—given his precarious health at the time, and what was to follow—that may well have been the case. For my money, there's something less invigorating about *Vu de l'extérieur* than his usual output, and it's an album that I've never really appreciated as much as I'd like to. The production of the follow-up is muddied by too many musicians taking the sonic middle ground, a stark contrast to the stripped-out minimalism with violent flourishes that preceded it on *Melody Nelson*.

When Mike Patton worked with Vannier on 2019's *Corpse Flower*, he was struck by their different approaches to making music, which became something they had to work through and overcome. 'That was kind of tricky,' he told me, 'because I'm a dense guy and he's a sparse guy. I wouldn't say we sparred over it, but it was definitely something we had to think about. A lot of tracks on that record I had to pull way back from and just kind of let the music speak. That's a hard thing for me, so this was an education. Honestly, it really was.'

I tell Vannier that I find *Vu de l'extérieur* a little flat and cluttered, and his response is surprising: 'He asked lots of people to work with him on that album, but they said no.' Was Gainsbourg's stock low at the time, after the apparent failure of *Melody Nelson*? 'I don't know. The problem with Serge was that he wasn't a very honest guy. A lot of people hated him.' Conversely, Gainsbourg was popular in England, where session players queued up to work with him—and if a trip over to Paris was thrown into the bargain then even better. Though these musicians were spreading themselves thinly across sessions with some of France's biggest stars. 'We weren't just playing with Serge,' says Parker, 'Dougie, Hawky, Les Hurdle, and I used to go over there twice a year for Joe Dassin as well. Johnny Hallyday used to come over here. I worked a lot with Claude François—he was very uptight, very on edge, and his arranger, Jean-Claude Petit, was a real prima donna.'

'There was a great rivalry with French singers,' says Dougie Wright. 'I did all the stuff for Joe Dassin, and Joe used the same band all the time with Parker, Hawkshaw, Les Hurdle, and myself. They didn't have any love for each other, but that's showbiz.' Demand was high for these specific musicians, which sometimes meant Serge had to fall back on his go-to producer in France, Jean-Pierre Sabar. Sabar, or sometimes Sabard, would take care of soundtracks and one-off singles in the main, while Hawkshaw and the experienced London session men worked on the more serious album front.

The late 70s saw Gainsbourg making soft-porn soundtracks like *Goodbye Emmanuelle* and *Madame Claude* with Sabar, using French session musicians to try to sound like British session musicians imitating Jamaican reggae and American funk; this was music that was several removes from the original source, and it sounded like it. *Madame Claude* includes 'Yesterday Yes A Day'—which did well in Japan—a dismal single sung by Birkin with the most phoned-in pun of Serge's career. Apparently, Birkin wrote the words, possibly a first, and Serge came up with the title (which was enough to warrant him taking sole ownership). Gainsbourg had been offered the job of scoring *Emmanuelle* in 1974 but passed on it. Pierre Bachelet made the soundtrack instead, which led to further films in the *Emmanuelle* series and *The Story Of O.*

'He was furious to have not cottoned on to *Emmanuelle*,' says Birkin. 'He thought it was a really mediocre film and he didn't want anything to do with it, and then it was such a success! He loved the boy [Just Jaeckin] who made it, he was such a sweetheart, but Serge didn't think it would make any money as it wasn't erotic in any way. And then it was such a big hit that his eyes popped out and he said, *Oh merde!* thinking about all the shitty films he'd soundtracked that never went anywhere. He could hardly believe it. So he did *Goodbye Emmanuelle*. It was very unlike him not to spot the success of something, and he was very affronted that he'd missed out.'

Alan Parker has fond memories of working with Gainsbourg. He won over Parker and his wife with his dithery wit and comedy set pieces. 'When he came and stayed at our house, he had this little black book. My wife said to him, Is that all your girlfriends? He said, No, these are my jokes. He'd written them all down to jog his memory. I can't remember any of the jokes now, but he had us in hysterics in his droll way. Story jokes—some of them would last for twenty minutes. There was a build-up and then the punchline would finally come, and we'd be falling about.'

If Serge's unpopularity was a problem in France at that point, there was a far graver crisis to come. *Vu de l'exterieur* was almost in the can, and then his heart packed in. Serge was just forty-five years of age when he had his first heart attack. Given his lifestyle, it maybe shouldn't have been that much of a surprise, though it came as a shock to poor Serge himself, who'd assumed he was invincible up to that point. 'I remember him not being well,' says Parker. 'His record guy, Philippe Lerichomme, contacted me and told me what had happened. I tried getting hold of him but it was impossible, because he wasn't there—he was in the hospital—and I remember speaking to his daughter, Charlotte. God, you're jogging my memory now.'

Speaking to *Vanity Fair* in 2007, Jane revealed that even at death's door, Serge remained image conscious as the ambulance came to take him to hospital:

'When they carried him out of the Rue de Verneuil to go to the American Hospital, he insisted on taking his Hermès blanket, because he didn't like the one they had on the stretcher, and he also grabbed two cartons of Gitanes.' Unsurprisingly, he wasn't allowed to smoke at the hospital, so he requested that Jane bring him some Old Spice deodorant, which he then used to conceal the smell of cigarettes. 'And when he left the hospital, they pulled the bedside drawers open and there were all these little medicine bottles filled with water and cigarette butts.'

Gainsbourg was dismayed that his near-death experience wasn't bigger news. He invited *France-Soir* to attend his bedside, where he pledged to drink and smoke more. He was true to his word. 'Serge loved being in newspapers,' Jane told the *Telegraph* in 2009. 'Even when he had a heart attack and we were in the hospital, he managed to give an interview to *France-Soir*. *'I'm dying here and France didn't know about it*, he explained, when I asked him why he'd done it.'

Serge was in hospital for several weeks, which gave him time to think. He decided on a rebrand for the next record, which would be delayed until November. Symphonic rock outlier Gérard Manset had begun to refer to himself by his surname only from 1972 onwards, and Gainsbourg too would move forward under one singular moniker. It's not the first time he'd call himself by just the one name—on the chanson '69 année érotique', he self-referentially talks about riding on a ferry with a painting by his near namesake, but from now on he will sign off with just Gainsbourg, as would a painter.* In a note to Françoise Hardy, written on American Hospital headed paper, he congratulates her on the birth of her son, Thomas Dutronc, with his surname scrawled in large letters at the bottom. Acquiring a one-name epithet is a mysterious process that involves some kind of celebrity osmosis. It's normally only conferred because of some level of greatness, though some rotters slip through: Bowie, Madonna, Whitney, Dalí, Picasso, Sting, Pétain. With Gainsbourg, it made sense—it was what people called him anyway.

Why did Gainsbourg love being famous? Viewed from the twenty-first

---

* 'Gainsbourg et son Gainsborough / Ont pris le ferry-boat / De leur lit par le hublot …'

century, where fame as a commodity seems almost worthless, it's difficult to remember why anyone ever wanted to be famous, and yet reality TV is full of vacuous egos harvesting their fifteen minutes before being tossed onto the loser heap. Jane has her theories, and they mostly relate to a lack of self-worth going back to his childhood. 'He loved it!' she tells me. 'I think it's one of the most touching things, because he thought he was so ugly. I mean, surely he couldn't have done after Bardot, but he did when he was younger, and that counts for so much. And being on the cover of a magazine meant people were talking about you, and so then he existed. Somehow it isn't vain.'

Serge was addicted to newsstands like some people become addicted to fruit machines or gee-gees. 'He had to be in the newspapers,' she says. 'He couldn't understand when I attacked a newspaper, and it happened one time, just after I left him. *Paris Match* published a cover of a photo where they said *first Christmas without their father*, and it was a picture of me and the children in Normandy in little Laura Ashley print dresses, and behind us you could see the daisies. It had clearly been taken the summer before, so nothing to do with Christmas. Anyway, they put it on the cover, and I attacked the newspaper for it. And Serge said, *But why? You had all the covers. You won't get covers if you complain.* I said, Serge, I did it for you. I don't want covers like that. He thought it was dangerous to get at the press. He didn't realise I didn't want my photo taken when I was pregnant with Lou [Doillon], because I knew it would be hurtful to him. He didn't see it because, for him, a cover was a cover.'

'I love Gainsbourg,' says Guido Minksi from Acid Arab. 'Of course, being from France, it's obvious that you would love Gainsbourg, but there are also a lot of things I hate about him, too. He was always desperately trying to recreate his success. That was his main default.' Minski's favourite track from the back catalogue is what publications these days like to call a deep cut. It's from *Vu de l'extérieur*, but it's neither of the tracks that bookend the album, 'Je suis venu te dire que je m'en vais' or the pretty 'Sensuelle et sans suite', which switches delicately from a major to a minor key, and is in fact a tale about a rubber doll leaking during intercourse. Serge interjects 'crac' and 'pschitt' onomatopoeia as things go wrong with the inanimate latex effigy.

'I'm going for "Panpan cucul",' says Guido, 'because the arrangement for me is crazy good.' The title roughly translates as 'smacked-botty time'. The catchy verses trundle along to a lazy groove concluding with an emphatic double kick at the end of each line. Slide guitars and piano bass lines carry the tune, with clown horns interjected for comedic effect, auditory euphemisms pertaining to the sound of breaking wind. 'It's funny that album because it's all about ass.' says Minksi, laughing. 'Every song is about ass. You have to understand what relationship the ass has to every track. Sometimes it's about farting, sometimes it's about sodomy. Every song talks about ass. Even *Vu de l'extérieur* could be about looking at someone's ass.'

Also at play on the album is what Gonzales described as the '*goo-goo-goo ga-ga* Gainsbourg', including childish diminutives for defecation and urination. 'La poupée qui fait', about the one-year-old Charlotte, is written with the English meaning of the phonetic 'poopy' clearly in mind. It translates as 'The Doll Who Makes …', a play on the Michel Polnareff hit 'La poupée qui fait non', with 'pipi' and 'caca' the product. Anybody who has ever felt concerned about posting pictures of their children online because of what it might mean for them in later life will probably feel better after hearing 'La poupée qui fait', which must have caused Charlotte embarrassment over the years. Even if the author's intentions are sweet, his habitual funny way of showing it marks Gainsbourg out as an artist whose USP is always TMI.

Paul McCartney, who wrote a far nicer song for Charlotte years later ('Songbird In A Cage', on *Rest*), was arguably the greatest pop songwriter of the twentieth century, but he was thought by many to have lost his edge when he started writing songs about, and for, his children. The McCartney-esque landscape is surreal but still safe for children to inhabit and play in, but Gainsbourg manages to be inappropriate even when penning kid's songs. 'La poupée qui fait' would turn out to be the thin end of the wedge.*

---

* McCartney wrote 'Songbird In A Cage' for Charlotte Gainsbourg around 2011. It finally appeared on 2017's *Rest*, produced by SebastiAn, with the legendary Beatles man on bass.

There's nothing thin about 'Hippopodame', a song supposedly inspired by Serge's first wife, Elizabeth 'Lise' Levitsky. Lise claimed they continued to have sexual relations right up until his death in 1991, even though they broke up in the late 50s, which would at least explain why he was sharing recurrent tales of strained bedsprings in 1973. Serge sings about desiring his plump paramour's derriere, which is exemplified in the deliberately heavy-handed piano playing. I used to think 'Hippopodame' was a work of misogyny, but now I'm more inclined to believe it's Serge's strange celebration of the human form in all its variety, comparing the subject to a Rubens, who he adored. It's not fat shaming but fat fetishizing, though the gravity-thudding piano might suggest the track isn't entirely without mockery. *So what?* I hear some of you cry. Gainsbourg is having fun—a *cochon* in the proverbial *merde*. But to my mind, *Vu de l'extérieur* is a dirty protest, an assault on the senses of the few people still paying attention, punishing them for the lack of attention they might have paid to his masterpiece, *Histoire de Melody Nelson*. It's a stroppy smearing of the walls with a shitty stick, too often infantilising and lazy.

It's not something he'd grow out of with the release of this album. The whiff of excrement rears its turtle's head again on Jane Birkin's 1975 album *Lolita Go Home*, a curious hotchpotch of disco, rock, and Cole Porter songs, with many of the tunes written in collaboration between Serge and the film director Philippe Labro. Gainsbourg puts incongruous words into Jane's mouth about slipping in shit and being appalled by the smell, on the song 'La fille aux claquettes'.* He followed through with more scat-related content in 1980, firstly on Jacques Dutronc's album *Guerre et pets*. The title is a pun on *War & Peace* (*Guerre et paix*); it sounds the same phonetically, but it means *War & Farts*.

Also in 1980, Gainsbourg published *Evguénie Sokolov*, a novella about a man who uses his uncontrollable flatulence to create works of fine art before taking his own life. Although the singer killed off the character, he named a track after him on *Mauvaises nouvelles des étoiles*—an instrumental reggae song

---

* 'J'ai glissé dans la merde. C'est dégoûtant. Ce qui me gêne c'est l'odeur.'

with the melody replaced by the sound of breaking wind. Gainsbourg was actually praised for his style of writing and the vigorous research that went into his supposedly parabolic tale about the arts—*Evguénie Sokolov* took him six years to write, and he became an expert on all things gastrointestinal. The publisher whittled his five-hundred-page manuscript down to a fifth of its original size, which, to many, still seemed excessive for a story based on one puerile joke. 'It's the story of a flatulist who commits suicide by natural gas,' wrote French magazine *Les Inrockuptibles*. 'Er, what can we say? Gainsbourg was an immense songwriting talent.'*

---

* 'Une histoire de pétomane qui finit par se suicider au gaz naturel. Euh, comment dire, Gainsbourg est un immense auteur de chansons.'

9

NAZI ROCK
ROCK AROUND THE BUNKER (1975)

[Jewishness isn't a religion. No religion
grows a nose like that.*]

A concept album about the Third Reich was always going to be one of the most controversial of Serge Gainsbourg's career, and the cover art for *Rock Around The Bunker* may have looked very different had he had his way with the original concept.

'Serge asked me to come to his house, so I turned up with my assistant,' Tony Frank tells me as we drink coffee in a comfy corner of his office in the sixteenth arrondissement, one spring morning in 2019. 'He said, I've made an enlargement of a picture, I want you to put that on the wall behind me, and then I want you to do the lighting for me with shadows. And so I opened the enlargement and it was a black-and-white image of the Gestapo. Laughing, he says, Put that on the wall with some pins. Then he comes back with a Nazi jacket from the German army. He may have rented it from a movie. He opens it to reveal his gold chain. And I'm looking at him confused, because he's a Jew, and when he was a kid he wore the yellow star.'

Gainsbourg in a German army uniform in front of a backdrop of marching Nazi soldiers might have been a little *de trop* for Polygram. 'I took those pictures, but then I never heard any more news about the record cover,' Frank continues.

---

* 'Juif, ce n'est pas une religion. Aucune religion ne fait pousser un nez comme ça.' Serge Gainsbourg, *Pensées provocs et autres volutes* (Librairie Générale Française, 2007)

'And when it came out, it was a self-portrait instead. I didn't ask him why. Maybe he thought about it and decided against it, but I think it was more likely the record company said, We don't want you to do this.' Frank hid the negatives in a safe, at least until he published a posthumous photobook simply entitled *Serge Gainsbourg* in 2009. 'I asked the family if I could put that picture in the book. That was the only time I used it.' (It has subsequently appeared in a *Mojo* feature, and in 2019's *Le Gainsbook*). 'The first book also has pictures of him with Bambou where he's wearing a kippah on his head. He's not like Bob Dylan, who's Jewish and then he's Catholic and then he's a Christian. Maybe it's one of those strange things he did to provoke the press.'

The eventual cover of *Rock Around The Bunker* looks as though it was dashed off in a matter of minutes with a couple of felt-tip pens, perhaps done while Serge was sat across from a record executive, or even Philippe Lerichomme himself. The lettering is scribbled and shaded, and the self-portrait doodled inconspicuously in the centre, like a page from a notebook placed strategically by the phone to alleviate boredom. Serge was an inveterate doodler, though few of his sketches have survived. When I was looking through a collection of manuscripts of handwritten lyrics at the British Library, collected together by the writer and archivist Laurent Balandras, I was taken aback by a sketch Serge had drawn of Charlotte which, although it appeared to have been scribbled quickly, was rendered with precision, a great attention to detail as well as a loving father's eye. He clearly had a way of distilling the essence of a person's image in the way that good cartoonists do. Doodling on pink tissue paper, he presumably felt some pride in his creation, writing her name below the portrait.

Jacqueline Ginsburg mentioned her brother's cartoonist tendencies when I visited her at Avenue Baugard, adding that he spent a lot of time imitating the styles of Walt Disney and Tex Avery as a child. This continued into the 1980s, when he'd use his drawing abilities for laughs while travelling in the bus with his American musicians. With a limited lexicon of English words, it was a way he could communicate and make everyone laugh.

'For some reason he used to find pictures of people who looked like me in print,' says the saxophonist Stan Harrison, who played on Serge's last two studio albums, as well as all of the live outings from 1983 onward. 'So Serge found this picture from a two-bit little porn pamphlet, which somebody must have found somewhere and showed to him. And in this picture there's a guy having sex with a woman, coming from behind her, doggy style, and Serge takes out his pen and draws one little thing to do with his hair and then draws a strap and a sax on him, and all of a sudden there I am, having sex in that magazine. It was hysterically funny, and, in a funny sort of way, I was flattered that he was thinking of me.'

George Simms, Stan's bandmate on the *Love On The Beat* album (they'd also toured together on the *Serious Moonlight* tour with David Bowie in 1983), was at the table in the Brasserie Bofinger in Bastille when Serge drew a quick self-portrait then, as was his wont, screwed it up into a ball and tossed it away. He was rarely fond of his artistic work, paintings or doodles, and destroyed nearly all of them. 'We're just sitting there, and he picks up his briefcase and takes out a piece of A4 paper and his fountain pen and starts sketching something,' says Simms. 'And when he's done, he shows everyone a self-portrait of himself with his big nose and ears, with a smoking cigarette in his mouth and all his stubble on his face. And he looked at it and everyone went, Oh Serge, that's so great, wonderful, great job! He looked at it and said, No, no, this is shit! He took it and crumpled it up into a little ball and he threw it under the table.'

At the end of the meal, everyone stands to attention when Serge gets up. 'Serge stood up, that means we're done. It's time to go,' says George. 'Everybody else stood up, and I reached under the table and grabbed that little ball and stuck it in my pocket. It sat in a box in my mother's garage for twenty-five years.' A decade ago, George took it to Christie's in Paris. 'Because Serge didn't sign it, the only thing they're waiting for to authenticate it is for Bambou to come by—an eyewitness who was sitting next to Serge when he did that. Bambou and I were the only ones sitting at the table who weren't drinkers. Serge didn't sign it, but with her testimony we can tell our buying public that this is authenticated. And it'll help when we eventually sell it at auction.'

If Serge had the eye of a cartoonist, or even a satirist, he was surprisingly apolitical. George, who became close to Gainsbourg and Bambou during those years he was playing with American musicians—partly on account of the fact that he could speak French—says, 'He was never prejudiced against anything except tight-arsed conservatives with broomsticks up their ass.' Serge might have given that impression, but politically he was probably a liberal conservative himself, another paradox in a man who was so radical in other ways.

'He never voted,' says Jane Birkin. 'He voted once, actually, for Valéry Giscard d'Estaing, and I remember at the time being disappointed that he hadn't vote for somebody more leftist. But, in retrospect, Giscard was the one who got abortion laws abolished—he was sort of middle-of-the-road. I know why Serge thought he wouldn't be a cheat, because he was a rich man in his own right, and he was the minister of finance before. So he thought that he'd probably be good for the country and that he wouldn't swindle. He had enough money and he had a name, Giscard d'Estaing, which sounded sort of chic, which meant he wouldn't need to play dirty. That was what he probably thought.'

Gainsbourg received plenty of stick for voting for an establishment figure who represented the last vestiges of the Gaullist right, and who ended up defeating François Mitterrand in 1974 by a slender 1.6 percent margin in the second round. But if Serge's right-leaning centrism comes as a surprise, it may not seem as peculiar if we consider his upbringing. He had seen for himself first-hand what the hard right was capable of during the Occupation, and he had a lifelong fear of communism instilled in him by his parents, who had fled with their lives from Russia. Gainsbourg loved status, which would have complimented a belief in a paternalistic ruling class looking out for the lower orders to maintain a kind of social stability. He paid his taxes on time and with relish, and he despised anyone who didn't. For someone who enjoyed rebellion and unruly behaviour, he was a social conservative at his core. He was nonplussed by the May '68 uprising, and, despite a penchant for schoolboy pranks, never expressed any kinship with Guy Debord or the Situationists because of their ultra-left political leanings. What's more, Gainsbourg *was* the spectacle in French society.

'You have to remember Serge's family had left the Ukraine because of the pogroms there, and that's why he didn't like communism,' says Bruno

Blum, the music producer nicknamed Doc Reggae, who used to look after Gainsbourg's legacy at Universal France. 'That's why he refused anything to do with communism. That's why he didn't even like Mitterrand, because he had French communist ministers, although of course they were French communist ministers who did a great job at the time and weren't Stalinists at all. But, still, it was a taboo for him. That's why he was always in the centre of the political spectrum.'

Centrist dad he might have been, but in 1967 he recorded a song that one might consider ill-advised with hindsight—and was probably more politically charged than he realised at the time—after he was contacted by the Israeli Embassy in Paris and commissioned to write a song to pep up the Israel Defense Forces. The brief to pen something motivational arose from a misunderstanding; cultural attaché Avraham Scherman had heard a Hebrew version of 'Le poinçonneur des Lilas', which was performed by Les Frères Jacques when they went on tour in Israel, and so popular it proved that someone adapted the song into Hebrew when they left. Sherman had heard the Hebrew version and conflated the details in his mind, assuming Gainsbourg had written the original in Hebrew because he was Jewish. With a war between Israel and Egypt seeming likely, he asked to meet with Gainsbourg. Jacqueline Ginsburg told *France Culture* that he was flattered that they'd even thought of him at all, but the family have sought to distance themselves from the song ever since, with his older sister calling the Zionist cause 'grotesque'.

'Le sable et le soldat' ('The Sand And The Soldier') was recorded and sent to Tel Aviv on the eve of the Six Day War, although its fairly plodding, hymnal verse, laid over an unabating bass note set to a minor key, would have been unlikely to gee anyone into battle. If musically it's not the most inspiring of songs, lyrically it was a tinderbox waiting to be ignited. 'All the Goliaths emerging from the pyramids will back away from the Star of David,' he sings, provocatively.* Instead, the recording languished unplayed in the archives of the radio station Kol Yisrael for thirty-five years, forgotten about in the chaos

---

* 'Tous les Goliaths venus des pyramides, Reculeront devant l'étoile de David.'

that comes with conflict. The song has never been given an official release by the Gainsbourg estate, though it can be found easily enough on YouTube.

That aberration aside, Serge seemed far more at ease offending his listeners with songs about pederasty and shit than he did making outlandish political gestures and statements. That changed in early January 1975, when he released *Rock Around The Bunker*. 'Le sable et le soldat' notwithstanding, Serge had hitherto kept his Jewishness under wraps. His new album was a powerful statement of protest that attested strongly to his own ethnic identity—a position he may have felt he had to take, given a growing cultural ambiguity concerning collaborationism.

In 1969, the German-born, French-naturalised documentarian Marcel Ophüls made a groundbreaking four-and-a-half-hour documentary, *The Sorrow And The Pity* (*Le chagrin et la Pitié*), which featured interviews with SS officers, Free French resistance fighters, French politicians like Pierre Mendès France, and English politicians such as Anthony Eden. The film quietly and systematically goes about destroying the Gaullist myth of a unified national resistance during *les années noires*, and challenges the perceived binary choices made between *résistancisme* and *collaborationnisme*, proposing many grey areas instead. *The Sorrow And The Pity* presents the case that many French citizens vacillated and in some cases facilitated the Nazis.

The film was deemed so controversial that it was banned for years, though it did receive a limited run at the Quartier de l'Odéon in 1971. The oversubscribed showings were enough to precipitate a public debate among metropolitans regarding the war, which soon spread across the country. Memories that had been repressed for decades began to re-emerge. Few had dared to rock the boat or challenge a myth that had calcified over the years, save for the odd crusader like Jean-Paul Sartre, whose play *Morts sans sépultures* (*Men Without Shadows*) was met with short shrift from the public and critics alike when first performed in 1947. The épuration sauvage, or wild purge, after the war seemed mostly to single out and vilify women who'd had relationships with German officers, with their heads ceremonially shaved in city squares. Nearly seven thousand traitors were sentenced to death—around half in absentia—with only a tenth of those sentences carried out. Soon, France went back to pretending that everyone had done their bit to resist the Nazis.

A similar wishful thinking had pervaded German society, with older generations trying to convince themselves of their own innocence. Albert Speer became a postmodern celebrity by claiming his complicity had come from an ignorance of what the Third Reich was up to. He was released from Spandau prison in 1966 after being convicted at the Nuremberg trials, and he subsequently published diaries to roaring success. The thinking was that if he, so close to Hitler, didn't know what was really going on, then the reader, who didn't know Hitler personally, would be yet more innocent of the horrors of the gas chambers.

In 1971, Andrew Birkin had been travelling back and forth to Germany with the idea of making a documentary with Hitler's architect. How did Gainsbourg feel about him fraternizing with the enemy? 'We didn't make the film in the end, but I was meeting with Speer on and off for about a year in Germany,' Andrew says. 'Speer liked Jane, and he liked the song "Je t'aime", and so he asked if I could get him an autographed copy. And Serge was sort of quite chuffed. He certainly perceived the irony. And when he made *Rock Around The Bunker*, he said, Make sure you send Albert a copy—which I did.'

The reassessment of what the French got up to during the war, with *The Sorrow And The Pity* acting as catalyst, began to permeate French culture, and soon there was an artistic reaction to this new openness. It even was given a name: *La mode rétro*. *Retro* was a neologism, a diminutive of *rétrospectif*, which may even indicate a glibness in the nature of the nostalgic re-evaluation. The *mode rétro* provided social catharsis for a nation that had trouble remembering, and it was so pronounced that it unleashed a torrent of artistic soul searching, mainly in film and literature, although it influenced fashion too.

Soon there were a number of movies released that explored the ambiguities of involvement during the war, including 1974's Liliana Cavani's Italian-backed film *The Night Porter*—which Birkin briefly name checks in her *Munkey Diaries*, expressing an ambivalence—and Louis Malle's controversial, French-made *Lacombe, Lucien*. In both films, fallibility is mixed up with sexual desire to complicate the portrait of Nazis and collaborators as 'bad people'. The presentation of a shared humanity, no matter how flawed, rouses in us a sense of empathy with characters who nevertheless carried out abhorrent acts in the name of Hitler. For some who'd suffered in the war, this ambiguity that followed on from years of denial was all too much to bear.

'The *mode rétro* was a strange fascination with the existential nature of the Occupation,' says Jonathyne Briggs. 'The idea that everything seemed to be black and white, but there was all this grey there, right? And maybe we shouldn't be so quick to judge what people did … and I think Gainsbourg thought, *Wait a minute, we can judge because many of them are still around and they've benefitted from this, they sent people to die and nothing happened to them.*'

Malle's film in particular presents in Technicolor what Hannah Arendt called 'the banality of evil', as Lucien, having joined the Milice Française (French Militia) by accident, not long after trying to follow his brother into the resistance, then carries out brutal acts of violence against Jews he comes into contact with as a part of his job. The Milice was a paramilitary organisation created by the Vichy government to assist the Gestapo with fighting the French Resistance, rounding up Jewry and proving more dangerous than the Gestapo and SS with the advantage of local knowledge. The Vichy regime under Marshal Pétain was more than co-operative. The 1981 book *Vichy France And The Jews* states, 'When the Germans began systematic deportation and extermination of Jews in 1942, Vichy's rival antisemitism offered them more substantial help than they found anywhere else in western Europe, and more even than they received from such allies as Hungary and Romania.'[*]

In *Lacombe, Lucien*, complications arise when the protagonist, played by Pierre Blaise, falls in love with a Jewish girl, France Horn, portrayed by Aurore Clément. The seventeen-year-old country boy, good-looking and dim, appears not to recognise this conflict of interests. Malle chose a young non-actor for the part in order that he wouldn't betray any emotions when

---

[*] Michael R. Marrus and Robert O. Paxton, *Vichy France And The Jews* (republished by Stanford University Press, 2019)

carrying out orders—a decision that works chillingly well. 'The magic is in the intense curiosity and intelligence behind the film,' wrote Pauline Kael in her 1974 *New Yorker* review, 'in Malle's perception that the answers to our questions about how people with no interest in politics become active participants in brutal torture are to be found in Lucien's plump-cheeked, narrow-eyed face, and that showing us what this boy doesn't react to can be the most telling of all.'

There was clearly still a strong undercurrent loyal to Pétain in France who were galvanised by the ambiguity of the *mode rétro*; in 1973, extremists stole Pétain's coffin from the Île d'Yeu cemetery, where 'the lion of Verdun' had died in exile, and demanded that he be reburied in Douaumont cemetery with the decorated war dead. His remains were recovered by police a few days later, and he was interred back on his small island of shame.

*

'*Rock Around The Bunker* is so good!' says Jane Birkin. 'If there's anything funnier than Serge doing that—and he was about the only person who could—then I don't know what is. When he sang, "So put on your black stockings, guys, we're going to sing the Nazi Rock", it was just so impertinent. Eva Braun singing "Smoke Gets In Your Eyes". It's absolutely so funny, but it's gone out of sight. It didn't make any money and it's never mentioned.'

It's true that *Rock Around The Bunker* is another album that gets passed over, usually referenced only as one of Gainsbourg's three concept albums from the 70s. It's a pity for the reason that, after the laziness of *Vu de l'extérieur*, this may be the album that carries his most consistently brilliant lyrics, and it also includes some wonderfully dexterous vocal performances where he delivers the words in a kind of rat-a-tat flow, deploying all the sibilance and onomatopoeia he can muster. 'Tata teutonne' and 'Est-ce est-ce si bon?' rattle out with an alacritous urgency as the singer finally gets to have his say after four years of immense suffering as a child and another thirty years of keeping quiet about it. 'I think it's pretty self-explanatory,' Serge told the music writer Alain Pacadis,

'I lived through that era.'* *Rock Around The Bunker* would prove to be an exorcism and a dark cabaret all in one.

Mick Harvey had a noble stab at 'Est-ce est-ce si bon?' on his album *Delirium Tremens*, calling his version 'SS c'est bon', thus revealing the titular gag lots of English speakers might have missed otherwise. Serge's song is also a nod to Yves Montand's 'C'est si bon', which was covered by Eartha Kitt and Dean Martin. Just thinking about 'Est-ce est-ce si bon?' makes Harvey laugh. 'I did have a go,' he says, 'but that was really tough. That album doesn't offer up a lot of possibilities. For me, musically, it's so-so. But it's just so hilarious, the way he's alliterated the whole thing. It's just a brilliant piece of writing, really amazing.'

If the album is musically so-so, it might be because he's tapping into the fad for 50s rock'n'roll that permeated the 70s: teddy boys and hula-hoops, *Happy Days* and *Grease*, and glam-rock bands like Roxy Music and the New York Dolls and the French version, Gasoline, featuring the cross-dressing punk provocateur Alain Kan.† It might seem cognitively dissonant to write a 70s concept album about the 40s with the sounds of the 50s, but recreating the music that was popular during the war would have meant Gainsbourg revisiting jazz again, which he'd already explored over five or six albums without much success. Besides, combining two contemporary retro fads was very meta, and very Gainsbourg. And his session musicians, under the watchful eye of Alan Hawkshaw, could play this stuff with their eyes closed. 'We concentrated on the basic feel of the track rather than worrying about the lyrical content,' says Hawkshaw, 'but Serge told me he was taking a pop at the Nazis with *Rock Around the Bunker*, since he was Jewish. He once said to me, I wish you could understand the words, Alan. I said, I think it's probably better that I can't.'

The album kicks off with 'Nazi Rock', a high-kicking, vaudevillian bop that recreates the final hours of the Sturmabteilung, or S.A., a Babylonian orgy

---

* 'Je crois que c'est assez explicite: moi, j'ai vécu cette époque.'

† Kan was last seen getting on the Paris Métro at the Rue de la Pompe station in April 1990. He disappeared and has never been seen again. 'It's a great French rock mystery,' says Etienne Daho.

of sex, drugs, Weimarian rock'n'roll, and crossdressing. The fun never ends—until it does, of course—though *La nuit des long couteaux* never occurs in the actual song, so we're suspended in a pleasure dome before the inevitable pain. Gainsbourg's vocals are offset by cheery backing singing, including the voice of Clare Torrey of *The Dark Side Of The Moon* fame. These singers are irrepressibly jovial throughout, no matter the subject matter, a chorus of stiff upper lips. These British voices may even represent the Allies, who were more stringent in the face of the Nazi threat. No wonder nobody in France bought it.

'Tata teutonne' makes fun of a grotesque called Otto, a hermaphroditic auntie with firecracker farts who sucks their own nipples. 'He recoiled at what he saw as revisionist,' says Briggs. 'He wanted to remind people of the horror of Nazism and Nazi ideology, so he emphasised it with these grotesque figures. He's also thinking about it from the viewpoint of how a child looks at it—these cartoonish, flatulent authority figures.' The breezy 'SS In Uruguay' is a song about Nazis evading capture and heading for foreign, exotic climes. There must have been a feeling that the likes of Klaus Barbie and Josef Mengele would get away with unspeakable horrors sequestered in their South America hideaways, and, while neither was found eventually in Uruguay, it offered the best rhyming scheme.

This was the climate in France in which Gainsbourg wrote *Rock Around The Bunker*, and while he was never one to miss out on a trend, the *mode rétro* must have felt close to the bone when he went into the studio in 1974. It's to his credit that it's as high-spirited and irreverent as it is. Singing Eva Braun's favourite song, 'Smoke Gets In Your Eyes', in the guise of Hitler in a bunker full of teargas, is audacious and funny, and I like to imagine he was inspired to record the song by hearing the version by The Platters that's frequently used in Rainer Werner Fassbinder's 1972 masterpiece *The Bitter Tears Of Petra Von Kant*. Fassbinder only ever made one film set specifically during the Second World War (*Lili Marleen*), but the Nazis are everywhere in his pictures, often as the jackbooted elephants in the room, implicitly crawling out of the woodwork and surreptitiously showing their true colours when circumstances take a turn for the worse.

Born in 1945, Rainer grew up sensitive to the silence of complicity. He saw hypocrisy and extremism laying low in every echelon of society. 'I bet Serge absolutely loved Fassbinder,' says Raechel Leigh Carter, and I'm inclined to agree, though the best evidence we have to go on is that he cast Fassbinder's last muse, Barbara Sukowa, in 1983's *Equateur*. It's hardly a smoking gun, and Sukowa's agent sadly resisted my emails, though Fassbinder and Gainsbourg shared many characteristics: they were both hugely productive contrary to the stultifying effects of their addictions, and they lived to shock, offend, and wake people up.

*

Rock Around The Bunker is withering, but it isn't entirely without poignancy. The occupation of Paris would have commenced not long after Serge Gainsbourg's twelfth birthday, and in 1941 Jews were required to wear a yellow Star of David badge to identify themselves. Nazi propaganda was pasted on walls that enforced nasty stereotypes: accentuated features and lurid pallor, with *citoyens* informed that this was what the enemy within looked like. With the state apparatus against him, and the walls taunting his physiognomy, it's little wonder Lulu Ginsburg grew up with a complex about how he looked. His face alone could get him loaded into a truck to Drancy internment camp or deported to one of the extermination camps if he happened to look at someone the wrong way on any given day.

'My father complied with the request to register ourselves as Jews, but my mother saw the trouble that was ahead,' says Jacqueline. 'We were made to wear the yellow star, and Jews weren't allowed out after eight o'clock, but my mother defied the orders and refused to wear the badge. She had a fright on a train once when a German came into her carriage and shouted for everyone to get out. Had they checked her papers then, she would have been off to the concentration camp. She remained quietly defiant against the Nazis.'

Serge was forced to report to officers each day, with his yellow star as identification. He turned the situation on its head and wore it as a badge of honour, pretending he was a 'sheriff or marshall or big chief', as the lyrics of 'Yellow Star' attest. Then, in the same year, he was hit by a grave illness that nearly killed him. It meant he was whisked away from Paris. 'In 1941, he became very ill with tubercular peritonitis, an illness that killed nearly everyone it affected,' says Jacqueline. 'There was no cure—he just had to go to the country and breathe in lots of country air. He went to a small village with five hundred inhabitants outside of La Sarthe. It was a terrible time for him. He was hunched over with a stick and walked around like a little old man. It really aged him.'

Gainsbourg took a visit back to Sarthe—his first bolthole during the Occupation—with Birkin in 1973, and while everyone at the farm who'd helped him was now dead, he recognised the church spire, the houses, and the little room where he'd stayed from the outside. It all appeared as it was, only much smaller. 'I went into the church where Serge had painted cardboard angels one Christmas and the vicar hung them on each side of the church, not knowing it was a little Jewish boy who would soon be hunted down,' Birkin writes in her *Munkey Diaries*. 'Poor Serge,' she adds, 'I think he regretted having gone back.'

Later during the Occupation, the family were forced to split up, and the sisters found themselves at a convent in Limoges while Lucien was sent to the nearby commune Oradour-sur-Glane. 'They were separated and put in different schools,' says Charlotte Gainsbourg. 'So they had a sense of the danger, but maybe not the drama.' Liliane and Jacqueline found asylum with the nuns: 'It was a bit like an adventure for us at the time,' says Jacqueline, 'and we didn't quite realise the danger we were in. I had a teacher who was very encouraging with my studies, although there was an underlying sense that they were trying to convert us.'

'But the religious institutions for boys didn't want to keep Serge,' Jane writes in *Munkey Diaries*. 'It was too dangerous.' Having fled Paris, he was now called Lucien Gimbaud—his first change of identity, and he'd be required to play a character not unlike himself. Little Lucien Gimbaud, like the future Gainsbarre, wouldn't be good at not drawing attention to himself. At the local school, Saint-Léonard-de-Noblat, he was discovered writing poison pen letters calling the other pupils 'yokels' (péquenots) and 'peasants'. Jacqueline remembers another scare at Lucien's school: 'Some gendarmes turned up, and my brother was told to take an axe to the forest and say he was the son of a butcher if anyone asked.' Birkin says he spent several nights hiding in the trees, while other children came by to bring him food, 'like in a fairy tale'. His parents eventually came for him, and they fled.

'His sister has often described those times as very exciting, because they didn't have any losses in their immediate family,' says Charlotte. 'They don't really know who got killed in Russia because they left in 1917, so they lost track of anyone from that time. And with the children being very small, they found the whole experience of hiding very exciting.' Toward the end of the war, the family were eventually reunited in Limoges; then, once the Allies moved in, they were able to return to their home back in Paris.

Even after recording *Rock Around The Bunker*, Serge mostly suppressed the memories of the Occupation, and he only began to open up about his experiences there in interviews late into his career. The trial of Klaus Barbie and the eight-hour Holocaust documentary *Shoah* by Claude Lanzmann put the war back on the agenda again in the mid-80s, which may have triggered something in him which allowed him to talk.[*]

'I think to some extent the fact that he was in Occupied France during his later childhood, living under those conditions, reflected in his outlook,' says Andrew Birkin. 'It's really impossible today for anyone to imagine what that was like, to live under that Star of David cloud, never knowing if you're going to be shipped off at any minute.' Serge Gainsbourg and Andrew Bikin were close in the early years of his sister's relationship with the French singer, and they would get uproariously drunk together and confide in one another, such as the time they wet the baby's head when Charlotte was born. During one of these occasions, according to Jane's *Munkey Diaries*, they had a drunken falling

---

[*] The filmmaker Claude Lanzmann was the brother of the writer Jacques Lanzmann, who formed a songwriting partnership with Jacques Dutronc in the 60s, penning the lyrics to many of his best-known hits.

out and Serge went upstairs and cut an *A* into his arm, which he proceeded to show Andrew. The older Birkin became lachrymose at the sight of the blood and self-harm.

Andrew Birkin recalls one story that Serge told him from his time hiding in plain sight only a hundred or so miles west from Vichy, and from Clermont-Ferrand, where *The Sorrow And The Pity* documentary is set: 'I remember Serge telling me the pleasure he got at a time of great danger when they were hiding out in the south west of France. It wasn't Occupied France, but they still had to wear the Star of David, and his mother had told him to iron it and wear it with pride and make sure it was presentable. And of course he'd cover it up with a coat, but he couldn't resist walking into a restaurant once and suddenly opening his coat and exposing himself like a flasher, except he was exposing the Star of David, and the wonderful shocked reaction of all these bourgeois closet Nazi French.'

Incidentally, Clermont-Ferrand, where *The Sorrow And The Pity* debunked the Gaullist myth once and for all, also happens to be the town in which Invader struck in 2016. The street artist pasted a five-metre-tall ceramic-tiled Serge Gainsbourg with a smoking cigarette onto the side of a pink house, rendered in his recognisable style, a pastiche of 8-bit video-game art. It's not as obvious as a Banksy, at least until you notice the address. Invader's tiles sit at the intersection of Rue Serge Gainsbourg.

10

METAMORPHOSIS
L'HOMME À TÊTE DE CHOU (1976)

> [Man has created gods. The reverse is yet to be proven.*]

'When I met Serge, I was nineteen years old, I was with a gang of punks at Le Palace,' Caroline von Paulus, aka Bambou, told *Les Inrocks* in 2001. 'They were all fans of Gainsbourg and made me discover his music. I fell madly in love with *L'homme à tête de chou*. To me, it's what he did best on every level, much stronger than *Melody Nelson*. Before that, I knew "Je t'aime … moi non plus" and "La Javanaise" like everyone else. At fourteen, when I saw Serge on TV, I told myself, If I had to choose a dad, I would want one like that.'[†]

Jane Birkin and Charlotte Gainsbourg both express a deep love for *L'homme à tête de chou*, too, and both think it is comparable to *Histoire de Melody Nelson* in its brilliance. But even if the family are in agreement at the worth of 'Cabbage Head Man', the album has remained largely out of the reach of casual fans. The prog-rock underbelly, directed by Alan Hawkshaw,

---

* 'L'homme a créé des dieux; l'inverse reste à prouver.' Serge Gainsbourg, *Pensées provocs et autres volutes* (Librairie Générale Française, 2007)
† 'Quand j'ai rencontré Serge, j'avais 19 ans, j'étais avec la bande des punks du Palace. Ils étaient tous fans de Gainsbourg et m'ont fait découvrir sa musique. Je suis tombée folle amoureuse de *L'homme à la tête de chou*. Pour moi, c'est ce qu'il a fait de mieux à tous les niveaux, beaucoup plus fort que Melody Nelson. Avant ça, je connaissais "Je t'aime … moi non plus", "La Javanaise", comme tout le monde. A 14 ans, quand je voyais Serge à la télé, je me disais, Si je devais choisir un papa, j'en voudrais un comme ça.' *Les Inrocks*, 1981

is more than competent, but it doesn't stupefy in the way that those Vannier arrangements do. *Histoire de Melody Nelson* is rightfully seen as a masterpiece now, while its stronger narrative-driven counterpart exploring surrealism and madness has remained a fan's favourite. Like *Melody Nelson*, *L'homme à tête de chou* was largely jammed using the same core of musicians, and tracks like 'Aeroplanes' provide moments of smooth elegance, but overall it's more sonically temperate than its predecessor.

Lyrically, it shows its teeth, a fairy story with a shocking denouement. It all seems so much more plausible and brutal than Melody crashing in a plane, and not just because the cargo cults of Melanesia are hardly *en route* between Paris and the northeast of England.[*] In a fit of jealousy, the protagonist beats his girlfriend to death with a hotel fire extinguisher—the fact he has a cabbage for a head is mere detail.

L'homme à tête de chou was Gainsbourg's third concept album in five years— or fourth, if you count the one about posteriors. The idea arrived courtesy of a large talismanic sculpture waiting for him in an art gallery not far from his place. He'd pass it when coming to and from his favourite bars. The sculpture is made of bronze, and was conceived and created by the artist Claude Lalanne, with the body of a man and the head of a Savoy. The cabbage stares at Serge through the window of the Paul Facchetti gallery, and he forms an unlikely kinship with this brassican effigy. He can relate to having an unusual head that people point at or make rude comments about. So he wanders into the gallery and pulls out a roll of cash. The Cabbage Head Man, 'Half vegetable, half guy,' eventually goes home with him.[†] And so begins his most extraordinary and audacious lyrical creation, a concept album with a defined plot and a story as evocative as the darkest fairy tale. Franck Maubert believes *L'homme à tête de chou* is 'worthy of all the novels that he didn't write, all the paintings that he didn't paint.'[‡]

---

[*] Melody Nelson comes from Sunderland. According to Jane Birkin, Serge found the sound of the name exotic.

[†] 'Je suis l'homme à la tête de chou / Moitié légume moitié mec.'

[‡] 'Ça vaut tous les romans qu'il n'a pas écrits, toutes les toiles qu'il n'a pas peintes.'

'At first, he pissed me off,' Serge scribbled on a piece of paper in 1976, which was photocopied and sent out as a press release, 'then he thawed out and told me his story. He's a tabloid journalist who falls in love with a cute shampoo girl who cheats on him with some rockers. He kills her with a fire extinguisher, sinks into madness and loses his head … which has become a cabbage."* The heroine and love interest is Marilou, and the story as ever is a patchwork of sources—some familiar, some obscure. Apollinaire and Nabokov (naturally) mingle with references to the 1963 novel *A Love Affair* by the Italian writer Dino Buzzati, according to *Le Gainsbook*. 'Variations sur Marilou' is suffused with rock idols, too: Jimi Hendrix, Elvis Presley, T-Rex, Alice Cooper, Lou Reed, and Les Rolling Stones.

There's also something of the Ovidian myth about a man turning into a cabbage. If Kafka's *Metamorphosis* was loosely inspired by *Jove And Io*, then *L'homme à tête de chou* offers a modern twist on *Narcissus*, where a man is transformed by his own ugliness rather than dazzled by his own beauty. And there's some Lewis Carroll in there, too, and one imagines he was partial to a bit of Ovid as well. 'My Alice goes astray in the world of malice by Lewis Carroll,' snarls Serge at the end of 'Variations sur Marilou', invoking the name of the true father of surrealism (if we're discounting Hieronymus Bosch, John The Revelator, and the aforementioned Roman poet).

Carroll published *Alice's Adventures In Wonderland* thirty years before André Breton was even a twinkle in his father's eye, and more than half a century before he founded the Surrealists. Leaping forward another generation to 1969, Surrealism and Carroll came together in the most visually arresting way when one of the movement's rejects, Salvador Dalí, was invited by Random House to illustrate a special limited-edition version of *Alice's Adventures In Wonderland*. It was a marriage made in, well, Wonderland, between two fellow travellers working nearly a century apart. Dalí obliged with twelve beautiful

---

* 'Au début, il m'a fait la gueule, ensuite il s'est dégelé et m'a raconté son histoire : journaliste à scandale tombé amoureux d'une shampouineuse assez chou pour le tromper avec des rockers. Il la tue à coups d'extincteur, sombre dans la folie et perd la tête qui devient chou.'

heliogravures and an etching for the frontispiece. The watercolours are relatively tame and tasteful in the oeuvre of an artist who could bend minds, and prompted Breton to declare, in 1929, 'It is perhaps with Dalí that for the first time the windows of the mind are opened fully wide.' He was later kicked out of the Surrealists for 'the glorification of Hitlerian fascism' after Dalí painted *The Enigma Of Hitler* and made overtures about his ongoing fascination with the führer that bordered on the psychosexual and perhaps proved the mind can be too open.

Dalí had a profound effect on Gainsbourg, right down to the decor choices in Rue de Verneuil. Astrakhan, a jet-black furry material you normally find in coats, adorns the walls, a direct copy of the material in Dalí's apartment at 88 Rue de l'Université in Paris, which Serge and his first wife audaciously broke into in 1948. Lise was working as secretary to the Dadaist George Hugnet and got hold of Dalí's keys while he and his wife Gala were away in the USA. The Ginsburgs made love in every room as well as on top of some priceless works of art, though they apparently spared Gala's bed out of respect. Gainsbourg took note of the interior and stole a miniature vintage porn picture from Dalí's personal collection. Serge also fitted a very low bath in his apartment after seeing Dalí's tub. 'He'd put a sheet in it, which is a very sophisticated idea,' says Birkin. 'So when you have a bath, you're on a sheet, and when you come out of the bath you let the water out and you give the sheet to the laundry.' (Serge apparently had a sit-down bath about once every three months, and washed meticulously, stripped to the waist, each day.)

'He spent several nights there, and seeing all the luxury of that apartment changed him forever,' Pere Francesch says in an email. Pere is the author of a book that explores the relationship between Gainsbourg and Dalí.* 'Lucien Ginsburg was reborn surrounded by luxury, works of art, surreal aesthetics, and sex. Gainsbourg would often talk about his experiences in that apartment, sometimes with more embellishment than reality, but it was clearly a shock for him at the time. The emotions he felt in the Rue de l'Université apartment

---

* Per Francesch, *Gainsbourg i Dalí, moi non plus* (Edicions Cal·lígrafs, 2019)

would mark him forever. Dalí had a profound effect on him, according to Lévitzky in her biography *Lise et Lulu*. We must bear in mind that Gainsbourg was very young at that time. He was barely twenty years old and Dalí was about to return from a long stay in the United States, where he'd had many of his greatest successes as an artist. There are other aspects that unite Gainsbourg and Dalí. In their works there are recurring themes such as sexuality, eroticism, and scatology—although in the case of sexuality and eroticism, both lived out their fantasies in very different ways.'

And then there was advertising. Dalí's forays into commercial ventures were bold, and many considered them abominable at the time; and, for better or worse, they paved the way for others to follow and acted as a declaration to artists everywhere that they wouldn't need to starve for their art any longer. The Surrealists branded him with the anagrammatic nickname Avida Dollars—a burn that didn't seem to bother him much.* Dalí turned himself into a brand after he moved to the United States in 1936, paving the way for commercially minded Pop artists like Warhol, and, later, kitsch money-monsters like Jeff Koons.

The Spaniard famously designed the logo for Chupa Chups lollies and appeared in a French commercial for Lanvin declaring in his inimitable way with eyes abulge: 'I am crazy about Lanvin's chocolate!'† He made adverts for Alka-Seltzer, Braniff International Airways, and Veterano brandy. He designed magazine covers and shop windows for Fifth Avenue; he worked with Hitchcock and Disney; as a keen fan of dance, he created sets and costumes for a number of ballet productions. Late in life, he published a surrealist cookbook, *Les Diners de Gala*; he founded the 'Dalí Universe' to curate Dalí works from his personal collection in museums across the world that he mostly established in his lifetime; then, of course, there was his house at Portlligat, which he put much energy into making into a functioning reflection of himself. He moved out in 1982, after Gala died, and the Catalonian property is now another museum in tribute to the couple's memory.

* 'Avide à dollars', or greedy for dollars.
† 'Je suis fou du chocolat Lanvin.'

Gainsbourg took Dalí's lead making commercials. And then he made more commercials. And then he made some more still. A relatively unsuccessful filmmaker he might have been, but as an ad man—which he essentially was, on the side—it's quite possible that he made more money than he did in his career as a musician. He and Jane were brand ambassadors for Lee Cooper, but that barely scratches the surface. Companies he directed TV commercials for, or endorsed, include: Martini, Woolite, Lux, Danone, Roumillat, St Michael's, Alsa, Pentel, Anny Blatt, Konica, BaByliss, Lancôme, Tia Maria, Pepsodent, Palmolive, Bouvril, Gini Bitter, and House Of Caron. He got his friends on board too, including France Gall, Isabelle Adjani, Jacques Dutronc, and Françoise Hardy.

'My God, he made absolutely tonnes of them,' says Raechel Leigh Carter. 'He loved it because it was quick money. I wonder whether some of those ideas came from Pierre Grimblat, the director of *Slogan*, because he had a fantastic career in advertising before he went into films. Whereas Gainsbourg tried films and then got into advertising. He did those ones for Woolite with different stars in them. And Jane got into the adverts too—because, again, it was quick money. Her partner after Serge, Jacques Doillon, made adverts too. He saw it as selling his soul because it wasn't films, but it did raise funds to help make the next picture.'

Ah, the age-old conundrum about whether committing artistic work to commercial ventures is selling out or not, not that it unduly seemed to bother Serge any. As well as directing, he also wrote jingles, or in most cases adapted his own songs to fit products. Many of these have been collected on two bootleg LPs, *Sell Out* and *Gainsbourg For Sale*. 'Melody Lit Babar', a song that didn't make it onto *Melody Nelson*, did get used in Martini's 1970 publicity alongside 'Valse de Melody', a song that is arguably the centrepiece of the record. The fact that the latter was heard via an advertising campaign before the record had even been released seems staggering now. Conversely, Serge, who was clever at recycling his own material, would occasionally leave a quality song like 'Les petits lolos de Lola' in a Martini commercial and never come back for it.

Gainsbourg exhibited his own persona in many of these ads, including a memorable one for the men's fashion label Bayard, where he's clean-shaven and sat up attentively in a shiny suit. 'Bayard changes a man,' runs the strapline, followed by an additional exclamation of disbelief: 'N'est ce pas Mr. Gainsbourg!'* Serge was as happy in front of the camera as he was behind it. He exhibited his partners in photoshoots for *Lui*, the high-minded French equivalent of *Playboy*; he and Jane posed in some provocative pictures in 1974 for Francis Giacobetti, featuring some spanking, and in 1978 with 'King of Kink' Helmut Newton, with Serge dressed up and Jane predictably dressed down.

It was Bambou's turn to pose for the artbook *Bambou et la poupees* in 1981, and naked for *Lui* in 1982, with Serge taking the snaps, and she would end up being dragged from TV studio to TV studio in 1984 to pole-dance topless while he performed 'Love On The Beat' live to the French nation. As somebody who grew up in Great Britain with an inherent prudishness, this all seems like capricious and awkward behaviour. The French, we must remind ourselves, are more comfortable and open with nudity, and with sensuality, too, and Gainsbourg was an artist who celebrated the nude on his thousands of trips to the Louvre, where, lest we forget, he could happily go without cigarettes.

While studying at the Beaux-Arts in his late teens, Serge would while away his Sundays at the nearby museum admiring the work of Delacroix, Titian, and Uccello. He was wildly beguiled by a tableau of Saint Sebastian by the early Renaissance painter Andrea Mantegna that hangs in the museum. He described it as 'a kind of orgasm of suffering' and declared it the most beautiful picture he'd ever seen.† This androgynous image was a blessing and a curse for Gainsbourg in that it transfixed him but did nothing for his inferiority complex as a painter.

At the age of thirteen, he'd been enrolled in art classes by his father at

---

* 'Un Bayard ça vous change un homme.'
† 'une sorte d'orgasme dans la souffrance.' Bayon, *Serge Gainsbourg, mort ou vices* (Grasset, 1992)

L'Académie Montmartre, where he was tutored by André Lhote and Fernand Léger. He was impressed by Lhote but didn't like the radical Léger, with his didactic, socially conscious art. Gainsbourg was haughty toward the more well-known of the men, perhaps because he was a communist. It was an intense period that led up to his peritonitis diagnosis, and he later recalled painting a life model with an SS soldier standing metres away from him.

After the war ended, Serge was accepted at the Beaux-Arts to study architecture at the Gromort-Arretche; he then changed course a year in, distressed at the rigour required, and returned to his original plan to be a painter. Mediocrity unfortunately got in the way, or at least an awareness of his own limitations. The few brightly coloured canvases that didn't get destroyed or burnt by his own hand have a visual texture reminiscent of Pierre Bonnard, who, I have to admit, doesn't inspire me either.

'Yes, he wanted to be a painter,' says Charlotte Gainsbourg, 'and he destroyed everything he made because he wasn't good enough in his own eyes. We have a few of them—not very many, maybe five. You can see he had a sort of frustrated relationship with painting and drawing.' Her father had wanted to succeed as a painter partly to impress his own father, who had also wanted to be an artist. Ginsburg Sr. had thrown in the towel after a painting he'd done of a girl he was besotted with was stolen whilst he slept on the Trans-Siberian railway. In a further case of history repeating itself, both fell back on their musical training, playing pianos in bars, only with Serge it would transpire that he had something special up his sleeve.

Gainsbourg's first wife, Lise, is sceptical about this image of a furious Gainsbourg breaking canvases like his hero Francis Bacon and throwing them onto a bonfire. 'I'm often asked if I have any paintings from Lulu,' she writes. 'No, I don't have anything anymore. He used to say in interviews that he'd destroyed everything. We picture an auto-da-fé or dozens of paintings burning in a fireplace. Apparently there are only a few paintings left of his: a self-portrait, a portrait of a woman that went to auction a few years ago, and a painting of two children, which he gave to Juliette Gréco. There's believed to be this abundance of broken canvases to choose from but it's all legend. Lulu hardly painted anything. I honestly believe that in his whole life he only ever produced about ten paintings, fifteen at most, several of which are very small. He destroyed a few, it's true, but he really didn't paint very much.'*

Perhaps there was a safety in advertising that doesn't come with the same creative expectations as other arts? Or maybe he saw advertising as an *art mineur* in the same way he did the *chanson*? 'In France, they think advertisements are works of art sometimes,' says Chilly Gonzales, who lived in Paris for eight years. 'I've worked on adverts there and I'm like, *They think they're working on an Oscar-nominated film here, what the fuck is going on?* I think in France, especially, the whole *you've sold out* mentality never really flew. There's no indie-rock ethos; there's no punk-rock ethos, apart from in very small pockets. To them, Téléphone is a punk band.'

*

There's an argument that the French didn't need punk because they already had Gainsbourg to shock them and push the limits of decency. There were also weekly magazines like *Hara Kiri*—the precursor to *Charlie Hebdo*— and stand-up comics like Coluche. The attitude of punk was also firmly embedded in the music press, thanks to the shamanic music writer Yves Adrien, who became very influential on the Parisian music scene and in the demolished demi-monde of Les Halles, where he hung out distributing Mandrax. 'Yves Adrien was fascinated by Huysmans,' says Bertrand Burgalat. 'He worked at *Rock & Folk*, and he was instrumental in the punk scene in the early 70s.'

---

* 'On me demande souvent s'il me reste des tableaux de Lulu. Non, je ne possède plus rien. Il a déclaré dans les interviews qu'il a tout détruit. On imagine un autodafé, des dizaines de tableaux brûlés dans une cheminée. Et on dit qu'il ne reste que quelques tableaux de lui : un autoportrait, un portrait de femme passé en salle des ventes il y a quelques années et un tableau représentant deux enfants, qu'il a donné à Juliette Gréco. On en parle comme c'étaient les débris d'une production abondante. C'est une légende. En fait, Lulu n'a pas peint énormément plus. Je crois que, de toute sa vie, il n'a réalisé qu'une dizaine de tableaux, une quinzaine tout au plus, dont plusieurs sont de tout petit format. Il en a détruit quelques-uns, c'est vrai. Mais il n'a vraiment pas beaucoup peint.' Elisabeth 'Lise' Lévitzky with Bertrand Dicale, *Lise et Lulu* (First, 2010)

'Yves Adrien was a genius,' says Etienne Daho. 'He was very different. He wasn't a straight rock critic—he was always on the lookout for different kinds of artists. He was the first one to write articles about Grace Jones and Amanda Lear. He considered them rock icons.' In *England's Dreaming*, Jon Savage called rock critics like Adrien, Philippe Manœuvre, and Alain Pacadis 'the French punk aristocracy'; Malcolm McLaren and Vivienne Westwood were in turn called 'couturiers situationnistes' by the French punks before they'd even launched the Sex Pistols, which may give some indication of the direction ideas were flowing.

Twenty or so years older than most of the punks who hung out in the detritus of Châtelet in the shadow of the gothic edifice Saint-Eustache, Gainsbourg was seen as a godhead in many ways, but there was an element of distrust from the generic music press away from its star columnists. Serge was making some of the best music of his career on albums in the mid-70s, but he'd also released a string of terrible 45s, was appearing in Woolite laundry detergent commercials, had gone on record to say that he'd voted for Giscard—which many on the left couldn't forgive—and was regarded as a has-been by more people than not. Another gonzo writer, Patrick Eudeline, managed to secure a two-page spread in *Best* magazine in 1975 after a dressing down from his editor for his apparent lack of taste. 'Eudeline identified in Serge a concept that has become commonplace in rock criticism [but was missing from pop]: *Attitude*,' writes Marie-Dominique Lelièvre in *Gainsbourg sans filtre*. 'Asceticism to escape reality. Behaviour verging on the suicidal. An escalation of narcissism. A theatrical taste for artifice. Patrick Eudeline headlines his column *Le dandy*. The editor downgrades it to *Un* dandy.'*

Adrien, a stout defender of the deteriorated and derided dandy, passed the torch to Alain Pacadis from *Libération*, a bohemian writer who emerged from

---

* 'Patrick Eudeline définit un concept devenu par la suite lieu commun de la critique rock: l'attitude. Une ascèse pour échapper à la réalité … Un comportement au bord du suicide. Une surenchère narcissique. Un goût théâtral pour l'artifice. Patrick Eudeline titre sa chronique "Le dandy". Son rédacteur en chef rectifie à la baisse: Un dandy.' Marie-Dominique Lelièvre, *Gainsbourg sans filtre* (J'ai Lu, 1994)

the underground with a death wish. He got what he asked for in 1986 when his boyfriend strangled him. Although he only lived to thirty-six, he managed to squeeze in a memoir, *Itinéraire d'un dandy punk*, and he did more for the revitalisation of Gainsbourg's public image in print than anyone else. 'He was a fantastic journalist,' says Etienne Daho. 'He was very bright and very sweet. When he loved people, he defended them to the hilt. He was at every party— he was drunk and drugged up all the time, but he was very sweet, and we loved him dearly.'

'Pacadis was a lovable terrorist,' said Jacno, a punk musician turned electro pioneer who, like Gainsbourg, was a foppish provocateur with a fatal fondness for fags (he died in 2009, aged fifty-two). Answering questions in an interview book from 2006 with a titular nod to Pacadis—*Itinéraire du dandy pop*—he said the writer was a travelling tramp frequenting luxurious places: 'And it almost always turned into a scandal. Gainsbourg had adopted him as a drifting companion. For example, they showed up together at the Elysée Matignon and it ended up in an unfortunate vomiting episode.' According to Calypso Valois, Jacno's daughter, Gainsbourg had a name for Jacno—Beep Beep—because of the noise he made when he played the synthesizer.

'Yves Adrien is so much more than a rock critic,' says the musician and writer Jean-Emmanuel DeLuxe. 'In fact, he is even more than a rock star. He was able to influence a whole generation of people. I would say he is the Huysmans of the late twentieth century. Alain Pacadis was more like a nightclubbing dandy, but both were inseparable. Edwige Belmore, the queen of the Parisian punks, compared them to Batman and Robin. Adrien, Pacadis, and Philippe Manœuvre introduced Gainsbourg to this new punk paradigm and made their audience aware that the old man was still relevant.'

According to Lelièvre, Gainsbourg was invited to join the 'Junkie Club', a clique of peerless Parisian punks, in 1978. As someone who refrained from taking any drugs other than cigarettes and alcohol, Serge was made an honorary member. The mythical club was a bit like a twelve-step fellowship in that the members only knew each other by their first names; at one point, Yves and Alain presented to the gang a London teenager in a swastika T-shirt called Sid.

Other names, writes Marie-Dominique, included 'Elisabeth, Edwige, Paquita. And Caroline. Caroline von Paulus.'

*

In 1986, Gainsbourg walked into the premises of an advertising magazine called *Media* in order to do a shoot for an article that would compare him with Salvador Dalí. The photographer that day was Roberto Battistini, a twenty-six-year-old Corsican who was slightly overawed to be receiving one of France's most famous men to his studio. 'Dalí was the first artist to play with his image and who knew how to manipulate the media,' says Battistini. 'When he was on a TV show, he was always doing something unbelievable, and Serge Gainsbourg later did the same thing. When he burned a banknote on TV, it was very popular and very unpopular, if you see what I mean. So, at the magazine, we were comparing the two. Gainsbourg was like the new Salvador Dalí.'

They shot Serge on a Saturday, so that he could also appear on a TV show with studios a few hundred metres from *Media*'s offices. He arrived at midday and spent around seven hours being photographed in various costumes. In one picture he is wearing a beret and holding a baguette, for a tongue-in-cheek article playing on stereotypical images of the French. For the pièce de résistance, he would be made up as Dalí, complete with a moustache attached to his face with prosthetic make-up. 'There is no retouching in the picture, it's the real thing. We put a real moustache on Serge Gainsbourg, like in the movies,' says Roberto.

The famous 'Gainsbourg as Dalí' photograph is striking in its likeness to the artist he's paying upper lip service to. 'The first pictures didn't look right with what he was wearing, so I asked him to strip. And then it was very difficult for him, because I used a 6x6 camera with film—not digital like nowadays—with very strong lighting. I directed him like it was a film, telling him to say, *Je suis fou … du chocolat Lanvin!* like Dalí. And I was asking him to open his eyes, but when you open your eyes like that and there's a very big flash, you are stunned for a few minutes. It makes you blind. So it takes time.'

Roberto was impressed with Gainsbourg's commitment to the task in hand: 'He was very professional, very smart, very nice, and he let me do what I wanted to do. For me, this was unbelievable, because I was a very young photographer, and he was fifty-five and very famous.' Serge often went the country mile for photographers, apparently giving up drinking for days before William Klein shot him as a woman for the cover of *Love On The Beat*, in order to try to reduce the bags from under his eyes.

In 2011, Battistini had an epiphany about his photo when Christie's invited him to partake in a twenty-year commemoration of Gainsbourg's death with William Klein, Tony Frank, and around fifty other photographers for exhibitions in Paris and New York. 'Nobody had a picture like I did,' he says, 'and so I imagined the project *Gainsbourg Still Alive*.' Since 2012, Roberto has been collaborating with artists who reimagine his Gainsbourg as Dalí picture in their own style, which he then photographs and exhibits.

First of all he asked his friend, the German artist Peter Klasen, 'because he uses a lot of photography in his painting and works with aerosols.' Other artists who've worked with him include Ivan Messac, Hervé Di Rosa, Omar Ba, and Miguel Chevalier. He's hoping to get Gilbert and George on board. They would be perfect for Gainsbourg as their self-mythologising devotion to their own collective image is perhaps even more committed than he was to his. Serge, the eternal contradiction, was practically a living *gesamtkunstwerk* like them, except that he failed in the one area that's central in creating total art: at the end of the day, he just wasn't a good enough artist.

The Cabbage Head Man has taken on a strange life of his own without needing the man who brought him to the attention of the public and put his picture on the cover of the record. *L'homme à tête de chou*, like *Gainsbourg Still Alive*, continues to proliferate without the source. In 2008, it was turned into a ballet by the French dancer and choreographer Jean Claude Gallotta, in collaboration with cult French singer Alain Bashung, who performed his own version of *L'homme à tête de chou* for the production.

Gainsbourg had collaborated with Bashung on the wonderfully weird *Play blessures* album in 1982, a proto-coldwave experiment that sounds like avant-garde rockabilly, a record Bashung made to try to distance himself from his big hit 'Gaby oh Gaby'. The song had saved him from a decade and a half of struggling as a singer, but the success also caught him off guard, giving him the sort of commercial exposure he didn't much like. Bashung gave his lyricist, Boris Bergman, the week off. *Play blessures* was a commercial catastrophe, but its cult status has grown over the years, which one hopes pleased Bashung. He died in 2009 from lung cancer while the stage version of *L'homme à tête de chou* was still being made. The show must go on, and the production was well received, featuring fourteen dancers, Bashung's disembodied voice, plus nearly an hour of additional music by the Canadian musician Denis Clavaizolle.

'Alain spoke to me about this project and asked me to create new colours in a cinematographic spirit,' Denis told me by email. 'For me it's like the story for a movie so I wanted to recreate it like a movie score. So there are ten additional pieces of instrumental music for the dancers to express jealousy, craziness, murderousness, and so on, because it's a dance show that's eighty minutes long and the record only lasts for thirty-five minutes.' In 2011, Maison Barclay issued a posthumous version of Bashung's *L'homme à tête de chou* without Denis's additional compositions. It had a further sold-out run at the Théâtre du Rond-Point in Paris in September 2019.

Gainsbourg never performed the album himself, but he did bring 'Marilou sous la neige' into the setlist in the mid-1980s. The snow inferred in the title is actually fire-extinguisher foam, with which the protagonist covers Marilou's lifeless body, following what is often dubiously and euphemistically referred to as a crime of passion. It's a pretty melody with a title like a Brueghelian winterscape, juxtaposed with a gruesome homicide—a complexity that didn't translate to Serge's American musicians when he played the song at the Casino de Paris in 1985.

'My brother Steve didn't understand any French, apart from *bonjour*, and so when we were onstage, doing backing vocals for that song, he was swaying from side to side with a big smile on his face,' says backing singer George Simms. 'Serge took Steve aside and said, Steve, when I am singing this song and you are dancing—and he imitated someone dancing in a jolly way, smiling and tilting his head and smiling and waving and dancing. *No no no! You do not know this song. It is about a man who hits a girl on the head with a fire extinguisher and he wants to cover her up with the foam from the extinguisher, and that is why "Marilou sous la niege" is a song about someone who is dead. You do not want to be dancing to this song.* That became a running joke. Serge would sing it with a serious face, and then he'd break into a Steve dance.'

On *L'homme à tête de chou*, Serge tried on a character for size. Later, he would go further and invite a character in, an incarnation made of boozy nightmares. If we use Bowie for comparison again, Serge Gainsbourg (Lucien Ginsburg) is a persona like David Bowie (David Jones) is a persona, but there are detectable traces of the person in the persona. With Ziggy Stardust, Bowie invited an extra-terrestrial rock star to accompany him; with Serge, it would be a pugnacious *clochard* called Gainsbarre. In both cases, the creation would threaten to take them to the edge of madness, though Jean-Claude Vannier is not so sure: 'The Gainsbourg/Gainsbarre thing was just marketing,' he says, grumpily. 'I don't get involved with marketing.'

FAME

AUX ARMES ET CÆTERA (1979)

> There's a quote that I like: 'I put all my genius into my life; I put only my talent into my works.' It's by Oscar Wilde.*

Before he officially subdivided his alter ego into the sensitive Gainsbourg and the boorish Gainsbarre, Serge was suffering from another split-personality disorder in the public eye. There was the serious artiste Gainsbourg who wrote cerebral concept albums like *L'homme à tête de chou*, and then there was the attention-seeking Gainsbourg who would release 'monumental bullshit' like 'L'ami caouette' if he thought it would get him into the charts.† His instincts were normally correct about these things, meaning he had a run of novelty 45s that charted during the 70s right at a time when he was producing some of his finest material on albums. His desire to be loved and on television seemed to outweigh any artistic concerns he had, although given that he thought all pop songs could be filed under a category *l'art mineur*, ideas of credibility seemed to concern him less than most.

'When Serge was singing "L'ami Caouette", he accepted that he would do his worst as a trade-off for being on a TV show,' says Alain Chamfort, a French pop star Gainsbourg collaborated with on and off for around five years. 'He

---

* 'Il y a une citation qui me plaît bien: J'ai mis ma génie dans ma vie et mon talent dans mon œuvre. Elle est d'Oscar Wilde.' Serge Gainsbourg, *Pensées provocs et autres volutes* (Librairie Générale Française, 2007)

† In 1990 he called 'L'ami caouette' 'une connerie monumentale'.

would go and he would sing, do the playback, and he'd never be any good at lip-syncing. He'd be completely out. You'd see him on daytime TV, some very bad show, and he accepted it to be everywhere. He wanted people to see him. He wanted to be famous.'

'L'ami caouette' started life as a sketch for the *Sacha Show*, which he then took away and underlaid with a Caribbean beguine rhythm, then completed it visually for the TV performances with four gospel singers flanking him in striking red bodysuits, with one squeezing onto his lap on a piano stool. Even in such close proximity, Gainsbourg still found enough room to smoke a cigarette.

'L'ami caouette' was recorded with Serge's auxiliary go-to man Jean-Pierre Sabar, an arranger who picked up the slack when Alan Hawkshaw and the KPM all-stars were too busy. The 'My Lady Heroine' single was also recorded with Sabar; that song also charted, and it's even worse than 'L'ami caouette', if that's possible. With a 1950s-style rock'n'roll swing, it's a trite offering with little to recommend it. 'Oh my lady heroine,' sings Serge, 'my opium, my cocaine … / Did you come from the Far East or a Persian market?'* The main line of the song is actually filched from 'In A Persian Market' by the English symphonist Albert Ketèlbey—a surprising reference from a late composer who'd fallen out of favour in post-war times and spent his last days on the Isle of Wight, where he died in obscurity. Gainsbourg's knowledge of classical music was extensive enough that he didn't always need to steal recognisable motifs from Chopin or Beethoven—he could mine the tunes of recherché English melodists and pass them off as his own without most listeners realising.

The logical conclusion to all this pandering to the lowest common denominator came in the shape of a holiday hit, 'Sea, Sex And Sun'—a title that has passed into the English language, oddly enough. Serge's love of alliterative wordplay crossed with an elementary grasp of English makes it perfect tabloid fodder, especially in reference to out-of-control Club 18–30 holidays or debauched TV reality shows featuring perma-tanned holiday

---

* 'Oh my lady héroïne / Mon opium ma cocaïne / Es-tu venue d'Extrême Orient ou bien d'un marché persan.'

reps. It wasn't his first real attempt at disco—that was Jane Birkin's 'Lolita Go Home', recorded with Sabar in 1975. Hawkshaw and the crew were drafted in for 'Sea, Sex And Sun', although Serge had no idea what he wanted to do at first, according to the English session musician.

'I think that was when I went over to Paris to routine him,' says Hawkshaw, 'and the first day I got there we went out for dinner, and I said over dinner, What have you written? He said to me, Alan, I have written nothing. So the next day I turned up in the afternoon, because he wasn't a morning guy, and I think that's when we sat down and I started to come up with some ideas at the piano. Serge was not a man to be hurried. He liked to be inspired by something. He needed inspiration.'

Given that disco was everywhere in 1978, did Serge suggest making a very commercial hit song in line with what was in the charts at the time? 'No, he didn't—I would have suggested that,' says Hawkshaw. 'I'd been busy with Alec R. Costandinos, doing Cerrone and bands of his, and my own disco thing with Love De-Luxe too. So I was into disco—I quite liked disco. It was easy to hook onto those four beats in the bar on the bass drum—you could hang anything around that. I used to like orchestrating big strings for disco. I would have suggested that beat, definitely.'

The lyrics were knocked off in ten minutes on the corner of a table on the back of an envelope. The song certainly garnered attention; by Serge's own admission, it was a case of acting in haste, repenting at leisure. There was even a maxi-45 that came out in Serge's broken English, with him muttering, 'Excuse me, I am a Frenchman, and I'm afraid I don't speak very well English … but I … I think that you are the most pretty little girl I ever knew.' It probably makes more sense than the French verse, where you have a hirsute fifty-year-old Frenchman perving on about 'little bosoms of Bakelite' like he's hitting on a Barbie. The B-side, 'Mister Iceberg', is also—surprise, surprise—about an older man hitting on a little girl in white socks, but it is musically more worthy than the flip side.*

---

* 'Mister Iceberg aime les petites filles en socks.'

These compromised publicity splashes were doing little for Gainsbourg's reputation, and they were maybe even putting off his natural fanbase. Serge's career wasn't where he wanted it to be, and the hope of some reflected glory from younger, cooler artists was one way to improve his public profile. He was encouraged to work with Alain Chamfort by Jane Birkin, and he wrote all the lyrics for the Breton-born singer's third album, *Rock'n Rose*. Chamfort, real name Alain Le Govic, had started his musical career playing in Jacques Dutronc's backing band in the 60s, and his first record was produced by Claude François—Cloclo was meant to do the second, but he walked out on the project, apparently after a senseless argument about his protege's youth. It seems a strange sticking point to bring up at that time, as Chamfort couldn't help being ten years his junior, and he'd been even younger when they made his debut. Gainsbourg was twenty years older than Chamfort, and very happy at the time to be associated with a young buck troubling the French hit parade.

'It was around 1977, and Gainsbourg wasn't popular at that time,' Chamfort tells me, reclining on a terrace cafe in the eleventh arrondissement, drinking Café Allongé. 'I was more than twenty years younger than him, so he was happy that somebody of my generation had been to see him to ask him to write for them.' Chamfort had recorded music for his next record in Los Angeles with a group of session musicians who would later go on to form Toto, but he was drawing a blank where the words were concerned.

He phoned Serge, who he'd met in the green room of a TV show Jane was performing on. 'So I called him—why not?—and I went to Rue de Verneuil to make him listen to the recording session, and he was impressed with the musicians, so he said okay. And he told me that he was going through this difficult period and he didn't want to become Mr. Birkin. He was afraid because Jane's career was flying. She'd made two or three movies where she was at the very top, so he was a little bit jealous.'

Rock'n Rose flopped, and Serge sought to distance himself from Chamfort, though he would agree to write a couple of texts for his follow-up album, *Poses*, which came out in 1979. Birkin also chipped in with a lyric for the English-language 'Let Me Try It Again'. Chamfort had high hopes for one of the pacier instrumentals he'd entrusted to another lyricist, and when it didn't turn out the way he wanted it to, he asked Serge if he'd step in. 'A lot of people in Paris recognised his talent,' says Chamfort. 'Everyone was impressed by his talent.' Gainsbourg came up with a lyric for a song he called 'Adieu California': 'I didn't like it much,' says Chamfort, 'but it was the best I was going to get at that point. I put the voice on it, but I knew it wasn't right.' Gainsbourg promised he would try to write something else if an idea came to him.

In November '78 there'd been a big story in the French press involving a celebrated around-the-world sailor called Alain Colas, whose trimaran went missing in an area close to the Azores during the quadrennial Route du Rhum yacht race. Neither he nor his sailboat, *Manureva*, was ever recovered. Months later, Serge and Alain attended a boat race themselves with Jane Birkin, the latter having been invited to start the race. During dinner, one of the skippers brought up the *Manureva* story, and Serge had a lightbulb moment. 'It had only happened about six months before, so I was apprehensive,' says Alain. 'It's a little bit insensitive to sing about the death of somebody so soon after. He told me, No, no, it'll be a tribute. And so I recorded the new lyrics, and "Manureva" was a big hit.' The song was released in September 1979; in early 1980 it climbed to no.2 in the French charts, and it stayed there for a month.

Some coolness by association was conferred by the French rock band Bijou, who asked Gainsbourg to perform an old song with them that he'd written for Michèle Arnaud called 'Les papillons noirs' ('Black Butterflies'). The collaboration was instigated by Philips's press attaché, Jacky Jakubowicz, who later became a famous French kids TV presenter. Gainsbourg had been on the label for twenty years while Bijou were recent signings. 'It was a happy coincidence,' guitarist Vincent Palmer tells me over email, 'because as a compulsive record collector from a very early age, I was an absolute fan of everything that Serge ever did, from his own albums to all his collaborations and compositions for others.'

'Les papillons noirs' was such a recondite choice that Gainsbourg failed to recognise it when it was played to him. He relearnt it and was invited to join Bijou on the single, which he did on crutches after breaking his leg. He and the band became friends, and then one night when they were playing in Épernay, about an hour and a half out of Paris, Serge was cajoled into joining them onstage for the song. It prompted a massive ovation from the audience when he came out onto the stage. It was the first time he'd performed live in a decade and a half, give or take some badly mimed TV performances, and it would ultimately herald a return to gigging. Gainsbourg had assumed those days were behind him.

I put it to Palmer that Bijou played a role in Serge's career rejuvenation. 'I wouldn't say Serge's career was deadlocked,' he replies. 'It was a generational thing. Our collaboration allowed fans of Bijou, who were mostly young, to get to know him and discover a rebellious kindred spirit, which was difficult to imagine from somebody who could be their father. A phenomenon of identification became particularly evident.'

'I think he was quite wounded by the fact his records didn't sell,' Charlotte Gainsbourg tells me. 'It wasn't something he was comfortable with. I can't remember exactly how he felt, because I was too much of a kid at that time, but I remember how success really was important to him. When I was ten or eleven, when it started to really work, he became very, very successful. He was so happy, and it was a revolution for him.'

*

Aux armes et cætera, recorded with The Revolutionaries in Jamaica in 1979, dramatically changed the relationship between Serge Gainsbourg and France. He'd actually been planning another concept album about a man riding in the back of a London cab who has a heart attack: the guy's ticker stops working as the taximeter clicks away, and his life flashes before his eyes, the prelude to an operatic death. It's certainly a striking idea, with plenty of personal experience for the author to draw upon. Whether or not it would have had enough pump for an entire album we'll never know.

The story goes that the next step taken into the musical unknown was initiated by Gainsbourg's right-hand man, Philippe Lerichomme, the man in the shadows. Lerichomme was extremely important to Gainsbourg, and the subject of the very last song he ever wrote, 'Un homme dans l'ombre'.[*] From the 70s onward, Lerichomme looked after the interests of both Serge and Jane. In 1978, after having his arm twisted to find other artists to handle by his employer, Phonogram, he'd arranged to see a punk band at L'Olympia. 'He waited there and the artist never turned up,' says Jane, 'but he did hear someone playing Bob Marley in the nightclub underneath.' The dub bass reverberating from the sound system below caught Philippe's ear, and he went to investigate. 'He said, *What's that?* The man said Island Records. And Philippe rushed off to Le Drugstore, as it was in those days, he picked up every record he could find from Island and Bob Marley.[†] The following morning he was at Rue de Verneuil, saying, *This is what you must do.*'

Thanks to sound advice and some string-pulling from his friend, Island supremo Chris Blackwell, Lerichomme and Gainsbourg were soon booked onto a flight to Jamaica; they would spend half of January 1979 working with Sly Dunbar, Robbie Shakespeare, Ansel Collins, Uziah 'Sticky' Thompson, and Robbie 'Tights' Lyn—as well as the I Threes, featuring Rita Marley on backing vocals—at the Dynamic Sound Studios in Kingston.

It's a nice story, even if something doesn't quite add up. For a start, there's the implication that reggae is new to Lerichomme's ears, though Serge had already

---

* 'Un homme dans l'ombre' was written for a TV special Jane Birkin was doing to promote 'Amours des feintes'. Birkin: 'I told him he should write a song for Philippe and he said, No, Philippe doesn't like anyone writing songs about him, he'd be terribly embarrassed. He never likes to draw attention to himself. So I said to him, Well, people always say that, but perhaps he would, and if you don't do it I'll have a go—to which Serge looked very piqued. And so he wrote the most marvellous song about everything he thought about Philippe, who was the man in the shadows. The searchlight on the TV show found Philippe, who was up in the control room as usual, and he came down, and of course he was pleased.' The performance, with Serge at the piano and Birkin singing, took place on October 12 1990, and would prove to be one of Serge's last appearances in public. Like so many of the tunes that Gainsbourg wrote for TV, the song was never registered with SACEM. A microcassette recording of the song was auctioned in Nantes in 2013, though it received little publicity, with publications more interested in the fact that his smoked cigarette butts and toenail clippings were also up for grabs.
† The Drugstore in Saint-Germain-des-Pré was a late night hangout which dispensed records as well as pharmaceuticals into the night.

recorded 'Marilou Reggae' on *L'homme à tête de chou* with Alan Hawkshaw in 1976, as well as an entire reggae soundtrack to *Goodbye Emmanuelle* with Sabar in 1977. Admittedly, it wasn't reggae played by Jamaican musicians, like the albums with The Revolutionaries would be, but the idea that Lerichomme had an epiphany about a new musical genre at L'Olympia sounds like mythmaking to me. (I would have liked to ask Lerichomme, but he doesn't, as a rule, do interviews.)

'We'd already had a taste of a reggae track, as you said, but I don't think that influenced Serge to want to go out there,' says Alan Hawkshaw, with magnanimity. 'Serge would always go straight to the root, so, if he wanted to do reggae, he would go out to Jamaica to do it. He wouldn't necessarily want to do a reggae track in London—which we did, of course—but that's not really the way to do it. It's like when people go to Nashville to do country.'

Serge and Philippe flew out to Jamaica with Jane's father, David Birkin, in tow. Jane couldn't attend because of filming commitments. 'My father found himself in a studio with cockerels sitting on the mixing desk,' she says. The initial meeting between the French camp and the Jamaican camp was awkward. 'They didn't take any notice of Serge, thinking that Lerichomme was the musician and Serge was the producer, because he looked older. And then they were all mocking French music and saying nothing was very interesting. And then Robbie Shakespeare said, Except for that one with the chic moaning *Je t'aime, je t'aime* ... And Serge said, *It's me! I'm the one who did that.*'

There was an alternative version of this story put around by Serge at the time that it was his musical prowess that broke down barriers. 'The story Serge told all the time was that when they heard him play the piano, they knew he wasn't a wanker—they knew he was a real musician,' says Bruno Blum. 'That's the legend, but the true story is that he came in to meet the musicians, and he sang "Lola Rastaquouère" on the piano. And they said, Who are you? Do we know any songs of yours? and he said, Yeah, I'm the guy who wrote "Je t'aime ... moi non plus". And they went, *Wow*! They'd been playing it in bars. There are three reggae versions of that song—I have them here, all recorded in 1969. They knew that song and it was a big hit, and they went, *Right, this guy is a real pop star*. It's not because he played well.'

Whether it was Serge's virtuosity or Jane's moaning that was the icebreaker to precipitate productivity, there was little productivity from Serge himself during the first week of rehearsal. Sly once described to Bruno Blum how they all watched Serge at the piano and followed him in much the same way Miles Davis followed Louis Malle's *Ascenseur pour l'échafaud* on a screen, interpreting Jeanne Moreau's emotions live. The musicians took the lead from the mumbling French guy sitting at the piano, observing him like a film and taking his lead when the mood took him. 'So they got really into the vibe, which was rhythmic and poetic. He has a rhyme, a beat, a groove to his voice, and the music came from that.' The lyrics weren't coming so easily. Having had nothing written down throughout rehearsals, he pulled an all-nighter the evening before recording, lying on a bed with just some titles, some booze, and a black marker pen, legendarily scribbling all of the lyrics in one sitting.

'Philippe Lerichomme actually told me that he was the one who put the songs together,' says Blum. 'There were bits of scrap paper everywhere. And so he said, Which one is this? and he stuck them together with Sellotape. He'd say, Is this the song? and Serge would say yeah but then change his mind at the last minute.'

Bruno was hired by Lerichomme in the early 2000s to assist him with Universal's back catalogue, with much emphasis on Gainsbourg as a heritage act; Lerichomme was sacked by the label soon after. The pair had been friends, but these new circumstances thrust upon them made the relationship untenable. Blum released a number of dub-reggae versions from *Aux armes et cætera* and *Mauvais nouvelles des etoiles*, and he also beefed up the live recordings with the Revolutionaries and extended what was available. Furthermore, a three-CD collection with a book called *Gainsbourg In Dub* came out in 2015.

'Most artists wouldn't get anywhere if they didn't have a manager and someone working for them, and they know that. The Beatles wouldn't have gotten anywhere without Brian Epstein, and Philippe was doing that for Serge, who was a complete wacko, up all night, drunk, needing someone to put his papers together to record the songs. He was the complete 100 percent artist who could never get his shit together. And Philippe came there, put him in a taxi … I know it sounds like a cliché, but he was that guy who dealt with the record company, and he dealt with everything. Philippe always says he doesn't want to take any of the credit, but he *should* take the credit. He locked Serge in his room for *Aux armes et cætera*, and he said, Tomorrow morning I'm coming in and it's done. There were all sorts of bits of papers stuck on the wall with Sellotape, and Philippe took them all in a paper bag to the studio and then started taking out the bits of paper, saying, *Serge, what's this song? What's this one? What's this one?* He was like a nurse.' Philippe had received a producer's credit on every album from *L'homme à tête de chou* onward, but it was usually more for what he did behind the scenes than for what he did behind the mixing desk.

Despite the unorthodox and chaotic backstory, *Aux armes et cætera* caught the imagination of the public, and it's still by far Gainsbourg's biggest-selling album in France. 'French people I know think the lyrics on that album are great,' says Mick Harvey. When I mention how the lyrics were written, collectively and in a rush, he adds, 'He was great with words, what can I say? I know people who can do that—great writers. Nick Cave can improvise songs out of thin air, and they sound *written*. In rehearsals, it just seems to be there all in his head—he's processing the way the lines go together. It's amazing the way he can just improvise songs when you're having a little jam. He'll string together three verses in a row and it's on the spot, because it's about what's happening and it's incredible. So I could imagine that with Gainsbourg. He could just sit down and say, I know what I want to write—and do it. Because he'd had so much experience of working with words and handling words. But by that stage he'd clearly lost the will to bother with the music.'

Perhaps the fact Gainsbourg was so sonically hands-off is one of the unique strengths of *Aux armes*. Sly Dunbar is effusive with praise for the album when I call him in Jamaica: 'When I first heard this French guy who did "Je t'aime" was coming to Jamaica I was thinking, *What's he gonna do?* and *What does he know about reggae?* But the first one we did in Jamaica, to this day, I think it's one of the top five reggae albums of all time. Listen to "Lola Rastaquouère", "Daisy Temple", and all those songs—there are some wicked riddims, man. I was playing them a couple of days ago, and it sounds like it was yesterday.'

One of the factors that Sly enjoys so much is the rawness to the record, which came from inexperience. Gainsbourg and Lerichomme were two men entering into a world where they had no sense of the sonic protocols: 'It was really and truly raw. They produced it, but they didn't really know what they wanted. So we made sure that the riddims and everything else was okay, and there were no overdubs. The only thing added was the backing vocals.' Contrast the dryness of the production with, say, Lee 'Scratch' Perry's 1976 classic *Super Ape*, with its horn sections, ghost voices, sound effects, hand drums, backward snare and hi-hat treatments, and so on.

One song that has undergone an interesting evolution is 'Marilou Reggae', which started life on *L'homme à tête de chou*, as previously mentioned. It got the raw reggae treatment on *Aux armes* as 'Marilou Reggae Dub', and then later was remixed by Bruno Blum and Solgie Hamilton for release in 2003. The latter is a much smoother experience, with some rattling sub bass and refracted echo. The decision by Blum to remix all of these tracks when he landed his job at Universal was a sound one, given that—to quote David Toop—dub 'anticipated remix culture'.*

While I'm at Blum's place around the corner from Porte de Pantin, he plays me some unreleased tracks from the vaults, including Gainsbourg singing James Brown's 'Sex Machine'. It sounds like a surefire hit to my ears, but Universal France doesn't appear to be in any hurry to release it. There are ethical questions about it, of course: the vocal track has been isolated from a recording of Serge messing around on a TV show—a recording dredged up from the vaults, chopped up and laid over a supporting funk track played at a later date by some of the best session players in Paris. You suspect Serge would have sanctioned the scraping of the bottom of barrels to keep him in the

---

* David Toop, *Ocean Of Sound: Aether Talk, Ambient Sound And Imaginary Worlds* (Serpent's Tail, 2001)

spotlight, though 'Sex Machine' is a classier update than that implies. If he had any objections, it might be the use of French session players when he usually insisted on British.

As for a French star going to Jamaica and appropriating the indigenous spoils, becoming an exponent of a new subgenre called 'Freggae', Dunbar has no misgivings about it. He believes that Serge was instrumental in opening up the incipient reggae market in France and taking it to the mainstream. 'The first album was a template for reggae in France. He was the one who made it become the national music. What he got was the real reggae—he didn't get some water-wash thing. It wasn't recorded in Paris or London—he came down to Jamaica, it was mixed here, then he went back to France. If he was alive today, the groove would be massive, man!'

Keyboard player Ansel Collins, who scored a no.1 hit in the UK with 'Double Barrel' in 1970, is also thankful for Serge's contribution to the reggae story, and he has no resentments about Gainsbourg taking native Jamaican music and profiting from it. 'We was happy that they came, you know!' he says over the phone from the Caribbean island. 'Music is for everyone, not for Jamaicans alone. I think everyone outside of Jamaica appreciates the music more than Jamaicans. In Africa and everywhere, no doubt about it. In Jamaica, they're not big into culture and music.'

Gainsbourg assimilates his way into the groove intuitively from the off, referencing his past and signposting the future with opener, 'Javanaise Remake'. He dices the words so they spill out even more rhythmically than on the original. He may have left the Jamaican artists to get on with the music while he got on with the words, but there's an alchemical reaction between his voice and their instruments that must have sounded amazingly fresh in 1979. Lou Doillon, Jane's third daughter, who often refers to Serge as 'Papa deux', told me in an interview for *Huck* magazine that she likes to hear his reggae tunes in unexpected places: 'Like in a bar a couple of weeks ago, I heard some songs I'd never heard from that album [*Aux armes et cætera*] before. It's always good when you have two things that collide. I love it when Lana Del Rey works with rappers. I suddenly find it very interesting, this kind of Lana

Turner figure arriving on a rap song. I love those confrontations, so Serge doing reggae is something that's unexpected and really cool.'*

The whole Fifth Republic was confronted with the unexpected in 1979, when Serge Gainsbourg appeared on television singing the national anthem. Rouget de Lisle's words being arrogated by a Jew with the help of black Caribbean islanders from five thousand miles away, some of them Rastafarians, was an affront to conservatives and nationalists.

'I love "Aux armes et cætera" because of what it did,' says Sparks singer Russell Mael enthusiastically. 'It was so blasphemous in a way! It received such negative critiques at the time, because he was doing a reggae version of the French national anthem. It was such a great move, and I liked the audacity of doing that song that offended a lot of French people.'

'I like his approach on "Aux armes et cætera",' Tony Allen told me a few months before he died. Allen, the famous Afrobeat percussionist, had lived in Paris since 1982, with his last home situated in the business district of La Défense. 'He's not singing a melody on that track, he's blending his talking style with the melody. It's a great track, and I remember years later thinking I'd like to meet this guy and for us to jam together. I was going to ask him. I was thinking about it and then I went to Lagos, and before I came back, he was dead.'

Not everyone was impressed with the audaciousness of 'Aux armes et cætera'. The columnist Michel Droit wrote an antisemitic polemic in *La Figaro* enforcing old prejudicial tropes levelled at Jews for centuries. Serge called him 'tout droit' (straight); Droit was an old-school establishment figure who later killed his guide in a shooting accident while on a hunting safari in central Africa.

'Serge was actually shocked by the response to *Aux armes et cætera*,' says Jane. 'Michel Droit wrote something about how being in the same atmosphere as Serge was like breathing in a tunnel with someone's exhaust pipe leaking. In other words, he was poison. And that he brought no good things to his

---

* 'The French are never happy with who they've elected,' HuckMag.com, January 30 2019.

coreligionnaire [the religion he's affiliated with]. First I'd ever heard of that, which in other words meant his other Jewish brothers. He was bringing them into disrepute by having dared to sing this anthem.' Serge began to receive hate mail. 'He kept lots of insulting letters in his attaché case. There was one that he liked to bring out that said he had eyes like an electrocuted toad. Serge was delighted by it. Even Michel Droit, even all the fuss that he caused, he had some fun with it.'

'When I was growing up, we still had antisemitic writing on the wall that he'd erase,' says Charlotte. 'There was a lot of graffiti, and there would be some nasty ones that he would get rid of. It's hard to remember what it was like—I mean, there's still a big antisemitism problem in France, but now he's looked at as kind of part of the French pantheon. He's part of the French culture, and he's very respected, but when I was growing up, he was still considered dirty and on drugs—even though he didn't do any drugs. He was this reviled man, and on top of it all he was Jewish. I really remember that as being very ruining. And at one point I remember my mother talking about some political guy, Droit, who said he was dirt, and that was very … he talked about that more than the war.'

An interregnum of more than a decade-and-a-half, where Gainsbourg had been absent from concert halls, had now drawn to a close. He was on the road again thanks to his pals from Bijou, who'd helped him conquer his stage fright by inviting him to join them for a rendition of 'Les papillons noirs' on a starry night in Épernay. There'd hitherto been little demand for his live return, due to a relative lack of success, but with a no.1 album and a clamour for the new Freggae king, he went on a tour of France with the Revolutionaries as his backing band. Everything was going swimmingly until the tour rolled into Strasbourg, situated in the northeast of France, the traditional heartland where the Front National often do quite well. Hotels were forced to drag their guests out onto the lawns at midnight because of bomb scares that turned out to be hoaxes. Then a number of paramilitaries turned up at the venue, and the show suddenly looked in doubt. What happened next has passed into legend.

'I can't forget that night!' says Ansel Collins. 'Someone said they're gonna storm the stage or something like that. We didn't perform that night.' In Birkin's *Munkey Diaries*, she says the band were spooked and refused to go to the venue to play.

We didn't go on,' says Dunbar. 'He told us to stay, because he didn't want anything being done to us. He went and he came back, and we left right after he came offstage. We drove from Strasbourg to the next town. Serge was a nice person. Chain-smoked cigarettes. Keep on smoking, never stop smoking!'

'When he sang it in front of the parachutists in Strasbourg, he left the Jamaican musicians in the coach who said they had enough problems at home,' says Jane. 'Serge and I whizzed across to the concert hall, and then Serge went on. We watched him from behind, and he was extraordinary. He sang "La Marseillaise" on his own in front of them. It's in a situation like that that you see someone do something out of bravura and courage. And the parachutists were all there in the first or second rows, and they didn't know what to do—whether to stand up or take their berets off—because he was doing the original version. So the atmosphere was extremely dangerous at the time.'

*

Serge somehow went from courageous to cowardly in a short space of time, characteristically snatching defeat from the jaws of victory. From triumph to despair in a few easy steps—the self-sabotage of an alcoholic about to pass into the fourth stage of dependence, where noticeable physical and psychological changes occur.

'He stuck up for me, wouldn't hear a word against me,' says Jane. 'He said it was all his fault because he got plastered too often, and that he punched me up too often. He took it all on himself. Which wasn't true.' In her diaries, Birkin recounts the first time Gainsbourg hit her in the left eye, back in 1970, and passes it off as a 'terrible scene'. Like so many victims of domestic violence, she seems to blame herself. As for why they separated, the truth of the matter was more prosaic, according to Birkin: 'We got into a rather boring pattern of being plastered every night. Me, like him, at the Elysée Matignon. And then there were all those people who used to tempt him with more drink, and a piano would come up through the floor, and they'd get him to play. And I used to get so bored around three o'clock in the morning, waiting until they'd close the joint, and then I'd take him back to make sure that nothing happened to him.'

Having a good time had become so routine that nobody checked to see if they were still having fun. 'After "Mineurva", around 1980, Jane left him,' says Alain Chamfort. 'And he was very, very sad. Destroyed. He was violent and drunk every night. I think it was because *Aux armes et cætera* was so successful. He went so long waiting for success to happen that, when it arrived, he was in the nightclubs every night with Jane, and they'd come back at four or five o'clock in the morning. It was the beginning of Gainsbarre as a construct, and Jane, little by little, couldn't accept the change in him.'

'Once I pushed him a bit too hard as he was trying to get his key in the lock,' says Jane. 'I pushed him, and it opened up his eyebrow. The next morning, he went, *Where did I get this from?* and I said, You couldn't get your key in the lock, and he said, It's a funny thing because drunk people don't normally do themselves that much harm. I don't know whether I ever owned up to the fact I gave him a little jolt. He was just too annoying.'

Birkin had become close to Jacques Doillon, the director of the film *La fille prodigue*, which they'd been making at that time. 'Serge was observing their relationship, but he didn't think anyone could …' Chamfort stops for a moment. 'He always thought that he was stronger, you know. He didn't think that Jane would ever leave him. He almost pushed Jane into the arms of Jacques Doillon. And Jane left. Afterwards, every day, he was crying, always *blah blah blah blah, I'm sad!* Okay, but he was responsible.'

'Keith Richards got himself a nurse,' says Bruno Blum. 'Two guys are always following him saying, Don't give him drugs. I would say Serge after *Aux armes*, when he got a lot of money, was almost the same. Jane left because of his drinking, and he went bad.'

'Having known him before his albums became really successful, I would have defined him as someone of great restraint, very classy, with a lot of finesse,' says Vincent Palmer of Bijou. 'Whereas from 1979 onward, after he became immensely popular, Serge seemed to have just one desire: to fuck around in all directions. It's as if he wanted to take revenge for all those years where he lacked recognition.'

As has been alluded to, a new person would enter his life when Jane left him: *Gainsbarre*. A persona he could hide behind and perhaps be protected by. A tangible creation where he could lay the blame for his defects of character at this other person's door. Adopting a persona is in a sense a denial of the self, and there are few people more delusional than those with an active addiction, a state that I have first-hand experience of. It's a grand idea, to invent a persona that becomes an extension of that person in order that they might perform better or assuage human anxieties, perhaps becoming an Übermensch in the process (it was certainly that Nietzschean idea that propelled Bowie). Some performers even forget the person they are completely, lost in a Stanislavskian reverie. I wanted to know how it feels to perform under a pseudonym with a character of one's own creation, so I asked performers of various stripes what a persona did for them.

First up, the comedian Graham Fellows, who had a big hit with 'Gordon Is A Moron' as Jilted John in 1978, and is best known as the performer John Shuttleworth—who Graham says is a character he has come to trust over the years. 'At the Edinburgh Fringe in 2006, I had a bit of a wobble when I had some memory loss, and I had to pack in my show,' he says. 'I was doing a newer character called Dave Tordoff, who was an ignorant builder who liked wearing bling. So it all went a bit pear-shaped, and I've been very weary of losing my memory, and I have had some hypnosis for that. It's worked—I don't catastrophise about it anymore. That wasn't Shuttleworth, though … I think John Shuttleworth would have protected me, somehow.'

'Maybe, by creating an alter ego, it's easy to think you've separated from it and you have control over it, but it's a weird feedback loop,' says Chilly Gonzales, whose real name is Jason Beck. 'I've never had a level of notoriety that caused me any *who am I?* moments in the mirror, and I'm thankful for that, but there have been moments. I didn't like people calling me by my first name for a very long time. I just felt better being Chilly Gonzales, because everyone was very respectful and did things for me. It was much easier to meet girls, and it felt like walking on air. Everyone called me Gonzo for a very long time, and if someone called me Jason it rankled me. It was a pretty strange denial of self, if you think about it.'

'It does protect you, I think,' says Will Oldham, who is better known as Bonnie 'Prince' Billy. 'Take someone who uses their own name—Paul Simon, for instance. I don't know how that entertainer separates personal identity from professional identity. If I sent Gainsbourg a letter, saying *I love Serge Gainsbourg*—he'd know exactly what I was talking about, because he knows who Serge Gainsbourg is. But if I sent Paul Simon a letter, saying *I love Paul Simon*, he wouldn't know what the fuck I was talking about, because who is Paul Simon? Paul Simon is all these different things, but Serge Gainsbourg isn't all these different things, he's this one thing, which is the creator of this cultural product, whether it's music or cinema.'

'It enhances some sides of you and pushes them forward,' says the singer Jehnny Beth. She was born Camille Berthomier, and traded under that name as an actress before she formed the band Savages and invented this new, tougher character. 'Nobody arrives like Gainsbourg. You go there and it's a journey, I think. But it demands quite a lot of courage to deny parts of yourself, because obviously people who know you well will say, But that's not you, that's not how I know you. Often, people who are figures like that, pop figures, end up quite lonely, because you push yourself to an area where you deny where you come from.'

At the age of fifty, Gainsbourg was finally a superstar. He'd attained everything he'd ever wanted and lost the love of his life in the process. He didn't have Jane anymore, but he had Gainsbarre, who grabbed people's attention and created headlines almost at will. This Faustian bargain would be played out in public to the fascination and occasional dismay of the French public right to the bitter end.

12

PROVOCATION

MAUVAISES NOUVELLES DES ÉTOILES (1981)

LOVE ON THE BEAT (1984)

> I'm a character and a myth. I have my look, I am the forerunner of neo-dandyism. And my two-day stubble requires a lot of care.*

In 1984, a half-cut Serge Gainsbourg burnt a 500 franc note on live TV, and the nation collectively gasped. Protesting the 74 percent tax he said he had to pay on his earnings, he lit up the money then attempted to put it out again so that there was just 26 percent left, to demonstrate the money he would take home after the government had taken its slice.† He and the host Jean-Louis Burgat discussed the legality of such a gesture. 'If I'm sent to jail, I don't care. At least I'll be on a diet,' he retorted.‡

'You do realise you'll provoke lots of people,' said Burgat.

'It's my money, I couldn't care less,' said Serge, holding the burning banknote for all to see.§ Serge had achieved peak *audimat*, the French word for

---

* 'Je suis un personnage, donc un mythe. J'ai mon look, je suis le précurseur du néo-dandysme. Et ma barbe de deux jours me demande beaucoup de soins.' Serge Gainsbourg, *Pensées provocs et autres volutes* (Librairie Générale Française, 2007)

† Somewhat ironically, the stub that was left recently sold at Sotheby's for five thousand euros.

‡ 'Si on me fout en taule, j'en n'ai rien à cirer … je serai au moins au régime.'

§ 'C'est mon pognon, j'en n'ai rien à cirer.'

TV ratings. It's a word Jane Birkin uses several times when I interview her, and furthermore it's what drove his dangerous alter ego, Gainsbarre. But before we get to Gainsbarre, we need to delve back further. The *billet enflammé* on French TV was far from an isolated incident.

The first recorded case of him burning money took place while he was making *Estouffade à la Caraïbe* (*The Looters*) in northern Colombia. The most memorable part of that production was when Gainsbourg was arrested for arson. 'He set fire to one of those hairy plants in a restaurant in South America when he was filming with Jean Seberg years before he met me,' says Jane. 'He set fire to the restaurant, actually. I don't know how they got him out of there, but he told them he didn't smoke. It was quite a dangerous place at the time. It was a kind of schoolboy prank that went wrong.'

'Serge loved to shock,' says Jane's brother, Andrew. 'That was part of his nature. I think it's probably the case with most artists. He wanted to shock people and wake them up a little bit, and part of the pleasure is in that ability to shock.' Andrew was there when Serge set fire to some Yugoslav dinars and was arrested in 1971. Jane and Serge were filming *Romance Of A Horse Thief* with Yul Bryner at the time, while the older Birkin was shooting the *Pied Piper* with David Puttnam. A division of the Yugoslav army was billeted in Vukovar, and the three of them were forced to stay in 'a horrible little bungeloid house', according to the brother Birkin. 'This was in the bar of a little village and Serge was getting a bit arseholed on whatever he was drinking. This money couldn't buy you anything, so he just set fire to it in front of whoever was there in the bar. And he was duly reported and nearly got thrown out as it was illegal, as it is in most countries. And then he repeated the gag on French television.'

As well as setting fire to money in bars and on TV, Serge's favourite party trick also involved toasting a tenner of someone else's money. 'I tried this out myself with David Puttnam's parents,' says Andrew, 'and his father was the senior bank manager at NatWest.' The trick involves taking a ten-pound note on loan from somebody at the table. 'And you'd pass it around and get everyone to remember the serial number. Very important that everyone remembers the number,' says Andrew. 'And then in front of everyone you'd set fire to it. But you're going to bring it back as the ashes fall on the plate, and you cover it with a napkin.' Suddenly Serge has forgotten the number. '*Ah shit, what was it again?* And of course there'd just be ashes. He'd pretend that he'd screwed up because he'd forgotten the magic word.' The *schadenfreudian* derivation of pleasure comes from the look on the victim's face when they suddenly realise their money is lying in cinders, and that's the end of the prank. 'The particular pleasure was seeing the look of horror on the face of someone like a bank manager. It was like burning a crucifix. So it turned into a bit of a party trick. There's a photograph in my book of him burning a note in a restaurant, with Jane and Charlotte looking on in horror.'*

Serge might have complained about paying too much tax, but he remained in Paris and paid them when others went offshore. He even seemed to take a perverse pleasure from it, and he made sure he was first in line. 'He disrespected people who didn't pay them,' says Jane Birkin. 'I remember Léo Ferré moving to Switzerland, and he thought that was most mediocre. And he used to run to the taxman who was in the adjacent street to Rue de Verneuil. He was always on time to pay his tax, and he thought, being an immigrant, one should always be extra diligent in paying one's tax on time. He was very straight that way, and he thought it was a terrible cheat not to do so. And he thought it was a terrible bore to go to Switzerland too, actually—he'd rather live in Paris and pay up. But he couldn't resist burning the banknote to show how much he paid in taxes, which was more than half. A sort of funny mixture or impertinence and truthfulness.'

In 1981, two years after the success of *Aux armes et cætera*, Gainsbourg gave the world a second instalment of reggae that didn't live up to its predecessor. 'Serge had done one reggae album, and it was such a success that he was tempted to do a second,' says Jane. 'Lerichomme said you must never repeat yourself. So he found himself repeating himself.'

'The second album was done in Nassau [in the Bahamas], and it was a little bit different,' remembers Sly Dunbar. 'The songs on the first one are better,

---

* Andrew Birkin, *Jane & Serge. A Family Album* (Taschen, 2013)

you know. The second one was done in Nassau, and the first one was done on the sly in Jamaica! It was good also, but the first one is the bomb!' The Revolutionaries were often at Compass Point Studios, making albums with artists signed to Island. 'We were like the house band—we did Joe Cocker's *Sheffield Steel* album, we did Grace Jones there, and we did some other singles and that. We'd go back every year to do Grace.'

Grace Jones's Compass Point trilogy rivals Bowie's Berlin trilogy and Tom Waits's Island trilogy as one of the best musical triptychs ever made (and all of these albums were released within the same decade, from 1977 to 1987). 'I remember talking to Chris Blackwell at the playback of the first session for *Warm Leatherette*, and he couldn't believe it,' says Sly. 'And then the next song was "Private Life", and when he heard it he said, My God, it's like magic—he couldn't believe the sound that came out of that session. You find that groove and it just happens in that moment, you cannot get it back—it's over!' That said, Grace Jones followed *Warm Leatherette* with *Nightclubbing*, an album that's even better than its predecessor. Serge would enjoy no such luck.

Mauvais nouvelles des étoiles came out in 1981. It was the album that followed the dissolution of his eleven-year love affair with Birkin. On the whole, like *Vu de l'extérieur*, it's an infantile affair, and it heralded another low ebb for its creator. *Gainsbarre*, the pugnacious brute of alter ego, shows up on 'Ecce homo'. He usually came out at night, often showing up for chat show appearances in place of his master—he was the foil Gainsbourg thought he needed, a scapegoat he could blame all of his misdemeanours on. Gainsbourg was the erudite songwriter, the sensitive soul, the genius; Gainsbarre, on the other hand, was bad news. *Mauvais nouvelles des étoiles* had a high-minded title, but most of the content therein was puerile.

The breaking-wind instrumental 'Evguénie Sokolov' referenced his own 1980 novella, a parabolic tale wherein he compares the production line of songs he writes to wild, tortured, rapturous farts. He spent years studying the alimentary canal like a doctor, but rather than helping people, he used it instead to write a self-referential book that very few people understood. That's not to say that there aren't moments in *Evguénie Sokolov* that aren't brilliant, or uproariously funny, it's just pitiable that someone so sophisticated could go to such great lengths to deliver something so utterly juvenile.

'Having been declared all-round champion,' he writes, 'I was nicknamed the Scent-Bottle, Whizz-Bang, the Gunner, the Artificer, the Artillery-man, Ding-Dong, the Trench-Mortar, the Gas-Bomb, the Bazooka, Big Bertha, Rocket, High Wind, the Blower, the Anesthetist, the Blow-Pipe, the Leak, All-Spice, the Goat, the Skunk, Pit-Gas, Gasogene, Wind in the Willows, Arsenic and Old Lace, Borgia, Zephyr, Sweet Violet, Windy-Windy, Mister Pong, Fart Minor, Stinker, Pipe-Line, Gas Container, Gun-Cotton, Arse Wind, Gas-Oil and the Big One, not to mention other terms I have now forgotten.'*

'He had a lot of different facets to his character, one of which was the ability to indulge in boyish or childlike activities, which is why I got on with him, because I can be the same,' says Andrew Birkin. 'He was also quite sophisticated on one level.'

The album's title was inspired by the work of one of his favourite artists, Paul Klee. Serge was an art collector on occasion, and one of his prize possessions was one of Klee's 1913 drawings, *Schlimme Botschaft von den Sternen* (German for *Bad Message From The Stars*). In his 1986 interview with Maubert, which is printed in full in *Gainsbourg à rebours*, he'd intimated that part of his love for Klee came from the fact that he too was a gifted musician who'd struggled to decide between painting and playing. 'Klee was a violinist of a professional calibre. His inspirations were comic, elegiac, tragic,' said Gainsbourg. 'It was Klee who said, Neither servant nor master, the artist is pure intermediary.'

Klee made endless philosophical pronouncements in his diaries, kept between 1897 and 1918, which his biographer Susanna Partch claims helped

---

* 'Déclaré champion toutes caté pas loin, et l'air gories l'on me surnomme l'Embaumeur, la Bombarde, le Canon—nier, l'Artificier, l'Artilleur, le Baroudeur, le Mortier, Bombe à gaz, Bazooka, Bertha, Roquette, la Bourrasque, le Souffleur, l'Anesthésiste, le Chalumeau, la Fuite, l'Odorant, le Bouc, Putois, Grisou, Gazogène, l'Éolien, la Voisin, Bor—gia, Zéphir, Violette, Vent-Vent, Mister Poum, Prout-Cadet, Cocotte, Gazoduc, Campingaz, Fulmicoton, Vent de cul, Gasoil, Perlouse, j'en oublie certainement.' Serge Gainsbourg, John and Doreen Weightman (translation), *Evguénie Sokolov* (TamTam Books, 1998)

cultivate 'the image he wished the public to have of him', and the self-mythologising of his own maverick tendencies was probably written with an eye on posterity too.[*] The Swiss-German expressionist had forged his own creative identity around the time of the First World War, and though not immune to the influence of cubism, his geometric shapes appear to defy uniformity, breaking free in order to convey the recalcitrant spirit of their creator. He did manage to hold down a good job at the Bauhaus during the 1920s, and he was paid well by Walter Gropius, but he found he couldn't serve two masters. Klee wasn't Jewish, but the Nazis decided he was nonetheless, and it would have appealed to Gainsbourg that Klee was blacklisted by Hitler as a degenerate artist. It's conjecture, but it's likely Klee's battle with his family over his ambitions to become an artist, and their desire for him to keep the family business alive and carry on fiddling, would have resonated too.

The album opens with an 'Overseas Telegram', which comes via the 'Post Office Anglais'. We can presume this one is about Jane, especially as she sang an unrecognisably schmaltzy version on her 1983 album *Baby Alone In Babylone*, a collection of songs written by Serge about their breakup. The reiteration of the word 'telegram' at the end of most lines could be construed as laziness, but Serge was clearly enamoured enough with the words to recycle them two years later.

The reiteration of lines comes again on 'Toi Mourir' and 'Mickey Maousse', which could be seen as an attempt to give the I Threes something to do, but given the childish content, it again suggests indolence on Serge's part. 'Mickey Maousse' brings the Walt Disney character into disrepute by bringing him into contact with Serge's squirting phallus. Bob Marley was supposed to be furious on his deathbed that his wife Rita (one of the I Threes) had been duped into singing such filth.

'Juif et dieu' stirs things up further: a thumb in the eye to his racist detractors, it points out that Einstein, Karl Marx, and—most germane in the context of the title—Jesus were all Jews. But the most indelible song on

---

[*] Susanna Partsch, *Paul Klee 1879–1940* (Taschen, 1990)

the album, and there aren't many, is the self-mythologising 'Ecce homo', in which Serge lays out the itinerancy and dingy habitats of Mr. Gainsbarre, the nightclubs and the boozing, and even the attire, with mentions of the denim and his three-day stubble. He'll tour TV studios in a crumpled shirt and army jacket, showing off his dark sunglasses, his lank hair, and his stubbly face, grubby and shiny with booze sweat.

'Ecce homo is the bad guy,' says Bruno Blum. 'Gainsbarre is the new Judas: *My name's Gainsbarre, you'll find me in bars.*' While Blum was making dub versions of the songs with Solgie Hamilton, he came across an unused verse hiding in one of the tracks. Time was against the mixing crew, and Solgie put his foot down and said Blum could do only one mix per track for the cash he was being paid. 'The holy grail of Gainsbourg is to find previously unreleased tracks, because of his songwriting, and I'm sitting there and none of the Jamaicans understand anything from his vocal, so they don't know it's a completely different lyric. Instead of Gainsbarre being born, it's Serge Gainsbourg dying. It's like the best poem he's ever written in his life. And so I tell Solgie we've got to mix this. And he's like, *What! Do what!? Bomboclaat! You never respect a deal! I knew it!*'

Serge rattles off an uncharacteristically mystical verse about wanting to 'drown in the liquid' and recoil backward like Arthur Rimbaud.[*] 'Ah man, great lyrics, some of the best work he's ever done. And I told Bambou about it, and she said she didn't know about the verse but that he had had a vision of the future, and, if he'd done that, he knew that one day someone would find it and release it after his death. This is all done on purpose.' The track with the extra verse is called 'Ecce homo et cætera'.

*

In 1980, the now reclusive writer and savant Yves Adrien published *NovöVision*, a book that helped to invent the 1980s in France. *Le Monde* was dazzled by the elegance of Adrien's writing, calling him the don of 'lightning phrases and

---

[*] 'Oh comme j'aimerais noyé dans le liquide / Descendre à reculons comme Arthur Rimbaud.'

luminous words, with a keen sense of aesthetics and layout. He plays with the printed press, with words which only take on meaning by their form, or their setting … behind his dandyism hides a vision of a cynical, lucid world.'[*] Twenty years later, *Les Inrocks* was still calling him 'the magi of the French language', and his presence is still keenly felt forty years after he retired and left the world his final offering. It's high praise, but he did arguably invent punk in 1973, and then got bored before everyone else caught up.

Adrien is still alive and contactable by post, but arranging something isn't easy. 'You could contact him, but he might say, *We can meet 3rd April 2021 at 17h25*, because he'd need to see if it was okay with the stars,' says Bertrand Burgalat, laughing. 'It's completely genuine with him, though, and he was a very important aesthete.' Gainsbourg certainly thought so. *NovöVision* arrived not long before Gainsbarre, with its mystical influence keenly absorbed by the French pop star. To be a true Novö, according to Adrien, you have to be a 'dissident of everything, including, and above all, yourself', and he urged readers to 'escape from yourself, cross the wall, invent a double on which you project your conflicts.'[†] 'I'll be your mirror,' says Adrien—the Novö is the slave to the reflection of oneself, the perfect Polaroid of yourself.

Jane left Serge the same year, driven away by his out-of-control drunken behaviour and violence, and moved in with the film director Jacques Doillon. Sat in an empty house, Serge saw this as his chance to reinvent himself without changing. The words of Adrien and the abandonment by Jane, taking the kids with her, created a perfect storm for Gainsbarre to come into existence. He became the perfect Polaroid of himself, an inverted devil or 'novömatik infrared'. *NovöVision* was one of the books spotted on his shelves by Marie-

[*] 'Yves Adrien a le don des phrases-éclairs et des mots lumineux, le sens de l'esthétique et de la mise en page. Il joue avec l'imprimerie, avec ces mots qui ne prennent un sens que par leur forme, ou leur place, et se gave de ponctuations. Derrière son dandysme se cache une vision du monde cynique, lucide.' Yves Adrien, *NovöVision: Les confessions d'un cobaye du siècle* (Éditions Les Humanoïdes Associés, 1980)

[†] 'Être dissident de tout, y compris, et surtout, de soi-même … C'est 'échapper de soi-même, passer le mur, s'inventer un double sur lequel on projette ses conflits.'

Dominique Lelièvre when she had a walk around Rue de Verneuil, and there's also an impressive life-size portrait of Gainsbourg by Stefan de Jaeger on the wall made up entirely of Polaroids.

Gainsbourg was a fan of Polaroid pictures, as was Bambou, who also had a smaller, less imposing portrait done by Jaeger. And then there were Gainsbourg's personal Polaroids, which he displayed backstage at his Casino de Paris residency in 1986, including photos of his lovers Birkin, Bambou, Bardot, Deneuve …

'Yeah, I met him on just the one occasion, at one of his concerts in Paris. We met backstage and it was really special,' says Russell Mael, who entered a Pullman Wagon of Gainsbourg's ephemera, with intimate photos pinned up in the dressing room and his favourite armchair from home sitting in the corner. 'We'd been invited to come back and say hello after the show. The show was really special—he was playing many nights at the venue, so he'd set up his dressing room. At the time, he was no longer with Jane Birkin, but he had Polaroids of her attached to the walls of his dressing room, and it was unique and odd because he was with his later companion, Bambou. It was strange and really cool … what you'd expect from him really.' I ask if they were naked Polaroids. 'Yeah, yeah,' he says bashfully. 'I left that part out.'

Gainsbourg could be reached sometimes if you caught him early enough in the day, before he started on the pastis, but once Serge started drinking, Gainsbarre would be summoned hence. 'I spent five years hanging out with him. He called me almost every day to go with him to drink,' admits Étienne Daho, laughing. Among the many things they would have talked about, Daho and Gainsbourg shared a devotion for the works of Francis Bacon—at least whilst they were still *compos mentis.*[*] 'It was very interesting, but only when we were together. Then the third person would come along, the person who appeared at the end of his life, Gainsbarre. It was a mask. And so he was very,

---

[*] Gainsbourg never met Bacon, although Jane bumped into him in the street in Paris when he had an exhibition at the Grand Palais in 1971, a huge honour for a living artist. She got Bacon to autograph a 100-franc note for Serge.

very different. I didn't like Gainsbarre very much but I liked Gainsbourg.' As Serge said himself, 'When Gainsbarre drinks, Gainsbourg leaves.'*

The chat shows beckoned, and the ante was upped with each appearance. Serge got what he wanted—at a price. *Audimat.* Everyone was talking about him. Jane remembers a time he had to go to Cannes on his own, because Philippe Lerichomme was with his children. It was unusual, she says, because Philippe was always with Serge: 'He was pounced upon by television people who were only too glad to give him a few drinks because then he'd be funnier, and then you'd have *audimat* when he'd say the most stupid things during the interview. He was plastered, and we were thinking, *Oh, no, why didn't someone stop him?* So he rang up Lerichomme afterward, saying, Did you see the television? Philippe said yes, because it'd been live. And you thought I was awful? Philippe said yes. So Serge complained, *Well, it's your fault, because you should have been with me!* He had a childish way, a petulance. Philippe always knew whether he should have one drink or two, but no more, and he used to run to be with Serge during the commercial breaks, so nobody had a chance to fill him up with more. He took care of him all the time. Serge wasn't like that at the beginning, of course.'

In 1986, Serge called singer Catherine Ringer a 'whore' on live TV. *Audimat.* Ringer had made some adult films with names like *Sexual Penetrations* and *Porno's Girls* before her husband-and-wife duo Les Rita Mitsouko took off. Her previous career was alluded to on a late-night Canal+ show *Mon Zénith à moi*, and Gainsbourg, who was sat next to her on the sofa, decided to take the moral high ground. The guy who wrote 'Je t'aime... moi non plus' and 'Lemon Incest' was suddenly speaking for the arbiters of decency, a hypocritical position from a contrary man who loved to shock but also harboured a deep-seated conservatism. Even the way he said it, 'Vous êtes une pute', was a peculiar mixture of the formal 'vous' and the immensely disrespectful 'pute' (whore).

'What do you want to know about that?' asked Ringer, defensively, when the *New York Times* brought it up in 2011. I requested an interview with

---

* 'Quand Gainsbarre se bourre, Gainsbourg se barre.'

Ringer for this book, but after some toing and froing of emails with her record company, her agent decided it would be a bad idea. 'I was surprised how he turned on me,' she told the *NYT*, 'but he was typically a kind of dirty guy, so I asked him how he could speak to me like that, considering I'd thought of him as a pretty dirty guy since I was a kid. But I wasn't angry with him because I knew he was always like that, wanting to be provocative. And I still love his music.' Les Rita Mitsouko would go on to cover 'L'hôtel particulier' on 1993's *Système D*, a sign perhaps that there were no hard feelings.

Ringer was prepared for a potential outburst, having, like the rest of the world, seen his exchange with Whitney Houston a few months earlier. If Ringer says she was surprised by how he turned on her, she appeared in control, eliciting the sympathy of the studio audience and making Gainsbourg look foolish in the process. While this confrontation isn't famous around the world, it's a key intergenerational TV moment for the French, where a woman in her twenties stands up to the increasingly artistically wavering grotesque sat next to her. It's a symbolic changing of the guard, though few people outside of France know about it. Which brings us to Houston. That incident took place on the TV show *Champs-Elysées*, hosted by the journalist Michel Drucker, in 1986.

'The discomfort when you watch some of his 1958 TV performances—that same edginess was kind of how he was when he was sober and he needed a drink in his later life, toward the end,' says George Simms. 'Bambou and I pulled up two chairs in her apartment to watch Serge on *Champs-Elysées*. The day before, Serge and the band went down to the studio and we pre-taped the song we were doing. We recorded our performance, and Serge was sober during the take. And after we finished, Whitney Houston got up to do a prerecorded track and sang "Saving All My Love For You". She did it for the sound people, and we were down the front, just inches from Whitney. She sang for real, and it was angelic, it was just unbelievable. She was still sober then.'

By the magic of television, the prerecorded performance was broadcast to the nation, and then Gainsbourg appeared on the sofa as if the two had been shot together in real time. 'They edited the clip so it looked like he'd just finished singing with the band. But during the taping, Bambou said to me, Look at him, he's sober, he wants a drink. And then he comes out live and she says, Look at him, he's smashed. And he was. And then he said it.'

'I want to fuck her.'

Those five words have become as synonymous with Gainsbourg as Jane Birkin and three-day-old stubble. Preceding this moment, Serge had kissed Houston's hand and told her, 'You are superb.' He then called her a genius. Drucker, sensing an incident brewing, attempted to intervene, which didn't sit well with Serge. 'You are not Reagan, I am not Gorbachev, so don't try, eh?' he snapped, slurring his words, followed by the immortal line. After the shock, the host—caught in a car-crash moment—tries to think on his feet while sitting in his comfy chair, but Serge reiterates the line in French, causing much mirth with an audience who are now prepared for it. It's a clip that has been shared far and wide, and for some it's all they know Serge Gainsbourg for.

'Most of the band were watching in the hotel room when he said that, and we were like, *Oh my God*,' says Gary Georgett, laughing. 'No matter how many times you watch it, it never gets any less cringeworthy. I knew it was a big scandal because it made the *International Herald Tribune*!'

'I was terrified to turn my head to the left and see what Bambou's reaction would be,' says George Simms. 'And I looked at Bambou and instead of looking hurt, she just grinned and said, Yeah, that's Serge …'

*

Gainsbourg worked on another record with Alain Chamfort in the early 80s, but this time things would turn ugly. Chamfort had had the idea to take Serge out of Paris to get him writing and keep him away from the nightclubs, so the plan was that they would work in Los Angeles instead. Gainsbourg soon discovered that LA had bars and nightclubs too. 'We were in LA for two months to write the new songs. He called Bambou to join us, but he wasn't really working. And he gave me a list of song titles, but there weren't any words: "Chasseur d'Ivoire", "Bambou", "Malaise en malaisie". After we'd been in LA for five or six weeks, the record company called me to ask about the recording. *No, I have no lyrics.* The president of the company came, and we arranged a meeting together. He said, Okay, Serge has to write, it's becoming too expensive.'

Two days later, Chamfort found Serge sitting in the bar closest to the studio, writing ten different lyrics on ten separate sheets. 'He was not serious, and we started fighting,' says the normally genial Chamfort. 'It was angry. He left the house that we rented together in LA. He left the studio. There was no discussion.' One of the lyrics he wrote for Chamfort, 'Souviens-toi de m'oublier', ended up as the title track on his new pal Catherine Deneuve's album.

Deneuve stepped out with Gainsbourg at a difficult time in his life, propping him up in various ways that look above the call of duty when viewed retrospectively. The actress described their relationship as somewhere between an 'ami' and a 'copain', which loosely translates as 'fuck buddy'. They had a hit together with the schmaltzy, Sabar-produced 'Dieu fumeur de havanes' ('God Smokes Havanas') in 1980, and then followed it up in '81 with an album that was always going to risk being forgettable with a title like *Souviens-toi de m'oublier*, although the opening track, 'Digital Delay', is a fascinating cut-and-shut using 'Ford Mustang' as the engine.

'He was very lavish and very generous,' says Jane, 'but it didn't mean he couldn't be perfectly mean, and by mean I mean that he couldn't resist a clever word. Once he had the idea that it would be funny to say that Catherine Deneuve was *neufs et d'occasion* or new and second hand—well for someone who saved your life practically,' she admonishes, as if Serge were standing right there in the room. 'She had him in her apartment when I left him, and she'd been an angel. And she was mortified.'

Meanwhile, Chamfort found himself in the unusual position of singing an album of material about Serge's other girlfriend. Was it strange, singing those songs on *Amour, année zéro*? *'Oui!* The whole album is about Bambou. And then there are tracks like "Malaise en Malaisie" where Bambou for him was an exotic inspiration, so almost all of the songs are about her and his relationship with her. He didn't write these songs thinking about me,' says Chamfort, laughing.

*

Mauvaises nouvelles des étoiles was a relative failure, but *Love On The Beat* in 1984 proved Gainsbourg was a French superstar set to last the distance. Making a second reggae album had proven to be a mistake, so, being the musical replicant that he was, he went looking for a different direction and a style to suck up and absorb.

'I love him,' says Guido Minsky of Acid Arab, 'but there are also a lot of things I hate about him too. He was really a junkie for success. When he heard that reggae was going to be big, he went to Jamaica and recorded a reggae album. When he heard this French band called Chagrin d'amour had had great success in France, he said, I want that exact sound on my album, which he did with *Love On The Beat*. And some French singers were recording in New York? *Okay, I want to record in New York.* That was the sad thing about him … he was an attention whore.'

Grégory Ken and Valli Kligerman had had a major breakthrough with their first album under the name Chagrin d'amour in 1982. Their self-titled debut sold three million copies and was the first French rap record, albeit one that sounds quaintly naïve and amateurish in retrospect. If Serge wasn't ready to make the plunge into hip-hop just yet, the sheeny American synth-funk they'd harnessed was too irresistible for him to pass up.

He'd also had his head turned by David Bowie—now a huge international pop singer—whose *Serious Moonlight* tour featured two of the musicians he'd end up hiring: saxophonist Stan Harrison and backing singer George Simms of the Simms Brothers. Bowie also had Frank Simms on his tour; Serge got Steve Simms, but he must have assumed he had both brothers from the Bowie tour, because he would mention it to his audiences with pride. 'I know that Serge was intoxicated by the idea of how Bowie had had such an incredible 1983, where he'd shattered all these records and had so much publicity and so on, and I think he relished that,' says George.

The plan had been to get Nile Rodgers to produce the next album, though he was busy in 1984, working with Madonna and INXS. One album Gainsbourg had grown particularly enamoured with was 1983's *Trash It Up* by Southside Johnny & The Jukes, which was produced by Rodgers with Billy Rush from the band listed as associate producer. When Rodgers said he was unavailable, enquiries were made to sound out his assistant.

Gainsbourg had recorded 'New York USA' in 1964 having never been to the Big Apple. His first trip to the States came in 1970, when he and Birkin flew to Chicago to promote 'Je t'aime... moi non plus', which peaked at no.58 in the *Billboard* charts. Two decades later, the world had opened up, and you could fly from Paris to New York in three and a half hours via Concorde. Serge took off for the new world—or New Jersey, to be precise—in search of new sounds. He and Philippe Lerichomme travelled to meet Billy Rush, who put together a demo, and they deliberated and dithered in the hotel as the guitarist sweated on their decision. White smoke poured out of the conclave eventually.

'Billy had a studio in his home in New Jersey, and he'd demoed a couple of songs to show them how they'd do it,' says Stan Harrison. 'Lerichomme and Gainsbourg went back to their hotel room to audition them. I don't think Billy knew whether they were going to go with him, because his approach was different to how it would have sounded had they got Nile. Somebody had to make the decision on whether or not to go with him, and I wonder how much that decision was based on what Philippe thought as opposed to what Serge thought.'

Love On The Beat is a return to form, and the title track is Sebastien Tellier's favourite Gainsbourg song: 'It's the embodiment of the Gainsbourg style, as far as I'm concerned. I believe that he wanted to make a song like this from the very beginning of his career; it's a culmination! It's such an intimate song, it feels like being in bed with him.' For a whole new generation who didn't know any better, this *was* the sound of Gainsbourg. The title track is a pervy Franglais pun on the vulgar 'bite' in French, a slang word for penis. The sound of sadomasochistic screaming can also be heard throughout. The indecency would have tickled naughty children, and so Gainsbourg became a kind of wayward avuncular figure, drunk and shocking and an embarrassment to the grown-ups, which made the relationship all the more transgressive and delicious.

'In '86, I was sixteen, and back then I really loathed him,' says Jean-Emmanuel DeLuxe. 'It was only later, when I worked with April March—who is Gainsbourg's finest interpreter in my opinion, by the way—that I began to reassess him. To me, he was just the annoying drunk uncle who concocted these outbursts on French TV. And his latest music offerings, for me, were really substandard. I think that Gainsbourg was dead artistically after *L'homme à la tête de chou*. I really hated Gainsbarre, and my prejudices were even reinforced when my friends forced me to watch him play live. It was really an awful moment, with a drunk and senile Gainsbarre butchering his classic songs.'

'When I was a kid, Gainsbourg was a bit scandalous, and he became very famous with his worst albums from the reggae period on,' says Bertrand Burgalat. 'He'd become very lazy with his music because he was a bit bitter, I think. From the reggae period on he was huge, and the back catalogue and the 60s stuff was very hard to find at that time. People really knew Gainsbarre, but they didn't know Gainsbourg.'

'Bertrand is one hundred percent right,' says Jean-Emmanuel. 'Universal in France were too busy exploiting Gainsbarre's legacy to really care about Gainsbourg's finest work. In 2009, the US label Light In The Attic gave *Melody Nelson* the great vinyl reissue treatment; before that, the major label had eschewed vinyl for CDs, and their CD reissues were poorly done with no detailed booklets, substandard visuals, and so on. I think Universal France finally realised that there was some money to be made after they saw what was happening worldwide.'

In 1984, funky synth-pop ruled the waves, and Serge had assembled a band of American musicians to do it authentically. The *causes célèbres* this time would be homosexuality and incest. In the song 'Kiss Me Hardy', Serge comes out of a Francis Bacon painting to make love to another man.* And in the chorus of 'I'm The Boy', he claims to enjoy invisibility, while in the verses he

---

* 'D'un tableau de Francis Bacon / Je suis sorti / Faire l'amour avec un autre homme …'

sinks into a demimonde of kinky sex and leather: 'Whore among whores / I sink into the mire / Where barbarians embrace and the angels bleed.'*

'One song I really love is "I'm The Boy",' says Stan Harrison. 'I always thought that was beautiful, and you know what's really interesting? That opening melody is taken from the solo bassoon from Stravinsky's *The Rite Of Spring*. And that line "I'm the boy that can enjoy invisibility" comes from *Ulysses*. I've been reading a lot of classics that I neglected when I was younger, and I'm in the middle of *Ulysses* and suddenly that sentence jumps out at me. I couldn't believe that line came from Joyce. That is so cool: you put Stravinsky and James Joyce together and you come up with this.'

It's easy to look at *Love On The Beat* now, with its feminized sleeve shot by William Klein and songs about homosexuality in the midst of the AIDS crisis, and dismiss it as Serge pushing buttons for attention. But a closer look reveals chansons that are more sensitively and empathetically written than one might have given him credit for. Whether this empathy comes from experience is unclear, but there's some evidence to suggest that, on the Kinsey scale, Serge would unlikely score zero. He admitted to a predilection for girls with bodies like 'little guys' in a wide ranging interview with *Liberation*'s Bayon in 1981.† Voluminous breasts intimidated him; he preferred smaller bosoms and women with figures like prepubescent teenage boys, or like the tableau of Saint Sebastien in the Louvre. During his affair with Brigitte Bardot he may have got his wish, and more than he bargained for, when he shared a one-night stand with the famous transsexual Marie France, according to her autobiography, *Elle était une fois*. France, one of the most famous it-girls of her day, was born a boy in Oran, Algeria, in 1946. She moved to Paris in the early 60s and became a singer, dancer, actress, and socialite. Metropolitan Paris was largely accepting of her as a woman during her 70s heyday, and in the mid-80s she had corrective surgery, which she wrote about touchingly and with humour

---

* 'Putain parmi les putes / J'enfonce dans la fange / Où s'étreignent les brutes et se saignent les anges.'

† 'J'aime qu'une fille soit comme un petit gars, ouais.' Bayon, *Serge Gainsbourg, mort ou vices* (Grasset, 1992)

in her autobiography, throwing in a Courbet reference for good measure: 'During the summer of 1985, I went to see a famous magician from London. With the tip of his magic wand, he made the origin of the world appear on my body. Then one morning I woke up in the pink: Goodbye shocking pink cabbage!'*

In 1967, France was invited to dance on *Dent de lait, dent de loup* by the choreographer Valérie Camille, as part of a one-off France Gall TV special with a titular duet penned especially for the show by Gainsbourg. 'Dent de lait, dent de loup' ('Milk Teeth, Wolf Teeth') is another song that didn't make it onto an album by either artist, a spiky mid-60s mod-inspired banger that may well have been influenced by ? & The Mysterians' '96 Tears', which was around at the time. Go and find the title sequence on YouTube if you've not had the pleasure, and if you have your glasses on you may even spot Marie France's dancing in silver boots in the background.

France was overwhelmed by all the celebrities hanging out at the studio: Claude François, Eddy Mitchell, Sylvie Vartan, Marianne Faithfull … and Serge Gainsbourg, who's looking right at her through a crowd of dancers. Over the course of filming, he keeps her in his sights, then sidles up and sings in her ear. He invites her to join him and some friends for post-production drinks. 'The prospect of being alone in an apartment with several men didn't fill me with confidence,' she writes, 'but Serge immediately reassured me by placing me under his tender protection. Relieved, I agreed to follow him.'†

They give the technicians the slip and go out dancing with her girlfriends and drink whiskey. Then they end up at his temporary abode at the University: 'We end up naked and entwined in his bachelor apartment in the Cité des Artistes with a black grand piano and an all-white bed. He found me pretty

---

* 'Pendant l'été 1985, j'allai voir un célèbre magicien de Londres. Du bout de sa baguette magique, il fit apparaître l'origine du monde sur mon corps. Un matin nouveau, je me réveillai dans une rose: Goodbye chou rose shocking!' Marie France, *Elle était une fois* (Cercles, 2003)

† 'La perspective d'être seule dans un appartement avec plusieurs hommes ne me mettait pas en confiance. Serge me rassura immédiatement en me plaçant sous sa tendre protection. Soulagée, j'acceptai de le suivre.' Marie France, *Elle était une fois* (Cercles, 2003)

and unique, he was sensual and passionate. I surrendered to his caresses, his kisses, his sweet nothings.'* Years later, Bambou would tell France that her fragility had overwhelmed him. Serge also apparently took pride in the fact that France was the only person he cheated on during his three months with Bardot. 'Knowing that I was a nice memory for him delights me,' she writes.†

Back to *Love On The Beat*, which concludes with 'Lemon Incest', a duet between father and daughter. This chanson set to an old Chopin tune with an electro underbelly includes lyrics like 'The love we will never make together is the most beautiful, the rarest, the most disturbing'.‡ On top of that, Serge and his daughter shot a video with the pair of them lying in a bed in an embrace and papa *sans chemise*. Charlotte was thirteen at the time, and the public was suitably shocked, but not enough to stop it getting to no.2 in the French charts.

It seems remarkable now, through the prism of modern sensibilities, that such an idea didn't end his career. It's one of the greatest moments of sheer audacity in pop, and as such, it could be argued that it also represents boundary pushing artistry. And yet we don't see it like that—certainly not in the twenty-first century, where preservation of the sanctity and safety of children is doctrinaire. 'Lemon Incest' is a double whammy: a terrible taboo, and the sublimation of his teenage daughter in public.

Sexual sublimation is a Freudian term, you'll probably be unsurprised to learn: it could relate to celibate priests ploughing all their psychic energy into Jesus Christ the Lord, or new members of Alcoholics Anonymous handing their will over to an unspecified higher power while avoiding sexual relationships in the early stages of recovery; or it could concern a fifty-eight-year-old pop singer exploring carnal fantasies about his teenage daughter in his art rather than carrying them out in reality. Or perhaps it's all an elaborate bluff to bring

---

* 'Nous finîmes nus, enlacés, dans sa garçonnière de la Cité des artistes au piano à queue noir et au lit tout blanc. Il me trouvait jolie et unique, il était sensuel, ardent. Je m'abandonnais à ses caresses, ses baisers, ses petits mots d'amour.'

† 'Savoir que j'ai été pour lui un joli souvenir me ravit.'

‡ 'L'amour que nous n' f'rons jamais ensemble est le plus beau le rare le plus troublant.'

dark deeds like these out into the open and fire up debate about something forbidden that gets habitually suppressed.

'I did a version of "Lemon Incest" on the first record [*Intoxicated Man*] and the lyrics are deliberately going to the edge of being not okay,' says Mick Harvey. 'But it's also expressing a very deep love. It's not the way I feel about thirteen-year-old girls or a daughter, but some people do, and obviously he had mixed feelings about that, and he expressed them. That's pretty bold, actually. It's better to do it that way and be honest about it than to, you know, do what Jimmy Savile did.'

'When he'd done "Lemon Incest" with Charlotte, he pulled her onto the television to do a few shows, and you felt that Charlotte didn't really want to be there,' says Birkin. 'She was very young and looked shy, and suddenly Serge looked as if he was pushing a bit. The tide turned for a little bit, not for long. But as the song shocked quite a few people, a sort of murmur went round.'

'I remember at the time he was crying about it on the television,' says Françoise Cactus of Stereo Total. 'He was clearly drunk, but he was crying because he felt misunderstood. People said this record was about fucking children or something, which was completely stupid.'

'I've had to talk about this many times, and I do ask myself—with something like "Lemon Incest", which I participated in—I don't think we would be able to do it again now,' says Charlotte Gainsbourg. 'But at the same time it's quite weird, because we live in a world that's so sexually oriented. We feel very prudish, but sexual references are everywhere. So, in a way, it's much more vulgar than it was in his day, but at the same time that doesn't mean anything in regard to provocation. So, yes, I think he would be described as misogynistic and disrespectful, but I find it so sad that those things couldn't happen, because I think we need that provocation. We need that disrespectfulness.'

Serge clearly didn't feel he'd got his fingers burnt enough, because two years later he made *Charlotte For Ever*, a film starring Charlotte Gainsbourg in the lead role with a soundtrack of songs recorded by her with her papa and Billy Rush producing. There's nothing quite as provocative on the soundtrack as 'Lemon Incest'. Charlotte goes through the motions up close to the microphone—singing higher than her natural register, like most of the Gainsbourg women—but there's a detachment and a sense she'd probably rather be back at boarding school, hanging out with her friends, than taking part in this awkward charade. Yet it's a dynamic that makes it all the more compelling. And, given who's singing, daddy hasn't stinted on the material.

He's also half-inched two of the melodies, as is his wont, from Russia with love. The title track is mesmeric, with an atmospheric hum and a top line stolen from a ballet by the Russian composer Aram Khachaturian. He taps into his heritage further, borrowing from the Soviet Jewish composer Matvey Blanter on the delectable 'Zéro pointé vers l'infini', combining klezmer with a sheeny 80s electro-funk to surprisingly gorgeous effect. It's a fascinating touchstone in the Gainsbourg canon for both father and daughter.

Twenty years elapsed between Charlotte's debut album and her 2006 follow-up, *5:55*. Her fourth album, 2017's *Rest*, is the moment where she wrests creative control, making *Charlotte For Ever*—an album of acquiesce—an interesting document of that journey and metamorphosis. Curiously, her first album is still unavailable on streaming services, though she has been playing 'Lemon Incest' and the title track live in recent years, signifying a reconciliation with a record she participated in under mild emotional duress more than thirty years ago.

The 1986 film *Charlotte For Ever* is more problematic. It's difficult to watch, and not just because his daughter appears naked in a scene as she dances in the bathroom mirror. The setting in a dingy apartment wastes the talents of cinematographer Willy Kurant, who declared himself out after this picture. It's visually beige, slow-paced, and the script is leaden with too many references, literary and personal.

'He was going way over the top with being clever in that film,' says Raechel Leigh Carter. 'The references were intrusive, and I found it a bit irritating.' Aside from the highfalutin Benjamin Constant quotes, there's also a plot that deliberately imitates life, or an alternative version of reality. Serge plays an alcoholic screenwriter who's trying to win back the trust of his daughter, who despises him for his promiscuity and the part she feels he had in her mother's death. Gainsbourg played on a tragic scenario Jane had imagined, after he'd bought her a grey convertible Porsche in real life in 1981. 'That's how his wife dies in *Charlotte For Ever*,' says Carter. Perhaps this was wish fulfilment on Serge's part. Carter believes the focus on *Charlotte For Ever* is often about Gainsbourg feelings for his daughter, when the film really concerns her feelings about him: 'It's not really about his love for Charlotte; in a way it's about her being jealous of him wanting other people. It is tricky thinking that he did these nude scenes, but it's not what people think it is. I don't think it's a good film … that's the worst part.'

It's an indulgent hour and a half that epitomises the self-importance and petulance of an alcoholic who is allowed to get away with it. The reviews were bad, but again Serge was let off the hook, protected by the age-old tradition enshrined in French culture where the right to make art, no matter how transgressive, is protected. Looking back, does Charlotte feel her father went too far?

'Not with that film,' she protests. 'It made me uncomfortable because it was when I was at an age where I didn't want to share that private thing we had on film. Because I made films of my own, which felt like my own world, so at the time I didn't want to share it with my father. Up to then it was as though I had a double identity, and suddenly making a film meant I had to be the way I was with him, to be his daughter again, with a film crew present.

'A lot of the scenes made me feel uncomfortable. I didn't want to be naked. We were very, very shy with each other, so sometimes he was able to say in public what he wouldn't say in front of me. So a lot of the love declarations, thank God he said these things to the press sometimes. He said things that make me realise now how much he loved me. Hearing them and seeing them now, because he's not here anymore, makes them very precious to me.'

13

DECLINE

YOU'RE UNDER ARREST (1987)

[
I can count my friends on the fingers of
the left hand of Django Reinhardt.*
]

If Serge Gainsbourg became the *éminence grise* of French pop, then in 1954 he was the pseudonymous Julien Grix. The provincial Sorel in Stendhal's *Le rouge et le noir* is complex and bookish but also smouldering, a Machiavellian character who seeks to advance himself through cunning and deception with the backdrop of the July Revolution to give the story some vim. And given that Serge was sent off to La Sarthe region with his mother for restorative air when he was gravely ill with tuberculous peritonitis during the Occupation—a condition that very nearly killed him—one imagines the following description of the protagonist from the novel must have jumped out at him when he read it at a similar age: 'He was a slim youth of eighteen or nineteen, weak in appearance, with irregular but delicate features and an aquiline nose … In his childhood, his extremely pensive air and marked pallor had given his father the idea that he would not live, or would live only to be a burden upon his family.'

And Juan Gris was a maverick 'synthetic cubist'—a style and description he presumably made up for himself, which allowed him more visual nuance in his pictures, abandoning the prescribed simplified palette of colours. He was housemates with Picasso in the early twentieth century, and he made the jump

---

* 'Je compte mes amis sur les doigts de la main gauche de Django Reinhardt.' Serge
Gainsbourg, *Pensées provocs et autres volutes* (Librairie Générale Française, 2007)

to painting full time in 1911, after making a living as a cartoon satirist for the papers *L'Assiette au Beurre* and *Le Rire*. Gris loved mixed media and *papier collé*, a collage technique where paper is mixed with other non-paper media, like paint. Gris took the ideas of Georges Braques and Picasso and made them fun. He used vivacious colours and media that had a deliberate ephemerality.

The idea of boobytrapping his own art so that it gradually destroyed itself would have appealed to an artist like Gainsbourg, who had his own destructive impulses. 'Juan Gris or Francis Picabia stuck bits of newspaper on their canvases,' he told Franck Maubert. 'They knew very well that twenty years down the line the paper would fade. Let's ask one of these lads: *Do you think that you're going to pass into posterity?* Answer: *And what has posterity ever done for me?*'*

We find enshrined in this response some of Gainsbourg's wisdom and some of Gainsbarre's cynicism, and perhaps because of the many years of success eluding him, it was a default response he'd reiterated as a defence mechanism when asked about his legacy. In one sense he was right that he, The Beatles, Beethoven, and Guesch Patti will all be forgotten as the earth melts into the sun seven and a half billion years from now, and some sooner than others. Serge Gainsbourg may have failed as a painter; as an artist, his popularity grows steadily year on year in death.

Self-destruction is a requisite for any *poète maudit*. It is written into the code of dark romanticism and decadence that one must immolate to be authentic and do one's best to die young. This self-debasement by great writers and artists, slowly killing themselves and succumbing to a glorious death, mostly went unseen in the nineteenth century, even if it was reported. These artists were only really known by way of their medium, whether that was the written word or their paintings. In the late twentieth century there were cameras and television and newspapers and paparazzi, and the decline of an artist slowly

---

* 'Comme plus tard Juan Gris ou Francis Picabia collaient du papier journal sur la toile. Ils savaient pertinemment que vingt ans plus tard le papier ne tiendrait pas. On a demandé a un de ces lascars: Pensez vous que vous allez passer a la postérité? Réponse: Et qu'est-ce que la postérité a fait pour moi?' Franck Maubert, *Gainsbourg à rebours* (Fayard, 2013)

scrawling a very public suicide note became less glamorous than it once was because less is left to the imagination.

'He and Jacques Wolfsohn used to drink,' says Bertrand Burgalat. 'Wolfsohn had these incredible dinners at his apartment, and Catherine Deneuve was their friend. One night, Gainsbourg was there and he hit his head on a table, drunk. Two days later, Wolfsohn reads in the newspaper: *Gainsbourg Attacked by Fascists*. He said, I can't stand it! Serge had a sense for publicity.'

'He was an alcoholic by the end—a full on unstoppable alcoholic,' says Baxter Dury, 'and it just looks grotesque. I guess it was justifiable somehow. People just let that stuff go. I know that character. You see that in any alcoholic character who has too much power to wield.'

Retrospectively, it seems strange that people didn't try to intervene, though perhaps they did. The first step in twelve-step recovery is admitting that you're powerless over alcohol and that your life has become unmanageable. Serge had a manager, so his life wasn't unmanageable in that sense, and he never got as far as taking the first step and admitting his powerlessness—or, if he did, he kept it to himself and quickly carried on the way he'd been going. 'I got clean in NA,' says Bruno Blum. 'In fact, we went to see Serge to say you can clean up—if we can do it, you can do it—but he was too far gone. He wouldn't even try.'

According to Gilles Verlant, Serge started psychoanalysis toward the end of his life, and he also consulted with alcohol specialists three weeks before his death, but by then he'd been in and out of hospital numerous times, was suffering with diabetes and respiratory problems, and was going blind. He'd told TV audiences following a risky operation in April 1989 that he'd gone under the knife because of a little thing he'd picked up in Africa while filming *Equateur*, but he'd actually had part of his liver removed because of cancer caused by cirrhosis. Five years earlier, Tony Frank had seen where things were headed, though he hadn't realised quite how quickly it would start to go wrong.

'I stopped seeing him after the Casino de Paris,' says the photographer, who did a pre-show rehearsal in 1985 and then never saw Serge again. 'I didn't have a contract with him, and I couldn't bring myself to go to the first night of the show. And maybe at that point I started to work with Johnny Hallyday more.' Later, he ran into Bambou, who told him Serge had some news for him. 'What I regret is that I didn't see Gainsbourg at the end of his life. Bambou told me Gainsbourg had said, "What's with Tony? He left to go on tour with Johnny Hallyday. I'm sure we won't see him again." The last time I shot him he'd just started to be so drunk. Bad drinking. He was fat from the drinking— it was showing in his face. I'd say to him, Can you just turn a bit more so your face is more in the shadow? I told him to do things that I used to tell him to do and he'd say, *What? What? What?!* He was completely out of his mind. He said himself, Now I'm Gainsbarre. When he started to be Gainsbarre I stopped working with him, because it wasn't easy. His alcoholism was really depressing. But I really regretted it a few years later because I didn't know he was so close to death. If I'd known that, I would have tried to see him.'

George Simms remembers some stories he'd hear from out and about in Paris, where Serge's behaviour was tolerated by everyone because of who he was. 'The provocateur came out in spaces, either onstage or even going out to a restaurant with his band in tow. He was in charge, and he knew it. He didn't have to feed on that to survive, but he just enjoyed the humour of it, and he knew that he would hold court wherever he was, and he could say anything he wanted. God, he was always onstage when there was a reasonably sized audience around him.' George recalls a night when the pair of them went to a tiny brasserie opposite Rue de Verneuil. 'After a few minutes a couple walks in in front of us, and Serge screams out in a voice that everyone can hear, with no attempt to modulate his voice, It is the minister of culture and his ugly wife! And, sure enough, it was Jack Lang and his wife who were coming to sit and have dinner. They didn't say anything.

'After we were finished, he looked at the oil painting that was on the wall between us—it was an early nineteenth century still life with a vase and flowers and leaves. He said, Look at this, it's disgusting. So he stood up, took his lit cigarette, and held it against the canvas for twenty-five seconds. Of course, all the waiters were looking, and the owner is standing there with a grin on his face and his arms crossed, and Serge finally took the cigarette from the canvas and there's not one speck of damage. So he put the cigarette in his mouth, leaned over to the portrait with the glowering ember of the cigarette touching the canvas, and he kept sucking in air until it finally burned a hole in the canvas. And then we sat down, ate dessert, finished our drinks, and left.'

Simms says the owner was probably secretly delighted that Gainsbourg had burned a hole in his painting. 'Another night he stood up on a chair to grab a bottle off the shelf that was about a foot and a half from the ceiling of the restaurant we were in. There were all these ancient bottles of wine and Cognac, so he grabbed this bottle of 1896 Armagnac and put it in his briefcase and went on eating. Of course, everyone was looking—the waiters, the owner, and so on—and of course at the end of the night they put it on his bill. And for the next couple of weeks on the tour bus, when most of the band would be asleep, or Stan and Serge were playing chess, Serge would grab it and pass it around, and we'd drink this 1896 Armagnac right out of the bottle and put it back, and then do it again the next night.'

Touring was a civilised affair, according to members of the band. Serge travelled on the bus with his entourage rather than being driven separately in a car—a move that endeared him to his musicians. 'I'm not antisocial at all,' says Stan Harrison, 'but I do seem to require time where I'm not with people. And if I'm travelling with people six days a week, and then being with them onstage, sometimes I need a break. So we'd be on these long bus rides, and I'd be sitting on the seat turned to the window reading a book, carving out my own personal space. And Serge walked up to me at some point and he said to me, You read so much, when do you have time to think? I thought that was the greatest line.'

Bon mots could just as easily turn to *mots laids* when Gainsbarre showed up. 'He loved getting reactions and he loved offending,' says backing singer Curtis King Jr. 'I'll tell you one thing that happened: we were in a hotel restaurant, and he was speaking to this woman in French. And we were like, *Okay, Serge.* We could tell he was offending her, and she had been pleased to see him. Serge would do what Serge would do. He was saying something in French and she didn't look very pleased, so I asked him about it: Serge, what are you saying? He said, I'm telling her she's ugly. He said he loved doing that kind of stuff, to see what reaction he'd get back from someone. It wasn't out of meanness—he just enjoyed seeing people's reactions. I don't think he was a mean guy, I think he was a curious guy.'

In 1985, Gainsbourg toured like he'd never toured before. The band played a five-week residency at the Casino de Paris, six nights a week with one day off, with an extra week added due to popular demand. Their tour through France, Switzerland, and Belgium was just as rigorous, and Serge stood up to the punishment, creating a rapport with his musicians that none of them would forget. They all talk about how close knit the group became, and are replete with stories of Serge's generosity, as well as his mealtime madness.

'He would always remember people's birthdays,' says drummer Tony 'Thunder' Smith, who also played for many years with Lou Reed. 'It was uncanny, because he'd come up to you and say, Today is your birthday, Tony. The thing about Serge and Lou is that their bands were really their families. Serge and Lou would invite the entire group to everything, whether it was boring or it was fun, and if one of the family didn't attend, they'd be insulted, which was interesting.'

'You know what was really remarkable? I don't think any of us knew who he was,' says Stan Harrison. 'And as we discovered who he was, it became more remarkable that we were actually doing this. I consider him to be one of my favourite people I've ever worked with, and I had no idea who I was signing on with when I joined the band.'

With Serge, Paris opened up like an exquisite flower. 'One night we are at this very exclusive club with every major star in France in that club, and he said, *Tony, now you will always be recognised at this club. You don't have to come with me to the club, you can come to the club and they will know who you are. Yeah, yeah, it's sorted.* It was incredible, really incredible.'

'We went to a restaurant—I think it was the Bofinger—and we were treated like kings!' says Stan. 'I went there with a girlfriend or maybe another person in the band later in the week, and it was as if we didn't exist.'

After touring France, the band went their separate ways. They then reassembled three years later, with the core of the same group performing seven nights at the Zenith in March 1988. Gainsbourg had visibly gone downhill physically in that time. He could maintain focus, and he'd charge himself up with his own adrenalin, but health problems seemed to be upon him, with frequent trips to hospital for his heart and liver just around the corner. 'Between the Casino de Paris and the Zenith there was a huge difference in him,' says Gary Georgett. 'It was kind of scary, seeing how someone can go down that road.' Tony says he'd noticed it too, but praised his resilience: 'The funny thing about Serge was that he was always energetic, no matter if he was feeling bad or not. You'd never know he was ill. You'd never know anything—I mean, he was smoking all the time.'

Charlotte says that playing shows still took a lot out of her father, especially as someone who'd suffered for so long with stage fright. 'Even the last one was still a real trauma, and physically it was very demanding. He was very excited, and he wanted to do it, but it cost him a lot.'

Serge always managed to raise his game when the curtain went up. Curtis King Jr., who'd just come off tour with Duran Duran, recalls the moment playing at the Casino de Paris where he suddenly realised Gainsbourg's generational appeal swept right across the board in his homeland: 'We hadn't rehearsed with the pyrotechnics, so that was one big surprise. I heard these blasts going off behind me and could feel the heat, so I'm glad I was able to keep my composure. And secondly, I looked out into the crowd and it was like being at a Duran Duran concert. Serge came on after all the explosions, and I could see families out there, but I could also see these young girls screaming. Serge walked over to me when I finished my rap and whispered in my ear: *You see, here in France, I am something else.*'

*

Perhaps the biggest contrast between *Love On The Beat* and *You're Under Arrest* is the cover art, which is illustrative of how quickly the singer had physically diminished in the space of three years. If Gainsbourg was a hopeless dipsomaniac in 1984, he still had the last vestiges of a vanity streak. He'd been photographed blowing smoke rings done up in drag by his friend William

Klein. In order to decrease the valises under his eyes, he forewent alcohol for days ahead of the shoot in the hope that he would appear more glamorous. He had no such worries for *You're Under Arrest*, which features portrait and profile mugshots of a dishevelled scallywag with cuts to his nose and forehead, denim prison garb worn open at the neck. Suffering from acute neuralgia and living in the groggy hinterland where hangovers and benders become one and the same, it still didn't deter him from pursuing his favourite theme and indulging his Lolita complex one last time on record.

You're Under Arrest is another concept album about a relationship between an older man and a younger girl, this time set in the United States, which has defined statutory rape laws, unlike France. Samantha is a drug user, and Serge is arrested by two police officers while he's trying to locate her somewhere in the Bronx. It's unclear if the arrest is drug related, of a sexual nature, or if he's been charged with namedropping Bronski Beat in a song in an incongruous way because of a tortured Bronski / Bronx pun.*

The sleeve of *You're Under Arrest* features the words *détournements de mineures* next to Gainsbourg's mugshot, a clue that he's been charged with being a dirty old man. In New York, you can be banged up for having consensual sex with anyone under the age of seventeen. When I interviewed the *last chanteuse*, Anne Pigalle, in 2019, she said a curious thing that gave me pause for thought: 'I don't think the English are too into the idea of an older man with a younger girl.' I didn't follow up what seemed like an offhand remark at the time, but, as it had been uttered by a French woman, it did make me wonder about age mixing and our differing attitudes to intergenerational sex across the Channel.

Paul McCartney singing 'She was just seventeen / You know what I mean' in 1963, when he was twenty-one, seems acceptable enough; Ringo Starr singing 'You're sixteen, you're beautiful, and you're mine' in 1974, when he was thirty-four, is—to modern ears—more suspect. Whether it was considered

---

* Jimmy Somerville had been covering 'Comment te dire adieu' in his live sets, an old Patsy Cline number Françoise Hardy had made her own, which Serge wrote the French words for. Flattery had ensured Somerville was dragged into the Gainsbourgian universe like Orson Welles in *Superman* #62 or some other weird comic book cameo.

within the bounds of decency at the time, it's hard to say, although it did reach no.4 in the charts. Fast forward ten years, and Bill Wyman's much publicised relationship with the teenager Mandy Smith brought as much prurience as opprobrium from the UK tabloid press.

It's important to note that Gainsbourg's public relationships with younger women were never illegal, as Wyman's relationship with Smith was when it began (even if the age gap between him and Bambou was similarly immense). The scenarios he explored time and again were borderline, though, and it's hard to imagine British audiences being so lenient in allowing him to keep indulging those fantasies in his music, especially after a scandal like the one that had engulfed him with 'Lemon Incest'. We've certainly become more sensitive to lyrical content than we were: the title 'Barely Legal' by The Strokes raised no objections that I can remember in 2001, but there were plenty of concerns about the consensual grey areas of Robin Thicke's 'Blurred Lines' in 2013.

As I write this, it appears France is waking up to historic abuse in a way that it has hitherto been backwards in addressing. When the #MeToo movement began to spread virally online in 2017, following mounting allegations against Harvey Weinstein, France was considered slow to react, with hostility coming from Catherine Deneuve and radio host Brigitte Lahaie (whose earlier sex films Alain Gorageur had soundtracked). France did have its own hashtag, #BalanceTonPorc, or *denounce your pig*, though, and a gulf in thought between high society and the proletariat appears to be widening.

The Polish-French auteur Roman Polanski has been wanted in the USA for the statutory rape of a thirteen-year-old girl since 1977, but that didn't stop the French film industry awarding him best director at the 45th César Awards in February 2020. There were protests before, some rioting after, and the actress Adèle Haenel walked out of the ceremony, followed by two more attendees.

In another case that perhaps even better illustrates changing attitudes in France, the writer Gabriel Matzneff is finally the subject of a criminal investigation following decades of documenting his own paedophilia. Matzneff has remained a protected species since the 1960s, but all of that changed when

RELAX BABY BE COOL

one of his former lovers published her own account of their relationship called *Le Consentement (Consent)* in 2020. Vanessa Springora, head of the Juilliard publishing house, claims she was groomed at fourteen when Matzneff was fifty, and it was a book she says she felt forced to write after he was awarded the Renaudot literary prize in 2013. Matzneff's accounts of sex tourism in the Philippines with boys as young as eight hadn't seemed to unduly upset anyone, and he won the patronage of President François Mitterrand, as well as Yves Saint Laurent and his partner Pierre Bergé.

Matzneff's behaviour was called out once in 1990, by the Canadian writer Denise Bombardier, who challenged him on the legendary literary discussion programme *Apostrophe*, expressing the feeling that she must be from another planet listening to him talk about the 'seduction' of minors and nobody raising objections to it. The literary cognoscenti closed ranks in favour of their star writer. 'There seems to be an old weird culture that protects art there, so that if you can make delicate pastry or you can write like Serge then you can more or less do whatever the fuck you like,' says Baxter Dury, whose records do very well in France.

That may all be changing now, though. At the time of writing, Matzneff's three publishers have dropped him, a prestigious stipend paid by the government—which he'd received for half a century—has been revoked by the Ministry of Culture, his column in *Le Point* has been taken away, and he's facing ruin. Matzneff has had no need to hide in plain sight, though the anger over this story indicates a culture that is changing. A *New York Times* headline in February 2020 declared, 'A Pedophile Writer Is On Trial. So Are The French Elites.'

Matzneff is an extreme case, and while he wrote about his own predatory sexual behaviour, Gainsbourg explored grey areas in his art without acting upon them, to the best of our knowledge. There's humour in song titles like 'Suck Baby Suck' and 'Five Easy Pisseuses', too, but if French people were laughing about 'little white socks' and coercing post-pubescents into fellatio in 1987, they're not laughing now. Changing attitudes could endanger his legacy if public opinion hardens further.

On his Red Right Hand blog, Nick Cave recently responded to a fan asking about problematic historical lyrics, 'What songwriter could have predicted thirty years ago that the future would lose its sense of humour, its sense of playfulness, its sense of context, nuance and irony, and fall into the hands of a perpetually pissed off coterie of pearl-clutchers? How were we to know?'

And then there's art, increasingly battling against a culture of censorship. 'In many families there are bad uncles,' says Stereo Total's French singer Françoise Cactus. 'Many of the girls I know have had some shit happen in their youths—it's very common. But if an artist like Balthus makes a painting then it's completely taboo. This is something I can't appreciate. They're punishing the wrong people!' Françoise fell foul of the arbiters of public decency herself when she made a large crochet puppet called Wollita for an exhibition in Berlin in 2005. The giant puppet appears to be naked, with crocheted nipples and a flat chest, causing people to jump to all sorts of weird conclusions.

'The papers were screaming *Scandal*, *Puppet porno!*, *Child pornography!* and all this stuff. This is completely ridiculous, but there was a lot of trouble. I had a neo-Nazi urinate on the building and try to destroy everything. I was shut down, and children's charities came and I had to explain myself. It was a puppet!' Françoise was told if she wanted the exhibition to continue, the puppet would need a plaque next to it explaining the intentions of the piece. 'Now when you have an exhibition you have to explain to the idiots what they have to think about it all.'

Serge brought another of his versions of *Lolita* to the screen in 1990, the year before he died. If it's a better film than *Charlotte For Ever*, Serge's vision was sagging like the tired bags under his eyes. *Stan The Flasher* is just over an hour long, a mercifully short end to a so-so film career. His friend Claude Berri is convincing as the beleaguered child molester Stan; his wife is played by Aurore Clément, who'd made her acting debut as France Horn, the Jewish girl that Vichy collaborator Lucien is obsessed with in the 1974 *mode rétro* picture *Lacombe, Lucien*. Élodie Bouchez, a celebrated actor married to Daft Punk's Thomas Bangalter, is introduced to the world in this film as the object of Stan's desires. Apparently, Gainsbourg offered Élodie a pop career, but she demurred.

Raechel Leigh Carter is a staunch defender of the film's merits. '*Stan The Flasher* is an absolutely heartbreaking film,' she says. 'I just feel so sorry for him. I know not everyone would because he's a bit of a perv who touches that young girl. I just feel so sorry for him because he's so desperate. And when you see the description Serge gave to Stan, about him being a desperate poet, and misunderstood, and a misogynist who is dissatisfied with his body and being led into temptation and stuff like that, you just think, *It's Gainsbourg, isn't it?* Except Gainsbourg wasn't a paedophile—although some people think he was. He was clearly a desperately unhappy person and a bit misogynistic and misanthropic and down on his physicality and looking for love.'

The name Stan, which was also the name of Gainsbourg's character in *Charlotte For Ever*, may have come from a familiar source. 'We were in Paris, rehearsing *You're Under Arrest*, and then we took a break,' says sax maestro Stan Harrison, 'and he walks up to me and says, *I have this idea for a movie I'm going to make. It's about a guy who walks around with a trench coat and you only see him from the back, and in the end he falls down and he dies, and when he falls on the ground you can see his thing is really small. I'm going to name it after you, I'm going to call it Stan The Flasher.* I thought, *Oh, I love this story, thank you … I think. But that's never gonna happen.* And the next thing I know, there's a film called *Stan The Flasher* that he made, that he named after me. As weird as it is, I'm flattered to be a part of Serge Gainsbourg's history in that way.'

Gary Georgett flew back to Paris to record the soundtrack for the film, which is mostly made up of sparse keyboard tracks with a metronomic pulse. 'I spent all day with him, and then I go home to relax, turn on the TV, and there he is. They were opening up the Musee D'Orsay, and he was going through the paintings, and he came across one which was by one of Impressionists, I forget which. He said, *This is shit!* and he spat on the ground.'

*

You're Under Arrest attempts what Serge didn't quite have the wherewithal to try with *Love On The Beat*: rap. Chagrin d'amour had made a very French-sounding rap-funk record in 1982, whereas Serge waited until there was an

African American in the band before attempting it. The fact that Curtis King Jr. hadn't rapped in his life was neither here nor there. Gainsbourg was creating a facsimile of how hip-hop sounded in 1987 to the ears of a fifty-eight-year-old Frenchman, and he required a black American man to make it authentic. It wasn't an uncommon misapprehension, given that white rappers like The Beastie Boys were viewed with suspicion initially, and white MCs weren't really taken seriously until Eminem came along. Curtis's wife at the time, Brenda White King, was also a backing singer, though she wasn't asked or required to rap. (Only true hip-hop heads would have known about pioneering MCs like Roxanne Shanté and The Real Roxanne.)

'I call myself a jack of all trades, and being a backing singer calls for you to vocally be a chameleon,' says Curtis, on the phone from New Jersey. 'So, having been that guy, I said, *Okay, he wants me to rap*. As much as I didn't like rap, I started listening to it and developed a character.' Those lyrics—'You're under arrest / 'Cos you're the best / Slippety slam bah-boom bam …'—sound like a cipher. 'I came up with all that,' says Curtis, proudly. 'He really wanted me to be wild. I grew up in that whole era and the rap scene, so I just drew from that. I was just summoning the rappers from the street.'

Perhaps the most obvious thing to point out here is that you don't ordinarily get collared by the old bill for being 'the best'—it's the stuff of nursery rhymes from the 'Rapper's Delight' school of Learian nonsense, but that's mainly down to Serge's undisciplined grasp of English. There are also some stuttering 'G-G-G-G-Gainsbourg's thrown in, which sound as though they're performed in one take by King Jr. rather than by a sampler or a scratched record, which was how it was supposed to be done at the time. 'That was just me!' says Curtis, laughing. 'He kept saying, *Do more*, and each time I was just getting more creative.'

There's something gratifyingly quaint about what many see as a misstep. Serge certainly had enough confidence in his own talents to believe he could subsume any musical ideas old or new and bring them into his own creative domain, and he almost pulled it off. Anyone scoffing clearly has a short memory. This was an attempt at counterfeiting a commodified version of New

York hip-hop, but Serge had actually been rapping for years. 'You know what, he was a rapper,' says Curtis. 'He was nothing but a rapper in my view. From years ago, from the 60s. He always had this speaking rap thing going on.'

His inimitable Gallicised *sprechgesang* had become his most recognisable leitmotif from 'Manon' on, always with a burning Gitanes in hand. Serge would think like a hip-hop producer, purloining from the classical greats. 'Lemon Incest' took Chopin's 'Tristesse' and transposed it over a disco beat; 'Jane B' bastardised Prelude 28 and laid it over a cool jazz-rock shuffle. And as previously mentioned, sampling African musicians and trying to pass it off as his own demonstrated a very hip-hop kind of sensibility. So to suggest the title track from *You're Under Arrest* was a stab at what used to be called 'urban contemporary' would be wide of the mark; it was more the valediction of a career in experimentation by a proto-hip-hop master.

The emergence of hip-hop represented an important shift in youth culture, and Serge saw the anti-drugs bandwagon as another way of reaching out to *les mineurs*. Pop stars warning children about the perils of drugs—sometimes when they were on drugs—was prevalent in the 80s, and Gainsbourg had first-hand experience to draw upon from home. Bambou had kicked heroin by the time of *You're Under Arrest* and before the birth of Lulu, telling *Les Inrocks*: 'Lulu was born a week premature and was seven and a half pounds and in good health. The media wasn't happy that I didn't deliver an addicted baby. So we only got on the third page of *France-Soir*, which Serge was mad about. He said to me, When there's bad news they fuck us on the front page; when there's good news they fuck us on the third page.'*

Had she not been on drugs when they met then, she admits, the chances that they would have stayed together would have been slim. Both were suffering, with Serge disconsolate after shattering the image of the ostensible dream couple and losing the love of his life because of his behaviour. 'He knew

---

* 'Et Lulu est né à 8 mois et 3 semaines, 3kg 400, en pleine santé. Les médias n'ont pas été contents que je ne fasse pas un bébé accro. On s'est donc retrouvés seulement à la troisième page de France-Soir, Serge était fou furieux. Il me disait, Quand il y a des mauvaises nouvelles, ils nous foutent à la une, et quand il y en a des bonnes, ils nous foutent à la troisième page.'

he'd screwed up,' Bambou also told *Les Inrockutibles*, in a wide-ranging article that was published in April 2001. 'I met a broken man who didn't understand what was happening to him. He was looking for someone who'd take care of him, someone who understood him without needing to speak, who wasn't jealous and who tried to help him. Like he was helping me. The first thing he said to me after our first meeting was, Damn, the two of us are on the same wavelength. Afterwards, we just didn't leave each other.'* Bambou went on to say that she probably wouldn't have stuck around had she not been on drugs. She'd catch Gainsbourg crying every day and he'd wink at her and try to assure her: 'Don't worry, it's crocodile tears'. She knew he was a wounded man who continued to love Jane, irrespective of the fact they were now together.

'I would sit with him sometimes and he would say how he was really heartbroken over the love of his life, which was Jane Birkin,' says Curtis King Jr. 'He spoke about that almost daily. He really still loved her, he said. He loved Bambou, but he loved Jane. Some things just never change in your life.'

On *You're Under Arrest*, Serge decided to wage his own war on drugs. 'Aux enfants de la chance' is a moralistic plea to children everywhere to 'Just Say No'. Punters would hear it at the local PMU cafe as they bought another packet of Gauloises and dropped a hundred francs on a thoroughbred *cheval de course*. There's no doubt that Gainsbourg felt he was doing the public a service with this chanson—incidentally named after a bar his father used to play piano in—though whether he felt like a hypocrite as an alcoholic who hit a bottle of pastis—his drug of choice—every day at 11am, it's hard to say.

I would have loved to have talked to Bambou. She proved elusive and gives very few interviews, save for that moving, insightful Q&A in *Les Inrocks* from 2001. Their son Lulu is impossible to contact, too, and I tried various sources, and even resorted to dropping him a DM via Instagram on the advice

---

* 'Il savait qu'il avait déconné. J'ai rencontré un homme blessé qui ne comprenait pas ce qui lui arrivait. Il cherchait quelqu'un qui prenne soin de lui, qui le comprenne sans qu'on ait besoin de parler, qui ne soit pas jaloux, qui soit là pour l'aider. Comme lui m'aidait. La première chose qu'il m'ait dite après cette première rencontre, c'est, Putain, tous les deux on est sur la même longueur. Après, on ne s'est pas quittés.'

of Philippe HeNGo, a full-time Gainsbourg impersonator from Rouen. To no avail. To my mind, Lulu Gainsbourg is the Boo Radley figure of this book, a reclusive character who people can speculate upon and say unpleasant things about.

'I took pictures of Lulu,' says Tony Frank. 'He was awful. He's shy, too, but he's shy in a way I don't like. When I told him to stay still, he was making faces and everything. I couldn't take pictures. Bambou lives in her own house. I don't know what she's doing now, or how she lives.'

'Marc Lavoine and I wrote an album for Bambou about ten years ago, and then she decided she didn't want to do it,' says Bertrand Burgalat. 'Lulu doesn't have much talent and the other children don't have either, but he tried to look like Johnny Depp, and he did a stupid album'—*From Gainsbourg To Lulu* from 2011, recorded by Gainsbourg Jr. with Depp, Vanessa Paradis, Scarlett Johansson, Rufus Wainwright, and Iggy Pop, received a critical mauling when it came out. 'It was a tribute to Serge, with some of Lulu's songs, and some of Serge's songs, but a lot of people didn't take it like that,' says Gary Georgett, who played on a couple of tracks. 'They thought he was trying to capitalise on his name.'

'In France we now have this Royal Family,' says Burgalat. 'The Gainsbourgs are like the Kennedys now. That's our Royal Family. But it's always Lou Doillon and Charlotte Gainsbourg—the other children are completely rejected, and nobody talks about them.' The other children from his second marriage to Françoise-Antoinette Pancrazzi, Natacha and Paul, were also impossible to contact.

And so Jane continues to carry the torch, a responsibility she says she sometimes feels awkward about, given that she wasn't with Serge when he died. It's easy to see that the love she has for him remains undiminished, though. 'What the English probably don't know was that I was in England the day he died. I flew straight to CDG, and my luggage was still going round. I thought perhaps it wasn't true—perhaps when Jacqueline called my mother and then my mother called me, it was a mad panic, and I'd got the first flight back on a Sunday morning for nothing. And for a second I thought, *Everyone's moving in a normal way picking up their suitcases, therefore it can't be true.* And then I saw Lerichomme waiting for me, and then I thought, *Merde.*'

A Birkin solo show that had been planned for the Casino de Paris became 'a sort of mass', as Jane describes it. Taxi drivers were telling her they were coming to pay tribute. The posters in the street were changed from a picture of her legs in tennis shoes—'which suddenly looked like his feet and his tennis shoes'—to the drawing of the cover of *Amours des feintes*. He'd written the album for her, and he'd done a doodle on the cover lying in hospital in 1990. It was the last album of songs he wrote.

'I remember the last album he did with Jane Birkin, and to be quite frank I was pretty much co-writing the damn thing. He didn't have much written,' says Alan Parker. 'He came across to my studio in Woldingham. We had all the backing singers and all that, but he put Jane's voice on it back in Paris.'

Parker became close to Serge in his final years, and he'd stay with him and his wife at their farm while they worked on music together. Alan was my final interview, and I'd just discovered that the last collection of songs Serge ever wrote and recorded were done just up the hill from the cottage in which I type this, a mere five-minute drive in the car. It's a real 'and did those feet in ancient time …' moment in the creation of this book. I went to Paris in search of Serge in 2013 (and for love, let's not forget that), and back in Blighty I found the last piece of his history on my doorstep in Nowheresville, Surrey.

Anyway, back to Alan: 'I remember on the last album with Jane, he set out a minute of piano, it was all plinky-plonky, and he said, I want some sophisticated chords on this, Alan.' Alan laughs. 'So you sort of have to put it together for him, if you know what I mean.'

Up at Garage Studios with Parker, Serge sometimes alluded to an awareness that his dying day wasn't far away. 'In a bizarre sort of way, on the last couple of albums I worked with him on, I got quite close to him as a friend. He'd say, I know what I'm doing. What the hell? He wouldn't dream of stopping or cutting anything out. He refused to: *If I'm going to die, I'm going to die.*'

'When I used to say to him to stop because he might live longer, he'd say, God, what boring years they'd be—and perhaps for him that was true. To die at sixty-two is really so young,' says Jane, adding, 'I didn't know who I was for about twenty years. I was so plastered with Serge. And after Serge. It's weird not to be able to do that anymore, but that was our life.'

Birkin took to the stage on May 18 1991 at the Casino de Paris, having cancelled most of the material she had intended to do. 'And Philippe said I must sing all the songs on the last album, because that was his last work. And he said I should go onstage and sing "L'aquoiboniste" a cappella, with no musicians, because it was like a little portrait of him. And so I did. People were weeping. Philippe said there would be no encores because he was dead. After a while I thought I couldn't go on like that, because it's not really my place, as Bambou is his widow. I just didn't know where I was anymore. I put the microphone down and then I didn't sing for a number of years. I didn't have an author anymore.'

The night before Serge's death was Bambou's birthday. He gave her a heart-shaped diamond from Cartier, then spent the evening at home, as he did most nights during his final days, in front of the TV, alone. He did put in a call to an old friend, though. 'I didn't see him for years, because of course he was with Jane Birkin,' Anna Karina told me. 'And then he became very sick, and before that he was a little bit sloppy and all that. He wasn't elegant anymore, he was Mr. Gainsbarre. And one night he phoned me out of the blue and said, Anna, I want to make a picture. And I said, I want to talk to you about it, what about having lunch tomorrow? He tells me, I'll phone you back because I'm just out of the hospital.' Her famous eyes well up with tears. 'And I never got the phone call, because the next day he was dead.'

The final single to come out was, appropriately enough, a remix of 'Requiem pour un con', re-released in very Gainsbourgian circumstances. 'Serge was feeling ill, and he thought Philippe could remix it, and that way he'd have something on the radio,' says Jane. 'Because Serge was a little bit jealous of me being on the radio all the time, and the television, even though they were his songs. So Philippe did it and it came out the day he died. It was called "Requiem", so it was all very weird.'

There are two cover versions on *You're Under Arrest*; both echo from his childhood in the 1930s, and perhaps signal that the end was nigh, especially 'Gloomy Sunday', the Hungarian suicide song that is supposed to have led listeners to take their own lives after hearing it (there's no statistical evidence). It has been recorded over the years by Billie Holiday, Sinead O'Connor, Lydia Lunch, Marc Almond, The Associates, Anton LaVey, and Diamanda Galás, to name but a few, and the urban myths that surround it are numerous.

Whether Serge knew this would be his final album is doubtful, even if deep down he suspected it, but nevertheless a cover of Rezső Seress's 1933 song feels rather like the full stop of a career that was a long and beautifully written suicide note. 'And Serge had sung the song "Gloomy Sunday", and he said, *You'll see*,' says Jane Birkin, who arrived at CDG on a Sunday morning. 'I thought, *It can't be true—it's a Sunday, like in the song.*'

'"Gloomy Sunday" was written by a very obscure Hungarian Jewish composer,' says Jonathyne Briggs. 'And the Hungarian holocaust was very similar to the French holocaust in that there were these weird nationalist elements to it, where there were lots of French people who were interested in protecting French Jews but were complicit in sending refugee Jews away—it's kind of what happened in Hungary as well. I think Gainsbourg again is being very provocative choosing this song and putting it as the centrepiece of the album. People interpret it as a song about suicide and darkness, but it's also a song about the rise of fascism in Hungary in the 30s, and the sadness that this Jew feels watching society turn. That's how I'm interpreting Gainsbourg's decision to put this song on the album—an album, interestingly enough, about being under arrest, which is kind of what happened to the Jews in his youth. He was constantly under the threat of being arrested when he was a child.'

*

For the follow-up to *You're Under Arrest*, Gainsbourg had booked a studio in New Orleans, the birthplace of jazz, where he was intending to record his next album, *Moi m'aime, Bwana!* with The Neville Brothers. The studio and the musicians had been paid for, and Gary Georgett had a plane ticket in his hand, ready to fly to Paris to write with Gainsbourg. 'Philip sent me a note simply saying *Serge is dead*,' says Gary. 'It took me some time to get over that, but it's not something we were surprised at.'

Serge had assembled a few bits and pieces for the album that never was. Whether he had more in his head, or whether he was planning to wing it and write all ten lyrics on ten sheets of paper the night before, we'll never know. 'A ma peluche tropicale', which started out as a poem dedicated to Bambou and referenced lots of his antics from the past, was one song mooted for the record. Another was the title track. And he'd started the lyrics of a song called 'Christian Name Christian', which may have been part of a desert-island concept disc, with a diss track aimed at a recently deceased British character actor.

'It was going to be about *Mutiny On The Bounty*, because he wanted to write "Trevor Howard, coward",' reveals Birkin. 'I said, You can't say that, Trevor's awfully sweet. He told me that on the phone, and it was two days before dying, I suppose. I realised it was a sort of a mixture of *Mutiny On The Bounty* and Friday from Defoe. I don't know whether it was going to be a homosexual relationship, but it was going to be a man loving another man with Friday, and he never got to do it.' The mind boggles.

The final track on *You're Under Arrest* is 'Mon Légionnaire', originally recorded by Édith Piaf in 1936. The curtain comes down with a homoerotic nod to Madame Arthur, where it all began. Going out in style, Serge shot a video with a sailor's cap doffed to Fassbinder's *Querelle*, perhaps, only the love interest to whom he sings the song is a petit garçon aged just twelve. 'I'm not sure he would have got away with that these days,' Jane says. 'Perhaps that's a pity, in a way. "Lemon Incest" caused a bit of a racket at the time but not that much. But the clip that went with it, with Serge carrying Charlotte in his arms? It was all a bit outrageous, but everyone knew that was him too. So, could any of that have existed now? I don't know. But I think people rather long for it, because he would say what he thought, and he didn't really care what people thought.'

Which brings us to the end of the book, although I have a penultimate hypothetical question, and, in the interests of balance, it will be followed by two opposing answers to ponder upon.

DECLINE

Question: would there be enough space today for a provocateur like Gainsbourg?

Tony 'Thunder' Smith, who played with Gainsbourg and Lou Reed, doesn't think either of them could have survived in the twenty-first century without heavy censure: 'People are afraid to do anything! They think, *I can't say this or that*, to a point where you have to say, *This is insanity*. It's like being chained and put in prison with your words. You have to think really carefully about everything you say. But you have to say what you're thinking. That's progress. I don't think a Gainsbourg or a Lou Reed could exist in today's climate. I just don't.'

Chilly Gonzales has a different take. 'There's so much censure, but the people who are unapologetic don't get punished, right? The people who get punished are the ones who seem hypocritical because they pretend to be something; self-proclaimed male feminists caught behaving badly! It feels different to someone who we knew was a certain way all along. I'm guessing Gainsbourg would be more like a Kanye West, who goes unpunished because he's unapologetic.' To be fair, West isn't without his critics, though he was able to mount a bizarre campaign for the White House in 2020, with his thirty million Twitter followers anticipating his every move. The word 'cancelled' has a finality about it, and West certainly hasn't succumbed to cancellation, especially not with those numbers.

'You never know how someone would have been like on social media, because it's generational and all that kind of stuff, but it seems what social media does would fit him like a glove,' says Gonzales about Gainsbourg. 'How would he fare in a twenty-first-century world? My guess is that he would be doing a lot of music with rappers. Who knows what he would have done in this version of the music business?'

And, finally, what of Gainsbarre, the construct that swallowed Gainsbourg whole? The caricature he was forced to become, smoking and drinking and offending everyone and stalking through the snow in his Repettos, so he never went out of character—what of this celebrity Sisyphus, forever rolling a boulder up the hill in the pursuit of *audimat*? I'd like to leave the last word with Bambou, who didn't talk to me personally, but moved me with that honest, emotionally intelligent interview she gave to *Les Inrocks* in 2001. This is what she had to say about Gainsbarre, and I really hope every word of it is true:

'He invented Gainsbarre to protect himself and to hide the guy who was hurting … Gainsbarre didn't ring true because he was the complete opposite of Gainsbourg; a mask. Gainsbarre protected Gainsbourg, but at one point he ate him up. But it wasn't really the drunk guy we wanted to see, we wanted to find Gainsbourg.

'Gainsbarre existed, a transition, but he didn't hang around. When Serge became aware of what he was doing, he stopped. That is to say just after the birth of Lulu. The rare moments when he was happy were when he was with Lulu. At home, he no longer had anything to do with his public image, he no longer needed to provoke. With me, he was not Gainsbarre, he became little Lulu Ginsburg again.'*

---

* 'Il a inventé Gainsbarre pour se protéger, pour cacher l'homme blessé … Gainsbarre ne tenait pas la route, parce qu'il était tout l'opposé de Gainsbourg, un masque. Gainsbarre protégeait Gainsbourg, mais à un moment il l'a bouffé. Pourtant, ce n'est pas le mec bourré qu'on voulait voir, on voulait retrouver Gainsbourg. Gainsbarre existait, transitoire, mais il ne fallait pas qu'il reste là-dessus. Quand il en a pris conscience, il a arrêté. C'est-à-dire juste après la naissance de Lulu. Les rares moments où il était heureux, c'est quand il était avec Lulu. A la maison, il n'avait plus rien à voir avec l'image publique, il n'avait plus besoin de provoquer. Avec moi, il n'était pas Gainsbarre, il redevenait le petit Lulu Ginsburg.'

ACKNOWLEDGEMENTS

I'd like to thank some of the people who helped me form a better picture of the subject and threw up more questions than answers about one of the great pop chameleons. Jane Birkin was as gracious and delightful as you'd imagine, and she kindly put me in touch with Charlotte Gainsbourg and Serge's ninety-three-year-old sister, Jacqueline. Thanks to them, and to Andrew Birkin, too. Merci Jean-Claude Vannier for being a loveable grump and throwing some shade, and to the late, great Anna Karina and her husband, Dennis Berry.

The Society of Authors provided funding after I applied for a grant, and without them this book could have taken several more years. The British Library was also a great resource, and thanks to the BBC Archive in Caversham for allowing me to have a poke around. Thanks to my agent, Natalie Galustian at DHH.

A massive loving thank-you to Claire and Jean Genie, who've had to put up with me throughout the making of this book. And to Dr. Russell Williams, who came with me for a memorable meeting with Vannier, and was a sounding board who did me the honour of reading the book and pointing out my dodgy translations and the odd fanciful digression. Other people I'd like to say cheers to in no particular order, who helped in some way with the book, are: Stan Harrison, crack New Jersey saxophonist, who put me in touch with most of Serge's American musicians; Bertrand Burgalat, who helped me change direction slightly; Chilly Gonzales, who had some revelatory things to say; and Tony Frank, who hosted me at his offices in *le seizième* for a few hours. Bruno 'Doc Reggae' Blum was also fascinating and knew his onions, as did French professor of pop Jonathyne Briggs, and Raechel Leigh Carter knows her Gainsbourg films! Vadim Kosmos was another sounding board and a great source of obscure titbits, as was Jean-Emmanuel De-Luxe, who came in at the eleventh hour with important details about the peculiarities of French society.

Merci George Simms for the war stories and the insights about Bambou. Thank you Paul Sandell at KPM for his help in getting Dave Richmond, Alan Hawkshaw, and Alan Parker, who also deserve a cheer or three.

Thanks: Mick Harvey, Jonny Trunk, Mike Patton, Russell Mael, Étienne Daho, Beck, David Holmes, Kazu Makino, Rob Chapman, Leila Wimmer, Sly Dunbar, Ansel Collins, Mark Lanegan, Acid Arab, SebastiAn, Curtis King Jr., Joe Mount, Pierre Koralnik, Jehnny Beth, Johnny Hostile, the sadly departed Tony Allen, Vincent Palmer, Johnny Marr, Sebastien Tellier, Graham Fellows, Will Oldham, Baxter Dury, Pere Francesch, John Robb, Roberto Battistini, Laurent Balandras, Denis Clavaizolle, Paul Gorman, Françoise Cactus, Philippe HeNGo, François Guernier, Dougie Wright, Tony 'Thunder' Smith, Nicolas Godin, Soko, Andy Votel, Robin Scott, Roedelius, Anne Pigalle, Gary Georgett, John Kumnick, Alain Chamfort, Alex Paterson, Dom Thomas, Cerrone, and Gainsbourg For Kids.

Thanks to Tom and Nigel at Jawbone, and Adrian Harte who put me in touch. Cheers to Luke and John at the *Quietus*; Neil and the guys at *Electronic Sound*; Michael Hann when he was at the *Guardian*; Dom, Niall, and Cian at *Huck*; Phil Hebblethwaite when we did the *Stool Pigeon* together; Seb Emina at the *Happy Reader*; and anyone else who has indulged my interest over the years and allowed me to write about Gainsbourg.

Cheers David 'Rockfort' McKenna, Matt Robin for support and contacts, Benjamin Schoos, and Thomas Ducres. To my brothers, Matt and Jules. Peter Headen and Duffell, Kev Chesters, Dan Sherrington, Andrew Gallix, Lucretia and John, David Barnett, Adam Narkiewicz, Rory Lewarne, Emily Gosling, Andy Barding and Rhoda Bracewell, Frankie Poullain, Daryl Woollaston, Debbie Ball, Zoe Miller, Giovanna Ferrin, Clare Dingle, Lauren Barley, Ferreol at Record Makers, Jerry Ewing at *Prog*, Mark Brend, Alex Marshall, and many others I may have forgotten. Thanks to the Mason clan for all their support, too, especially to Pat, Chris, Lulu, and Kiki. God bless my dearly departed pal, Pascal. If I've not mentioned you by name and should have done then feel free to blank me in the street the next time our paths cross.

Translations in the book are mostly mine, but I should give special mention to Paul Knobloch, whose work for TamTam Books has been a massive help, and I was able to align his version of Gilles Verlant's *Gainsbourg* with Verlant's original tome. And thanks to John and Doreen Weightman, who translated *Evguénie Sokolov*—also for TamTam—and provided a memorable paragraph of euphemistic fart nicknames from the original French (see the chapter entitled *Provocation*). I'm not going to lie, Google played its part, too, so thank you Google. I was wary of writing another Verlant-based hagiography, so I consulted a number of French-language takes, including Franck Maubert's *Gainsbourg à rebours* and especially Marie-Dominique Lelièvre's *Gainsbourg sans filtre*, where she never lets her subject off the hook.

I'd like to thank VeeLite on the *Guardian* message board who, when I compared Gainsbourg to Kayne West in a mildly pointless *Guardian* article in 2017, following the death of Johnny Hallyday, said, 'May I politely suggest that someone comparing Kanye West to Serge Gainsbourg doesn't actually know who Serge Gainsbourg was.' I hope this book goes some way to redressing that assumption.

And thanks to the late, great Serge Gainsbourg himself, for being a source of fascination: brilliant and funny and tragic and sometimes pathetic, and enigmatic enough to make the search for answers a consuming one. And, above all, thanks for all the remarkable music.

INDEX

INDEX

INDEX